The Visitor's Guide
to
Bavaria

THE VISITOR'S GUIDE TO BAVARIA

George Wood

MPC

HUNTER
PUBLISHING INC

British Library Cataloguing in Publication Data:
Wood, George
The visitor's guide to Bavaria.
1. Bavaria (Germany)— Description and travel — Guide-books
I. Title
914.3' 304878   DD810.B34

Published by:
Moorland Publishing Co Ltd,
Moor Farm Road,
Airfield Estate,
Ashbourne,
Derbyshire DE6 1HD
England

ISBN 0 86190 202 5 (paperback)
ISBN 0 86190 203 3 (hardback)

Published in the USA by:
Hunter Publishing Inc.,
300 Raritan Centre Parkway,
CN94, Edison, NJ 08818

ISBN 1 55650 085 8

Printed by Butler and Tanner Ltd, Frome, Somerset.

Acknowledgements:
I would like to acknowledge the assistance given by many people in Britain and Germany in the preparation of this book. My wife read the manuscript and made many helpful suggestions, in particular, contributing background detail for the Mittenwald area. Ruth and Rudolf Schmidt in Bayreuth, Ursula and Wolfgang Winter in Heidelberg, and many others provided material and ideas. I must mention too, the comprehensive information provided by the *Fremdenverkehrsverbände* in Augsburg, Munich, Nuremberg, Regensburg and Starnberg.

Without all this help, my task would have been much more difficult and the end result much less comprehensive.

G. W.

CONTENTS

Grading of Walks

In much of Bavaria, altitude is of less importance than the nature of the terrain because the starting points for walks are themselves likely to be considerably above sea-level. Typically this could be 800–900m (2624–2952ft) in the Alpine regions, 500–600m (1640–1968ft) in the Lakes and Chiemgau and 500–800m (1640–2624ft) in the eastern border lands. The categories of walks you will see indicated in the margin of this guide should, therefore, be regarded more as an indication of the variations in altitude likely to be encountered and thus of the degree of effort which will be required.

H	Strenuous and usually wholly or partly above 1000m (3280ft)
M	Moderately strenuous
L	Less Strenuous and usually not above 1000m (3280ft)
⬩⬩	Well signed or waymarked
⬩⬩⬩	Easy to follow with the aid of a map
⬩⬩⬩⬩⬩	Requires careful map-reading
△	Least interest
△△	
△△△	
△△△△	Most interest

 Indicates start of walk

INTRODUCTION

The Country and its People

Bavaria, or Bayern to give its German name, is the largest of the German states or *Länder* which make up the Bundesrepublik Deutschland (German Federal Republic) or, as it is usually called, West Germany. The total land area is similar to that of Scotland, distances being very roughly 370km from north to south and the same from east to west. In the south and south-east, Bavaria shares a border of some 400km with Austria; on the eastern side is Czechoslovakia and in the north the Deutsche Demokratische Republik (DDR) or East Germany. The western border is shared with the *Länder* of Hessen and Baden-Württemberg.

The political history of Bavaria is more complex than that of most other European countries. Inevitably it is necessary to refer to the political background from time to time but for the general tourist and holidaymaker it will suffice, at this stage, to say that the former independent kingdom of Bavaria ceased to exist after World War I. It was absorbed into greater Germany at the end of March 1920, remaining after World War II in that part which became the Federal Republic. The last monarch was Ludwig III who does not appear to have been of particular significance. Several of his predecessors, however, had a profound influence on the development of their country, pride of place going, for the foreign visitor at least, to Ludwig II (ruled 1864–86).

Much of Bavaria is quite sparsely populated but there are several major centres of population of which Munich, the state capital, is the most important. The total population of Bavaria is around 10 million of whom well over half live in and around the principal cities and towns. The population of Bavaria is greater than that of Austria, Switzerland or Belgium. Whereas in Germany as a whole Catholics and Protes-

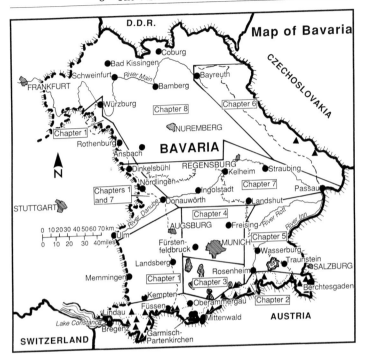

tants are more or less evenly divided, in Bavaria some 71 per cent are Catholic. Thirty-five per cent of the land area is forest, the 'Bavarian Forest' with the adjoining 'Bohemian Forest' on the Czech side of the border constituting the largest afforested area in Europe. The Alps occupy some 15 per cent of the land leaving just 50 per cent for all other purposes, the most important of which is agriculture. Dairy-farming is important nearly everywhere and in the mountain regions there are traditional ceremonies associated with the movement of cows to the high pastures in the spring and their return in autumn.

The popular impression is that Bavarians are great beer drinkers and this is true in some areas, particularly Munich with its great breweries and the *Oktoberfest*. Nevertheless, beer certainly takes second place in the great Franconian wine-producing area with vineyards mostly along the River Main. In the south-west corner of Lower Bavaria (Niederbayern), in the district known as the Hallertau, is the largest hop-growing area in all Europe.

Germany's highest mountains are to be found in the Bavarian Alps along the border with Austria with such giants as the Zugspitze (2963m, 9718ft), the Hochblassen (2706m, 8875ft) and the Watzmann (2713m, 8898ft) to name just a few of the many peaks over 2000m (6560ft). The rest of the state is by no means flat and there are some respectable summits along the Czechoslovakian border with the Dreisessel (1332m, 4368ft), the Rachel (1453m, 4765ft) and the Arber (1457m, 4778ft) all providing a stiff challenge for the rambler.

Bavaria's waterways have long been important commercial arteries. From west to east the River Danube, which has its source in the Black Forest, flows for some 350 of its total 2850km length in Bavaria while in the opposite direction the Main (pronounce it 'mine', rising near Bayreuth, wends its tortuous way westwards for an almost identical distance to leave Bavaria only when it reaches the outskirts of Frankfurt. Not surprising that for centuries men have dreamed of linking these two great rivers to create a major east–west waterway. It was Kaiser Karl der Grosse (Charlemagne) who in the year 793 started the digging of a canal which would have achieved this object albeit on a fairly modest scale. King Ludwig I revived the idea in the 1820s and eventually a through route was established but only for vessels up to 120 tons and 32m (105ft) long. After World War II the project for a major link was once again revived and at the time of writing work is all but complete on a system which will provide through transit for vessels up to 110m (360ft) long and a load capacity of more than 1500 tons. So at last the dream has been realised. The construction of the Rhein-Main-Donau-Kanal (Rhine-Main-Danube-Canal) between Bamberg on the Main and Kelheim on the Danube will enable large ships from northern France, the low countries, northern Germany and Switzerland to travel via an inland route to Austria, Czechoslovakia, the Balkan countries and the Black Sea. Many other rivers criss-cross the land, some being navigable to a greater or lesser extent. Most of them drain into either the Danube or the Main.

There are many attractive lakes, some of which are described later. Since Bavaria has no coastline the lakes and rivers are popular for bathing and all kinds of water activities but there are also dozens of attractive and well equipped swimming pools indoors and out, most of the latter being heated.

In an area as big as Bavaria, there are considerable variations of climate; the first thing that must be said is that the summers are usually warm or very warm and that the winters are severe. In the Alpine regions of the south, snow may persist for about 6 months of the year and in the east and north-east, even though the snow may not last as long, temperatures can remain low for many months with markedly longer winters and shorter summers in consequence. As one moves west and north-west the severest winter conditions are likely to be tempered a little by milder air coming in from the Atlantic and, of course, the vineyards which flourish along the River Main are further evidence of climatic variety.

The language of Bavaria is German and those with a knowledge of it are not likely to experience any difficulty. The *Bairisch* dialect — shared with Austria — has regional variations while the Regensburgers have their own distinctive speech. Then there is Swabian in the west — if anything even more of a puzzle than *Bairisch* — and Franconian in the north but all this need not worry the visitor unduly. English is widely understood since the British and American forces and families constitute large permanent English-speaking communities. Younger Germans often learn English as their first foreign language and will be anxious to try out their knowledge on English-speaking visitors.

The inhabitants are not all alike, of course. A Bavarian can also calls himself a Franconian or a Swabian for these areas have belonged to Bavaria since around 1800. The true Bavarian on the other hand, that is from Upper or Lower Bavaria or the Upper Palatinate, is a member of the same ancient race as the Austrians, though the latter are often reluctant to acknowledge this.The visitor who comes with a pre-conceived notion of a Bavarian as a beer-swilling, leather shorts-wearing yodeller will have to perform a rapid mental adjustment; and if his idea of a typical Bavarian house is a chalet with rocks on the roof he must be prepared for a lot of surprises.

Visiting Bavaria

Accommodation

Parts of Bavaria have long been popular tourist goals but since World War II the emphasis has been on Upper Bavaria with its mountains and winter sports facilities, made familiar by Olympic and other international events. Other areas have developed gradually over the years and there is now ample provision for holidaymakers everywhere with numerous camp sites and youth hostels, some of these in novel locations. In the chapters which follow it is not the intention to refer in detail to holiday accommodation. The reader may assume that in each place or the immediate vicinity there is a range of accommodation including hotels, inns, pensions, self-catering flats or bungalows and so on. Prices are generally modest but for the foreign visitor the 'value for money' depends largely on the international exchange rate prevailing at the time of the visit. Significant variations in the range in a particular place are mentioned. Needless to say, Germany's high accommodation standards prevail everywhere.

Architecture

If, as is likely, Bavaria has been entered via Frankfurt, an early stop might be made in the fine old town of Miltenberg on the River Main with its cluster of light, steep-gabled timbered buildings, picturesque squares and quickly changing scenes. Then later, 300km or so to the south-east, a visit might be made to Wasserburg on the River Inn; it could not be more different with its cubic, square-shouldered houses of stone, flat façades and sharply defined squares to be taken in at a glance. Again, these two might be compared with a typical Swabian town such as Mindelheim or Weissenhorn with wide pleasant streets bordered by a frieze of Swabian gabled houses. No other European country can display such a wide variety of architectural styles and this is not, of course, confined to domestic buildings. Public and particularly church architecture reflects the ebb and flow of many different cultures over more than a thousand years and here in Bavaria one can identify the influence which Italian, Spanish and Greek cultures, to name but a few, have had on the builders, architects, painters and sculptors who devoted a lifetime of work to their land.

To attempt even a brief description of every beautiful or interesting church would require several volumes and even mention of every one would be more than a book of this size could sustain.This book confines itself to some of the really outstanding edifices or those upon which the traveller will come quite naturally in following the suggested routes. Almost every church has a pamphlet or booklet describing the most important features and such publications are sometimes multilingual or have an English version.

From a church architecture point of view, 1803 was a momentous year for this was when the so-called 'secularisation' took place and the Catholic religious foundations in particular were dissolved by the Bavarian state and stripped of their assets. Great harm was done to the Church and not only were Bavarian religious traditions overturned but there were enormous losses of cultural value. Many churches of Catholic orders were demolished, valuable libraries were destroyed or sold for a pittance, church plate was melted down and the populations of the great religious houses dispersed. Even the famous baroque church at Wies was listed for demolition but was reprieved after representations from the farming community. That so much has survived for us to see today is nothing short of a miracle.

Architecture cannot fail to feature to some extent in the itinerary of every visitor. Bavaria is extremely rich in fine buildings both religious and secular and reference has been made to examples of the various styles as this fascinating country is explored. It may be helpful for the layman to be reminded of the main architectural styles which will be encountered:

Romanisch (Romanesque). Comprehensive term for the period 1000–1300 peaking between 1025 and 1125. Buildings typically have round arches to windows and doors, load-bearing columns with little ornamentation. Porches or portals often supported by columns and the half-circle between lintel and arch — the tympanum — may have thematic or decorative sculpture. Example: parish church in Altenstadt near Schongau.

Gotisch (Gothic). Twelfth to sixteenth centuries with three main stages, 'early' 1220–1300, 'peak' 1300–1400 and 'late' 1400–1500. The buildings seem to strive up towards heaven with pointed arches, soaring columns and towers. Ceiling vaults with ribs, nets or stars. Porches often decorated with carved figures and some use of brick as well as stone. Example: Frauenkirche in Munich. (*Neu-Gotisch* (neo-Gothic) is the term used to describe nineteenth- and twentieth-century buildings designed in the 'Gothic' style.)

Renaissance. The name comes from the Italian *rinascimento* (rebirth) and the style was founded upon Italian influence between about 1500 and 1620 and leaning towards Italian palaces of the period. Examples: Jesuit church of St Michael in Munich and the *Schloss* (palace) at Neuburg on the Danube.

Barock (baroque). The style of the seventeenth and eighteenth centuries with Italian origins. Free use of allegorical decorations in relief by means of stucco (pulverised marble and plaster) and adoption of relief effect by painting. Baroque is the outstanding art form of

Upper Bavaria. Examples: the *Klosterkirche* in Fürstenfeldbruck and the *Rathaus* (town hall) in Landsberg.

Rokoko (rococo). Playful development of baroque adopted in the eighteenth century, principally between 1720 and 1780. Much gilding and decoration with a shell motif. The form reached its peak in Upper Bavarian churches where with the aid of stucco, relief and painting, the impression of space, height etc is no longer limited by the physical dimensions of the building. Examples: church at Wies and the Amalienburg (Nymphenburg) in Munich

Klassizisimus (classicism). Revival of Greek and Roman principles at end of the eighteenth and beginning of the nineteenth centuries. Renunciation of colour and stucco and concentration on symmetry. Examples: Königsplatz in Munich and Walhalla near Regensburg.

Kirche is the usual word for church and, as in some of the examples above, is often incorporated with the name of the church as one word. A cathedral is *Dom* or occasionally *Münster*.

Festivals

Bavaria is a land of festivals and at almost any season there is some event which the traveller should endeavour to see or participate in. The mid-winter visitor will find much of interest with Christmas markets and numerous festivities from the beginning of December until Christmas Eve, Christmas itself and then New Year. The use of candles on Christmas trees is still common in Germany and adds a nice touch. New Year's Eve (*Sylvesterabend*) is a time for merry-making and every district has it own brand of activity with either a religious or a secular slant to the goings-on. Everywhere though, there is an atmosphere of expectation as midnight approaches and as soon as the clock strikes twelve the air is filled with noise as fire-crackers are let off, drums are beaten and voices are raised in excitement. All this is supposed to stem from ancient rites performed to drive away evil spirits at the opening of a new year. Nowadays it is largely a matter of having a traditional excuse for yet another evening of jollity, not that the fun-loving Bavarians really need any excuse.

In the New Year, 6 January is *Dreikönigstag*, Three Kings' Day (Epiphany) and some families wait until this day before adding the kings to the Christmas crib. By the ninth century the three kings, sometimes called the Magi, had acquired the names of Caspar or Kaspar, Melchior and Balthasar. The Christmas story of the visit of the kings to the baby Jesus is well known and prior to the Reformation which put a stop to the practice, many miracle plays were performed re-enacting the famous journey. In many Roman Catholic areas a modified form of the ceremonial has persisted in the form of *Sternsinger* (star singers) who don regal robes and go through the streets or from house to house collecting for charity. In the Bavarian Alps the group may be accompanied by others who form a procession and stop from time to time to sing carols appropriate to this time. Many superstitions are connected with Epiphany; to the visitor the most obvious is the chalk inscription often seen on the door lintel with the initials of the kings and the numerals of the year on either side written thus: 19C + M + B88. In rural areas the chalk marks often endure throughout the following year. Pre-lenten jollifications take various forms and names, with *Fasching* in Munich of particular interest. The church calendar provides numerous reasons for a holiday or festival and every town and village has its own special events to celebrate as well. Mention has been made of many of these later in the book.

Visitors may come across posters advertising a *Dult*. This word does not appear in many dictionaries; it is normally associated with a church anniversary, for example that of the consecration of the church. In Bavaria the meaning is often widened to include annual fairs and markets especially in places which do not have a permanent market or market day. The *Dult* is then something of a cross between a street market, a flea-market (*Flohmarkt*) and a jumble sale. Needless to say, no two are alike. Early May seems to be a favourite time for these fairs which may be called *Auedult* (meadow market) or *Maidult* (May market). There is also a *Hofdult* (court market) in Altötting in May-June, a *Frauendult* (women's market) in Pfaffenhofen (August) and even a *Nikolausdult* in Schrobenhausen on 6 December. Lists of public holidays and of some festivals and pageants are given at the back of the book.

Touring and Travel

A glance at the map reveals that Bavaria begins in the west just about 20km from the centre of Frankfurt and since that city is a focal point for travellers by road, rail or air this seems to be the logical place to start touring. The visitor not provided with his own car could hire a vehicle at Frankfurt for there is no doubt that with a car one can make much better use of the time available even though Bavaria is remarkably well served by the Deutsche Bundesbahn — Federal Railway —

and by some private lines and 'bus services.

Where, in the ensuing chapters, it is necessary to refer to distances, the metric versions have been used since these are what the visitor will find on signposts and maps. Where heights are mentioned both metric and imperial units have been used. In a few cases there are established English versions of place names as well as the German ones and in these cases both have been shown initially and thereafter the English form has been used. Other words which occur frequently such as *Rathaus* (town hall), *Kirche* (church), *Kloster* (monastery, nunnery, convent, etc), *Gasthof* (inn) etc have an English translation given the first time they arise and thereafter the German form has usually been used as being more helpful to the visitor not conversant with the language. The glossary in 'Further Information' can be consulted in case of doubt. Reference has been made to some of the gastronomic specialities of the various regions, best sought out in the old family inns rather than in modern 'chain' establishments. It should be noted that most restaurants and inns close for one day a week for their *Ruhetag* (rest day). If the *Ruhetag* of an establishment mentioned is known, this has been stated in the text.

An endeavour has been made to divide Bavaria into areas which can be fitted into a logical touring pattern. Most of the areas are too big to be covered from a single base and this guide generally assumes that a progressive tour will be made. This is not the best arrangement for families with children and they would find it better to establish themselves within reasonable distance of the sort of activities that they enjoy and confine themselves to one or two longer excursions to other places, paying due regard to the weather conditions — especially in summer — and the distances involved.

The whole of Bavaria is very good rambling country and much has been done to encourage the walker to see the best of the countryside. Numerous long-distance paths have been identified and thousands of walks have been marked by local authorities or rambling organisations, with details obtainable at local tourist information offices. Nevertheless, it is prudent to obtain a fairly large-scale map of the area if only to avoid missing something of interest and it is, of course, essential if one intends to depart from the waymarked paths. Nor has the cyclist been forgotten. Many parts are ideal for cycling and some hosts have bicycles available for the use of their guests. In any case, bicycles can be hired quite cheaply everywhere. (See 'Further Information'.)

The motorist will often wish to use his vehicle to reach the starting point of a walk and for his benefit many free *Wanderparkplätze* (walker's parking places) have been provided. These usually have a map showing the rambles in the vicinity with details of the waymarks, distances or time required for each walk. All such walks can be completed in one day, the majority being less than 10km. Some of these special car parks can be recognised by their distinctive blue 'P' sign with a pictogram of a couple of hikers. The motorist will also require a smaller scale map for his travels about the area and those available from filling stations are very suitable for this. For example, sheets 4, 5, 6 and 7 of the series issued by Aral cover the whole of Bavaria at a scale of l:400,000. Their filling stations also carry a series specially designed for the touring holidaymaker at a scale of l:200,000. For those with some knowledge of German there are many booklets obtainable locally giving detailed descriptions of walks. Walking is the single most popular activity and while a book of this size cannot contain a comprehensive catalogue of the rambling possibilities, most chapters will include details of walks which may be regarded as typical of the area.

Finally, a few tips for the travelling tourist. Plan the day's itinerary with care in order not to miss worthwhile sights which may not lie on the direct route. Don't attempt too much in one day — leave time for a leisurely meal, a quiet stroll, a swim or just a seat in the sun. Avoid the main tourist attractions at weekends and holidays. It is always quieter in spring or autumn; if visiting Bavaria in summer, plan your sightseeing if you can for mid-week and early in the morning or towards evening. Take care to be suitably clad for the weather. Especially in the mountains the weather can change very quickly so before setting out on a ramble or ski-tour check the weather prospects. The locals will usually know if the signs are favourable for their own district.

Wear sensible footwear for walking. Town shoes, sandals and high heels are of no use in the mountains. In hilly areas do not be tempted to leave a marked path for an attractive-looking short cut through meadows or woods.

When travelling from place to place without pre-booking, avoid big and crowded hotels and seek the more modest rural inns and *pensions*, many of which enjoy a local reputation for good food and regional specialities.

1 THE ROMANTIC ROAD AND ALLGÄU

The Romantic Road

The Romantic Road (Romantische Strasse) is the oldest and one of the longest of Germany's many tourist routes and runs from Würzburg in the north to Füssen on the fringe of the Alps in the south, a distance of some 350km. Würzburg can be reached by road or rail from Frankfurt in less than $1\frac{1}{2}$ hours.

A good starting point for exploring **Würzburg** (population 130,000) is the Court Garden (Hofgarten) attached to the Residenz — the home of the former prince-bishops of Würzburg. The square on the town side of the palace provides a lot of parking space but there is a 2-hour time limit here. Do not overlook the fantastic wrought-iron entrance gate at the east end of the building. The creator of this masterpiece, Johann Georg Ogg, is seen in a nearby statue dressed in his working clothes.

Then this magnificent palace, the creation of Balthasar Neumann (1687–1753), the most significant architect of south German baroque, must be inspected. Napoléon enviously described it as Europe's stateliest parsonage. At 13 years Balthasar was apprenticed in the trade of casting cannons and bells and when he was 24 came to Würzburg to work in Kopp's foundry. There he obtained his indenture for firework-making and in 1712 was allowed to arrange a great firework display for the visit of Kaiser (Emperor) Karl VI. A loan from his home town and the support of some well-wishers enabled him to give up manual work and study geometry, surveying and architecture. In 1714 he was accepted as an ensign in the prince's forces and between purely military duties worked with Greising on Kloster Ettal, visited Vienna and worked in Milan before he was promoted to engineer-captain and in 1719 built his first house in

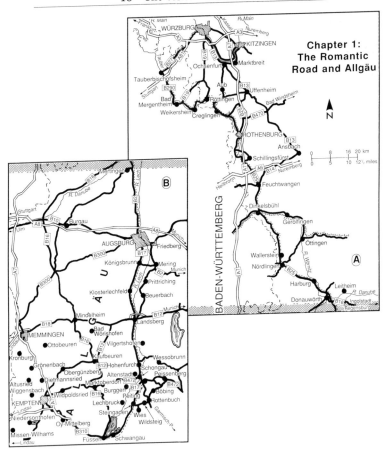

Chapter 1:
The Romantic
Road and Allgäu

Würzburg. Such was his meteoric rise to fame that the following year he was entrusted with the building of the Residenz and in 1722 with the oversight of all civic building in the city so that even where he was not responsible for the design, something of his taste and aptitude came through. When Friedrich Carl von Schönborn became prince-bishop of Bamberg and Würzburg in 1729 the completion of the still unfinished Residenz was authorised — it took until 1744 — and the now Lieutenant-Colonel Neumann was appointed director of all military, church and civil architecture in both bishoprics.

The splendid emperor's hall in the high central pavilion of the

PLACES OF INTEREST IN WÜRZBURG

Residenz (1720–44)
Magnificent baroque palace with lovely formal gardens.

Bavarian State Wine Cellars
Close to Residenz. Wine-tastings most days.

Stift-Haug-Kirche (1670–91)
Famous 'crucifixion' (1585) by Jacopo Tintoretto.

Cathedral (*Dom*)
Mixture of building styles and art, 855 to the present day.
Re-consecrated in 1967 after war damage.

Old Town Hall
Built about 1200, upper storeys added in fifteenth to sixteenth centuries. Colourful façade.

Old Bridge over River Main (1473–1543)
Baroque statues and fine view to Marienberg fortress.

Marienberg
Fortress (thirteenth century and later additions) overlooking city. Home of fine Main-Franconian Museum with large exhibition of Franconian art and culture. Riemenschneider Room.

Residenz has a ceiling painting (1751) by the famous artist G.B. Tiepolo. At performances during the annual Mozart festival in June this hall is lit by hundreds of candles and the walks in the garden are lined with hundreds of flickering coloured lights. Across the street from the main building are the Bavarian State Wine Cellars for this is the land of the esteemed Franconian wine with the greatest vineyards in all Bavaria. Wine-tastings (*Weinproben*) take place almost every day and visitors are cordially welcomed.

A route from the Residenz in the old town on the east side of the River Main to the Marienberg fortress on the west side can be devised to take in most of the important cultural sights of the city. The town scene is enhanced by the towers and cupolas of many churches; a little to the north through Theater-strasse which opens off the Residenzplatz (*Platz* means square) is the Stift-Haug-Kirche which should be visited if only to see the monumental crucifixion (1585) by Jacopo Tintoretto. Back towards the town centre is the Augustiner-kirche and the baroque façade of the Neumünster before reaching the Domplatz. St Kilian's *Dom* was only re-consecrated in 1967 after war damage. It contains elements of building styles and works of art from 855 to the present day. One of several contributions by Tilman Riemenschneider is his moving portrayal of Rudolf von Scherenberg as an old man. The ceiling of the choir is very fine and the rebuilt main

Entrance to the Residenz garden, Würzburg

and side aisles are visually rather disappointing in comparison. There are fine examples of modern work but the mixture of old and new is not to everybody's taste.

Several more churches in the immediate vicinity are worthy of inspection but if time is limited the visitor should now make his way down towards the river, past the Marktplatz (Market Place) to the Altes Rathaus (old town hall) and then on to the Alte Mainbrücke (old Main bridge) to enjoy what is undoubtedly the most photographed Würzburg view, that of the Marienberg fortress on the hill above vineyards and as foreground the baroque figures of bishops and early saints upon the bridge itself. The figures include that of St Johann Nepomuk. He is the patron saint of bridges and also of Bohemia where he lived in the fourteenth century and was chaplain to Queen Sophia. Her husband Wenceslas suspected Sophia of infidelity and wanted Nepomuk to disclose what she had said in the confessional. When the priest refused to do this the king had him bound and thrown into the river from the highest bridge in Prague. Nothing happened to prove the Queen's innocence nor did any divine intervention save Nepomuk's life but the onlookers saw a remarkable sight. When the drowning priest came to the surface for the third time he was wearing a glittering gold halo in which were five gleaming stars. As here in

A gallery in the Mainfränkisches Museum, Würzburg

Würzburg Nepomuk is often easily recognised wearing his halo with the five stars as he stands watch on many bridges in central and western Europe. Another of the figures on the bridge is St Kilian after whom the cathedral is named.

Motor vehicles no longer use the old bridge but signs over either of the other bridges in the city will lead the motorist quickly up to the Marienberg fortress.The pedestrian may take the more strenuous approach by zig-zag paths. The fortress, home of the dukes of Franconia and sometimes of the prince-bishops can be visited and there is a *Gaststätte* (restaurant) here.

The splendid Mainfränkisches (Main-Franconian) Museum is housed in the fortress. Galleries with various themes lead to the Riemenschneider Room with many examples of this craftsman's work. Tilman Riemenschneider (1440–1531) of Würzburg produced altarpieces, sepulchres, reliefs and statues for churches and dignitaries. He also helped to run the city, serving variously as councillor, judge, tax-collector, head of local defence and finally *Bürgermeister* (mayor), the highest civic post. In 1525 his peace and prosperity were shattered when the Peasant's Revolt against the ruling princes erupted across Germany. Riemenschneider stood firm with other councillors in refusing to send troops to quell the uprising but the revolt failed and he was imprisoned. Eventually released he died 6 years later at the age of 71. The museum houses many of his works, often brought back from locations far away to make this significant collection in his home town. The centrepiece is his sculpture *Eva* which some consider his finest work. Without doubt the title 'Master Carver of the Middle Ages' is well deserved.

Music plays an important part in the cultural life of Würzburg and in addition to the Mozart festival there is a 'baroque' festival in May as well as many occasional concerts, recitals and so on. There is a Kilian Folk Festival in July and the Wine-producer's Festival lasts for about 10 days, end of September to the beginning of October. Würzburg is an excellent centre for touring and a booklet describing possible itineraries for day excursions is available from the information office near the *Hauptbahnhof* (main railway station). Würzburg is also a starting or calling point for various cruises up and down the River Main, mostly during the summer months.

The Romantic Road leaves Würzburg as Bundesstrasse (Federal Road) No 8 (such main roads will henceforth be identified only by the prefix 'B') and in the suburb of **Höchberg** one must watch for signs stating 'Romantische Strasse' and join B27 towards Tauberbischofsheim. However, this town, together with other places of interest such as Bad Mergentheim and Weikersheim on this part of the road actually lie outside the Bavarian border.

The traveller wishing to remain within Bavaria should leave Würzburg via Mergentheimer Strasse (B19) and head directly south for Röttingen (about 30km) to join the Romantische Strasse as it follows the pretty little River Tauber. **Röttingen** with 1660 inhabitants is little more than a substantial village. The baroque *Rathaus* (town hall) presides over the small market place which presents a fairly unspoiled medieval scene. There is a small historical exhibition in the lobby. The old town wall has seven towers and the new bridge over the Tauber is once again under the eye of Nepomuk. There is an archaeological trail and also a rather surprising one with the theme of sundials which are found in considerable numbers in this area. For about 5 weeks in July-August there is a theatre festival here which attracts its audience from a wide area. About 10km north-east of Röttingen the parish church in the village of **Aub** has a crucifixion group by Riemenschneider and the 1482 *Rathaus* overlooks a pleasant little square which has a notable baroque pillar surmounted by a gilded figure of the Virgin Mary.

PLACES OF INTEREST IN AND NEAR RÖTTINGEN

RÖTTINGEN
Town Hall and Market Place
Unspoiled medieval scene.

BIEBEREHREN (4km E)
Kreuzberg
Hill with Stations of the Cross, chapel and fine view.

AUB (10km NE)
Parish Church
Crucifixion group by Riemenschneider.

Town Hall (1482) and **Baroque Virgin Mary Pillar**

In this valley there are signs — a bicycle above the words 'Liebliches Taubertal' (Lovely Tauber Valley) — which mark the line of a 100km cycle ramble between Wertheim where the Tauber enters the Main west of Würzburg and Rothenburg, a peaceful route equally available to the walker but not, of course, entirely within Bavaria. From Röttingen only a few minutes are needed to reach **Bieberehren**. Turn off the main road here and cross the river to the foot of the Kreuzberg, a modest hill surmounted by a chapel to which the approach — 274 steps — is flanked by the Stations of the Cross in a series of very detailed reliefs. From the chapel there is an extensive view eastwards over the valley.

Back on the Romantische Strasse pass through the village of **Klingen** and upon crossing the Tauber once again the route leaves Bavaria briefly as the road crosses a spur of neighbouring Baden-Württemberg. This does, however, provide an opportunity to stop in the attractive little town of **Creglingen** where one of Tilman Riemenschneider's most famous masterpieces, the Marienalter, can be seen in the Herrgottskirche (Church of the Lord God).

About 6km beyond Creglingen the Romantische Strasse re-enters Bavaria for the third and last time and after about 17km if time permits, a brief halt should be made in the village of **Detwang** on the outskirts of Rothenburg to visit the little 1000-year-old church of St Peter and St Paul. There is much of interest but the main attraction is another famous work by Riemenschneider, his Altar of the Holy Cross. It was originally made in 1508 for St Michael's Chapel in Rothenburg and was moved to Detwang in 1653. After being in the hands of the Teutonic Order the church became the Lutheran (Protestant) parish church in 1544.

After a few minutes cross the river and climb steeply up to the walls

The ring wall at Rothenburg

of **Rothenburg ob der Tauber** (Rothenburg above the Tauber). The town walls are complete (total length 2.5km) and ample free car parks are available outside them. As one approaches Rothenburg today it must look much as it has done to travellers over the centuries for little has changed. So must the invading Swedish mercenaries of General Tilly have seen it in 1633; but they fully intended to ravage and destroy the town to take revenge upon the citizens for their stubborn defence. Tilly rode into the market place and, having lined up Bürgermeister Nusch and the town councillors before him, demanded wine before giving the soldiers leave to do their worst. He was handed a large silver cup and drank deeply; 'How much does this cup hold?' he demanded of Nusch. Upon learning that it held more than 3 litres he challenged the Bürgermeister to drain it in a single draught saying that if he did so, the city and the lives of the people would be spared. The cup was refilled and handed to the trembling Nusch who put it to his lips and drank steadily until it was drained. To the mayor's surprise, General Tilly kept his word and Rothenburg was saved. The story is remembered each year at Whitsuntide when it is the subject of a folk-play; and every day at 11 o'clock crowds gather in the market place to see the drama re-enacted — albeit rather stiffly

PLACES OF INTEREST IN ROTHENBURG

Town Walls and Towers
The well preserved walls can be followed right round the town (2.5km).

St Jakob's Church
(1311–1471)
Works of art including three Riemenschneider altars.

Kriminalmuseum
History of crime and punishment. Rather gruesome collection of instruments of torture.

Doll and Toy Museum
Dolls from 1780 to 1940 and other toys.

Town Hall
A fine thirteenth- and sixteenth-century building and a remarkable bird's eye view from the tower.

Puppet Theatre
Performances for various age groups.

— by wooden busts of Tilly and Nusch in windows either side of the clock on the front of the Hall of Councillors.

More than 300 years were to pass before the town was again threatened with destruction when, during the closing stages of World War II, General Devers was planning an assault with his American troops. By chance an American citizen working with the army knew and loved the city and he was able to persuade Devers to spare it if a surrender could be arranged. The civilian himself worked out the surrender terms and the following day Rothenburg was declared an open city. Its beauties are enjoyed today because of this intervention by J.J. McCloy who was later to become the US High Commissioner in Germany and, fittingly, Honorary Patron of Rothenburg.

It cannot be denied that Rothenburg (population 12,500) is a perfect gem and in summer it is very crowded. The discerning traveller is advised to come at a quiet time of year to enjoy the many delights. Then he can stroll through the pleasant old streets, walk the walls or enjoy a leisurely meal in one of the excellent hostelries in the town. St Jakob's church (1311–1471) has many works of art including three Riemenschneider altars; there is a fine organ on which there are regular recitals in the summer. The medieval Kriminalmuseum has a gruesome collection of instruments of torture from all over Europe and traces the history of crime and punishment — not for the squeamish. The Puppen- und Spielzeug (doll and toy) Museum has dolls from 1780 to 1940 and many other toys. The tower of the *Rathaus* (thirteenth and sixteenth century) provides a wonderful bird's eye view of the town and surrounding countryside. The little Puppet Theatre has shows to appeal to various age groups. But above all, Rothenburg is a place for walking and looking.

From a base in or near Rothenburg many worthwhile excursions are possible. The motorist could reach the Main Valley towns of Ochsenfurt and Marktbreit comfortably in half an hour and Würzburg itself in less than an hour. **Uffenheim** is a pleasant town and has a highly superior camp/caravan site adjacent to the large, modern, heated outdoor swimming pool. To the north-east on the edge of the Naturpark Steigerwald, **Bad Windsheim** (population 12,000) is noted specially for the Fränkisches-Freiland open-air museum in which houses and farms have been re-erected to display the life-style and conditions of the Franconian countryside from the fourteenth century to the present. No dead museum this; the houses are assembled in three tiny villages and rural life carries on as in the past. Here also are the Ochsenhof-Museum, local history and art housed in a former grain store dating from 1537 and the Vorgeschichts-museum, a branch of the pre-history museum in Munich telling the geological and geographical history of this area.

East of Rothenburg on the southern fringe of the Naturpark Frankenhöhe is **Ansbach**, the *Kreisstadt* (administrative centre) of this area with close on 50,000 inhabitants. The *Schloss* (palace) is the former Margrave's residence, started in 1713 on the site of an earlier palace. The great hall is two storeys high with a musicians' gallery along one side and a ceiling fresco by C. Carlone. The *Spiegel-kabinett* (mirror chamber) is remarkable with its many framed mirrors and valuable groups of porcelain figures and vases by many great European manufacturers. The present design of the *Hofgarten* was created in the first half of the eighteenth century and it has a 110m-long (360ft) orangery. The Margrave's museum is concerned particu-larly with the natural history of central Franconia from the earliest times until the end of the Roman period. The earliest parts of the former collegiate church of St Gumbertus date from the thirteenth century but it has been extensively altered over the intervening centuries; its three prominent towers have now become the emblem of the town.

Back on the Romantische Strasse, **Schillingsfürst** (population 2400) lies to the east of the road some 12km south of Rothenburg. The small baroque-style *Schloss* is the former residence of the princes of Hohenlohe-Schillingsfürst. It occupies a good vantage point on a spur

PLACES OF INTEREST TO VISIT FROM ROTHENBURG

UFFENHEIM
20km N. Interesting small town. Fine swimming pool.

BAD WINDSHEIM
25km NW. Noted for its extensive Franconian open-air museum.

ANSBACH
35km E. Busy larger town with much to see including former Margrave's palace.

SCHILLINGSFÜRST
12km S. Richly decorated baroque palace with furniture, tapestries and porcelain.

DETWANG
2km down Tauber valley. 1000-year-old church of St Peter and St Paul. Riemenschneider's altar of the Holy Cross.

of the Franconian upland which falls quite sharply here to the south. The rooms in the *Schloss* are decorated with liberal stucco and contain fine furniture and porcelain. The unique oxen-treadmill in one of the outbuildings should not be missed.

Since Rothenburg the Romantic Road has been the B25 and the next stop is at **Feuchtwangen** some 40km away, a pleasant little town (population 10,500) which suffers a little from the proximity of Rothenburg. It does not make too much of its designation as a health resort but there is plenty to interest the visitor. Legend has it that Karl der Grosse (Charlemagne) founded the *Kloster* here after, arriving exhausted from the hunt, he was led by a dove to a spring which is now marked by the little dove fountain. A more substantial historical fact is that monks, probably from Hirsau in the Black Forest, founded a Christian establishment here in 817 from which developed the present collegiate church. This Romanesque building is of considerable interest to the historian but the casual visitor will be particularly attracted to the altar to St Mary created by Michael Wohlgemuth, the teacher of Albrecht Dürer. Both this church and the neighbouring St John's are now Protestant buildings. St John's is first documented as the parish church in 1257 but parts of it are much older. The altar, baptismal font, tabernacle and pulpit are all fifteenth century and the crucifix seventeenth century.

Every corner of Feuchtwangen is steeped in history and the visitor will find his stay more interesting if he arms himself first with explanatory leaflets from the information office in the market place. Roman-style architecture is at its best in the 800-year-old cloisters which become the location of the open-air theatre in the summer months.

*St George's
Church,
Dinkelsbühl*

After the Old Town Festival at the beginning of June, the 'most beautiful little open-air stage in Germany' opens in the middle of that month and from then until the beginning of August the actors perform either the sombre *Tragedy of Florian Geyer*, a story of the peasant revolt or the colourful *Merry Wives of Windsor*. The *Heimatmuseum* here is of outstanding interest and contains many examples of the varied and often amusing folk-culture of the district.

Only 13km separate Feuchtwangen from **Dinkelsbühl**, yet another charming medieval town. Free car parking is outside the old town walls and perhaps the first feature of note is the picturesque array of towers, many of them of unusual design. A little smaller than

---

PLACES OF INTEREST IN FEUCHTWANGEN

Former Collegiate Church
Thirteenth century. St Mary altar (1483) by Albrecht Dürer's teacher M. Wohlgemuth.

St John's Church
Very old with valuable contents from fifteenth and seventeenth centuries.

800-Year-Old Romanesque Cloisters
Scene of open-air theatre in summer.

Heimatmuseum
Folk culture of the district. One of the better local museums.

Dinkelsbühl

Rothenburg, Dinkelsbühl gives the impression of living much more in the present and is obviously a centre for the local population as well as a tourist resort, with old houses, fountains, churches, walls and towers. Do not allow modern shop-fronts to detract from the glories above them. In the market place note the Deutsches Haus Hotel (1440), considered to be one of the finest half-timbered houses in southern Germany. Visit the sixteenth-century Ratstrinkstube, the former councillors' taproom. Outstanding amongst the town's several churches is the Catholic parish church of St George. It is an important Gothic building erected between 1448–99, the finest example of a south German hall church. The three aisles have a common height of 22.5m (74ft), exactly the same as the width of the church which is 77m (252ft) long. Amongst several altars there is one presented by the shoe-makers' guild and dedicated to St Crispin, patron saint of cobblers the world over.

Dinkelsbühl has a remarkably lively programme of entertainments and activities for its guests. Musical and theatrical presentations are numerous and in the summer months there is a special programme of events for children and young teenagers. Various festivals also feature in the yearly round, the most famous being the Dinkelsbühl *Kinderzeche*, children's festival, another reminder of General Tilly and the Swedish hordes. It was in 1632 that this town was besieged

PLACES OF INTEREST IN DINKELSBÜHL AND NÖRDLINGEN

DINKELSBÜHL
Town Walls and Towers

Deutsches Haus (1440)
Considered one of the finest half-timbered houses in south Germany.

St George's Church (1448–99)
Magnificent Gothic. Fine example of a south German hall church.

NÖRDLINGEN
Town Walls and Towers

St George's Church (1444–1508)

94m-high (308ft) tower named Daniel.

Former Carmelite Monastery St Salvator
Notable fifteenth-century wall frescos and high altar.

Rathaus
Fourteenth-century town hall with external Renaissance staircase (1618). *Bundesstube* with old wall paintings.

Town Museum
Housed in the Spital zum Heiligen Geist (1518–64). Building and contents both of interest.

and, like Rothenburg the following year, held out stubbornly against the invaders. In the end there were not enough able-bodied men left to man the battlements. Most mayors would have sent a civic dignitary to Tilly to plead for clemency but the Dinkelsbühlers had another idea. The gates were opened and a small boy marched out followed by the entire child population of the town. Each child carried flowers and they marched solemnly towards the enemy camp. The general's heart softened and he spared the town. Every year since then, except in times of disaster the *Kinderzeche* has been celebrated each July and is now a fine folk festival with music, dancing and a representation of the town's patron St George slaying the famous dragon. It is easy to get out into the countryside to the east of Dinkelsbühl and the visitor may wish to explore some of the territory described in Chapter 7.

Continue southwards along the Romantische Strasse leaving Franconia and entering Swabia to pause in **Wallerstein** nearly 30km south of Dinkelsbühl and perhaps climb the 65m-high (213ft) Burgfelsen, a rocky outcrop with splendid views over the area known as the Ries. The castle (with porcelain museum) and its gardens may be visited; there are various festivals and an autumn fair. Most visitors will, however, be anxious to hurry on the few kilometres to **Nördlingen**, an exciting medieval town of some 20,000 inhabitants.

PLACES OF INTEREST FROM NÖRDLINGEN TO DONAUWÖRTH

HARBURG
On B25 17km SE of Nördlingen. Attractive little town dominated by big castle. Conducted tours.

Town Museum
Works by Riemenschneider, also tapestries and ivories.

Town Hall and ancient bridge over River Wörnitz

FÜNFSTETTEN
8km NE of Harburg. Terminal of steam museum railway to Monheim, 7km further east on B2.

Fifteen million years ago an enormous meteorite struck the earth and created the 25km-wide shallow crater of which Nördlingen is the central point. The geological puzzle about the origins of this 'crater' was solved as a spin-off of the training of NASA astronauts in the area. There has been a settlement here since earliest history but of immediate interest is the remarkably intact town wall of 1327, still in its original state with five gates and eleven towers. The complete circuit of the town on the wall is a modest stroll of 3.5km and is a useful introduction to the narrow streets and alleys which can then be explored at leisure.

Right in the centre is the town church of St George with its 94m-high (308ft) tower called Daniel. There are sufficient sights here to occupy the tourist for quite a long time including the fourteenth-century church of St Salvator, the Reichstadtmuseum which includes a fine art gallery and the 700-year-old *Rathaus* with its famous external staircase. Every third year (1990, 1993, etc) in September there is a historical festival in honour of the city walls. Cars are banished from the old town which is given over to merry-making. Regular events in Nördlingen include concerts and theatrical productions during the winter months, a medieval spring festival on a Monday in May with a procession of school children, Nördlingen Fair in the fortnight after Whitsun, horse-racing in July and open-air theatre in July and August. Details and exact dates for all these events are available from the Städt. Verkehrsamt, Marktplatz 2, 8860 Nördlingen. Nördlingen is served by rail and it may be mentioned here that all principal places now on the route south are readily accessible by public transport.

From Nördlingen the route turns south-east and in about 17km reaches **Harburg**, the name of both the town (population 5600) and

PLACES OF INTEREST IN AND AROUND DONAUWÖRTH

Parish Church of the Assumption (1444–61)
Late Gothic hall church. Fifteenth-century stained glass windows.

Church of the Holy Cross (1717–20)
Heiliges-Kreuz-Strasse. Fine baroque church by J. Schmuzer.

Fuggerhaus (1539)
Reichsstrasse. Beautiful Renaissance building with large portico.

Hintermeierhaus or Gerberhaus
Im Ried 103. Old fifteenth-century half-timbered house now the *Heimatmuseum*.

Schloss
At Leitheim 8km E of town centre. Noted for chamber music concerts by candlelight May to October.

of the impressive castle above. This is no ruin but the biggest surviving castle in south Germany. Building took place from the twelfth to the eighteenth centuries, some of it in the baroque style. Conducted tours of the complex include the church, ramparts, keep, etc and take place daily except between 1 January and 15 March when the castle is closed to the public. The town museum contains works by Tilman Riemenschneider and a collection of tapestries as well as Norman ivory work. The stately *Rathaus* is one of a number of fine timbered buildings and the ancient stone bridge over the River Wörnitz is also not to be missed. If this attractive little town has become rather overshadowed by its bigger neighbours — Rothenburg, Dinkelsbühl and Nördlingen — this at least means that it is a more peaceful place to linger. Leisure hours can be spent in many different ways — fishing in or boating on the Wörnitz; swimming in the Ozon-Hallenbad with its sauna, tennis, bowling and above all, walking, for Harburg is at the centre of a network of well marked footpaths.

It is about 20km from Harburg to **Donauwörth** (population 20,000) where the Wörnitz feeds into the Danube (Donau). It is a very popular centre lying at the crossing of the Romantische Strasse with the east-west route along the famous river (described in a later chapter). As the cultural and economic capital of northern Swabia (Schwaben) there is a rich and varied choice of entertainment and activity for visitors. The essential sights to be seen include the parish church built 1444–61, the significant baroque Church of the Holy Cross, the treasures of which include the most famous monstrance of the craftsman Anton Betle (1716), the Fuggerhaus (1539) and the

The Residenz at
Würzburg

Statue of St Johann
Nepomuk, Würzburg

Wörnitz Tower, Dinkelsbühl

Hintermeierhaus (late fifteenth century), now the *Heimatmuseum*. The Reichstrasse is one of the most beautiful streetscapes in southern Germany. June and July are the months of festivity here, a folk festival, *Schwäbischwerder* children's day and the Reichstrasse festival all following in rather quick succession. Between May and October there are classical chamber music concerts by candlelight in the *Schloss* at nearby **Leitheim**; advance booking is essential. Dates and details of events are available from the Städt. Verkehrsamt, Rathaus, 8850 Donauwörth. Needless to say, the usual range of activities is available and the tourist office can provide suggestions for cycle touring. There is a large caravan park about 8km south of the town at **Mertingen** on the fringe of the Augsburg Nature Park.

From Donauwörth B2 becomes the Romantische Strasse and there is nothing of special interest in the 43km to Augsburg. The motorist could, if he wished, make a wide sweep to the west and explore some of the Augsburg Nature Park before heading for the city itself.

Augsburg is one of the biggest centres outside Munich. The name derives from its founder, the Roman Emperor Augustus. It has been a trade and travel focal point for the whole of its 2000-year history. It is not a place to be dismissed in a few words. Its $1/4$ million inhabitants see to it that culture and progress go hand in hand as befits the place which produced such sons as Mozart, the Holbeins and Brecht. Here, early aviator Soloman Idler tried to fly in 1635, Rudolf Diesel invented and tested his revolutionary internal combustion engine at the end of the last century and Willy Messerschmidt had his aircraft factory, one of his machines having been the first to break the sound barrier in 1943. It was the home of Hans Holbein the Elder whose paintings are in the cathedral. Hans Fugger was a village weaver who arrived in the fourteenth century and never looked back. The family prospered and became bankers of international repute, like the Rothschilds of a much later age. The Fuggers put their wealth to good use and charitable purposes including the Fuggerei, a little town within a town: 106 houses were built for citizens and workers 'of good repute' and let to them in 1525 for a 'peppercorn' rent which their successors still enjoy today. In fact in modern terms it works out at DM 1.71 per year!

As discovered in Würzburg, all the main sights are to be found within a very compact area in the centre of the city and once again the advice to motorists is to park the car and explore on foot. The *Dom*

The Ladies' Courtyard at the Fuggerhaus, Augsburg

makes a good starting point; the first cathedral was built in the tenth century on the site of the earliest Roman settlement. In 1047–63 it was rebuilt as a triple-naved Romanesque basilica and from 1320 was Gothicized and widened to five naves with the addition of five chapels at the east end. Apart from size, the casual sightseer may not find the exterior particularly exciting. Inside however, it is a different matter. Under the west choir is the old crypt from 1060 and from the same period are five windows containing what is reputed to be the oldest stained glass in the world. Supported by two lions, an early bishop's throne is thought to date from about 1100, a monumental piece of interior architecture. Of particular interest and value are the paintings of Hans Holbein the Elder (1465–1524) and one by G. Petel painted about 1630.

A short walk northwards from the cathedral is the birthplace of Leopold Mozart, father of Wolfgang Amadeus. The house is now a museum and memorial to this famous musical family. Returning past the *Dom* take the opportunity of seeing the former bishops' Residenz built and added to over the long period 1508–1773 and perhaps rest for a while in the pleasant *Hofgarten* laid out in 1739. The church of St Anna is outwardly insignificant but contains the family vault and chapel of the Fugger family built in the style of the Florentine and Venetian Renaissance. Restoration work was carried out under the direction of Elias Holl (1573–1646), the city architect who had such a great influence on many buildings still in existence today and, indeed, on the layout of the town itself. He was responsible for the magnificent *Rathaus* started at the beginning of the Thirty Years' War and topped out in 1618. With its seven storeys it was a veritable skyscraper — never before had anybody dared to go to such heights. The building was seriously damaged in World War II but has been fully restored and presents a fine picture across the square with twin onion-domes flanking a central gable. The nearby Zeughaus as its name suggests, was originally an arsenal. Built between 1602–7 it too was the concept of E. Holl and is the earliest example of a baroque façade in Germany. Almost next door is the Fuggerhaus (1512–15) with its courtyards and next again is the Schaezler-Palais (1765–7) the most beautiful rococo building in Augsburg with a grandiose banqueting hall.

At the south end of the old town — at the opposite pole to the *Dom*, so to speak — is St Ulrich's *Münster,* a Catholic late Gothic church, the foundation stone of which was laid by Emperor Maximilian I in 1500. The church contains a number of interesting relics associated with the history of Augsburg. Back towards the old town centre is the former Dominican church of St Magdalene housing the museum of pre-history and relics of the Roman occupation. Built 1513–15 as a double-naved church with a row of chapels along each side and decorated during the years 1716–24 in elegant rococo stucco by the Feuchtmayers, it makes a fine setting for the historical exhibits. Many of the towers which once formed part of the town fortifications are still standing. A little way east from the Roman museum and across the Stadtbach (town brook) is one of these, the Volgeltor, where a left turn leads into the Fuggerei, the unique little 'town within a town' already mentioned.

Augsburg also has a wide variety of entertainment especially for music-lovers. From October to June, the Stadttheater presents opera, operetta, ballet, drama and orchestral music. The Comedy Theatre also functions during the same period but is probably more suited to the native taste. Everyone could enjoy the shows at the puppet theatre near the Rotes Tor — one of the towers — at the south end of the old town. Here too, is the open-air theatre where operas and

PLACES OF INTEREST IN AND AROUND AUGSBURG

Cathedral (1046–63 and 1320)
Very old stained glass. Paintings by Hans Holbein the Elder.

Former Bishops' Residenz(1508–1733)
Pleasant baroque *Hofgarten* (1739).

Church of St Anna
Annaplatz. Built, enlarged and restored 1321–1616. Rococo interior 1747–9. Family vault and chapel of Fugger family.

Town Hall (1618)
A very imposing baroque *Rathaus* by E. Holl.

Zeughaus (1602–7)
Zeughausplatz. Also by E. Holl with first baroque façade in Germany by J. Heinz.

Schaezler-Palais (1765–7)
Maximilianstrasse 46. A most beautiful rococo building with grandiose banqueting hall.

Churches of St Ulrich and St Anna (St Ulrich's Minster)
Ulrichsplatz 19. One of the huge altars incorporates the Christmas crib scene. Baroque preaching hall (1710).

Former Dominican Church of St Magdalene (1513–15)
Elegant rococo stucco (1716–24). Now a museum of prehistoric and Roman periods.

Fuggerei
The 'town within a town' built about 1525. 106 houses built for citizens and workers 'of good repute'.

FRIEDBERG
(6km E of Augsburg city centre)
Town Walls and Towers

Pilgrimage Church Unseres Herrn Ruhe
E of town. Beautiful eighteenth-century baroque building. First class stucco.

Castle
Mainly 1552 and mid-seventeenth century

Town Hall (1670–80)
Lovely building influenced by E. Holl.

KLOSTERLECHFELD
(24km S of Augsburg)
Pilgrimage and Klosterkirche Maria Hilf (1603)
The Pantheon in Rome was used as the pattern for this fine church by E. Holl. Rococo interior.

operettas are performed in June and July when there is also the Augsburger Mozartsommer, a series of chamber music concerts held in the banqueting hall of the Schaezler-Palais.

Friedberg (population 26,500) is on a short spur just a few kilometres along the B300 east of Augsburg; in spite of its charming townscape it is not as crowded as some of its better-known neighbours. It is significant that one of the 'sights' here is the silhouette of

Augsburg seen in the west from the town wall. The eighteenth-century pilgrimage church Unseres Herrn Ruhe is claimed to be one of the most beautiful places of worship built in the Bavarian baroque manner. It is reached through a leafy walk at the east end of the town and has an unusually richly decorated interior with mighty reddish-grey marble columns with golden capitals and delicate rose stucco work by F.X. Feuchtmayer. The cupola painting in the choir is by C.D. Asam. Little is left of the original thirteenth-century castle but later additions, the tower from 1552 and works from the middle of the seventeenth century still overlook the town and today house the excellent *Heimatmuseum*. The *Rathaus* (1670–80) was built by a pupil of Elias Holl, famed for his work in Augsburg, and the hand of the master is very evident in this lovely building. A folk festival takes place here at the beginning of August.

To continue southwards, return towards Augsburg but avoid going right into the city again by turning left after about 3km into the B2 (signed Fürstenfeldbruck and München) and follow this for 11km to **Mering**, there turn right towards Königsbrunn (8km) to rejoin the Romantische Strasse (now B17) after crossing the River Lech. The map reveals that the Lech marks the eastern edge of the area known as Allgäu and a little of the country between the river and the western boundary of Bavaria is explored later in this chapter while the country east of the Lech will be the subject of Chapter 3. The 26km to Landsberg can be covered as quickly as the heavy traffic permits for there is not too much of outstanding interest on this section. **Kloster-lechfeld** about midway deserves a brief mention though. The pilgrimage and Klosterkirche Maria Hilf was built in 1603 by Elias Holl from Augsburg as a result of a bequest made by the patrician widow Regina Imhoff of that town. Holl adopted the Pantheon in Rome as his pattern for this impressive church with its cylindrical form and cupola. A main aisle was added later and the adjacent *Kloster* was built by the Franciscans in 1666–9. The interior of the church is decorated in the rococo style. Unless one intends to visit Klosterlechfeld, however, a more pleasant route from Mering is by the road on the east side of the river, reaching Landsberg via Prittriching and Beuerbach.

For a little while now the route has been in Upper Bavaria (Oberbayern). **Landsberg**, in a rather wild and romantic setting, is a town of 19,000 inhabitants, one of the main entrances being the Bayertor (Bavarian Gate), erected in the fifteenth century and considered to be one of the finest town gates in southern Germany. The

Landsberg market place

beautiful *Marktplatz* is dominated by the *Rathaus* (1699–1702) which has first class external stucco by Dominikus Zimmermann who was *Bürgermeister* here from 1759 to 1764; he was also responsible for the interior decoration. There is a gallery containing the works of the Anglo-German artist Sir Hubert von Herkomer (1849–1914). In front of the *Rathaus* the elaborate fountain with a statue of Mary dates from 1783. The citadel here is the place where Adolf Hitler was imprisoned in 1924 and wrote *Mein Kampf*; ironically, Nazi war criminals were also incarcerated here awaiting trial in Nuremberg after World War II.

Outstanding amongst the churches of Landsberg is Mariae Himmelfahrt (Assumption of the Blessed Virgin), the parish church. This mighty fifteenth-century basilica replaced a thirteenth-century building on the same site. The baroque interior is of a rarely seen richness and the eye is drawn towards the vast high altar with its figures of Joseph and Joachim and the three archangels. Unusually, the windows flanking the altar are of stained glass and this seems to enhance rather than detract from the gilded reliefs. St Johannes-Kirche (1741) was built to plans drawn up by D. Zimmermann and has a number of interesting features. The former Jesuit *Kloster* church of the Holy Cross was built 1752–4 and replaced an earlier one built to plans of Elias Holl less than 200 years earlier. The rococo decoration of the present building includes work by several notable craftsmen, D. Zimmermann being responsible for the stucco in the sacristy. It is interesting to note the way in which many of the craftsmen of earlier centuries worked in a comparatively small area. Riemenschneider was almost exclusively active in the Tauber valley and here in the Lech valley, Holl and Zimmermann have had a significant influence on architectural trends.

Landsberg is one of many places with a traditional Christmas market (*Christkindlmarkt*); there is also a theatre and concerts are given in the *Rathaus* and in some of the churches. A visit to the town tourist office at Hauptplatz 1 or to the area office (Von-Kühlmann-Strasse 15) will reveal that, in the area soon to be reached, activities like walking, cycling and water sports are very popular. The area office publishes an annual guide to more than fifty *Hobbyferien*, that is, holiday packages with a particular theme. This is not the place for a catalogue of the holidays on offer but a few examples will indicate the sort of thing available. The term *Hobby* is given a rather broad interpretation. Seven-day cycling holidays offer a choice between bed and breakfast in private houses or in traditional inns and include hire of cycles or tandems and provision of route maps. A variation combines a modest cycle tour (230km) with professional tuition in sketching of landscape and architecture, no previous experience necessary. The cycle tours can often be made *ohne Gepäck*, ie without luggage, which is forwarded independently to the next overnight stop. In an area with several designated long-distance paths it is useful to know that rambles can also be made on the *ohne Gepäck* basis. One arrangement based on the Lech-Höhenweg has the option of 2 days cycle touring in addition to the walking days.

In general, the touring holidays are not 'conducted', the participants are provided with maps, accommodation vouchers, etc to make their own way from place to place. They are therefore specially suitable for couples or family groups but if one wishes to be included in a larger party this can be arranged sometimes. A quick look at some of the other possibilities in the programme: a 3-day visit to Landsberg for the *Christkindlmarkt* at the beginning of December, watercolour painting, glass-painting, bowling, riding and sailing. There is even a *Hochzeit* (wedding) offer which includes accommodation in the romantic old town, civil and church ceremonies, a horse-drawn coach to the church and dinner by candlelight and the *Flitterwochen*, a week's honeymoon (priced for two!) could well provide newly-weds with a unique and memorable start to married life.

The basic Lech-Höhenweg closely follows the river all the way from Landsberg to Füssen and good waymarking makes it unnecessary to give a detailed description of the route here but the content of the 7-day *ohne Gepäck* package may be of interest to those contemplating such a holiday:

Day 1. Reception in Landsberg in the evening, descriptive slide show and distribution of maps, vouchers, etc. Day 2. Guided tour of Landsberg and transport to a restaurant at Zollhaus 10km north of the town for lunch, returning on foot along the river bank. Day 3. Continue southwards on east bank of river and cross to Hohenwart/Römerkessel; 'bus excursion to Kloster Wessobrunn with guided tour of the monastery and to the pilgrimage church at Vilgertshofen (see Chapter 3). Day 4. On the east, and later the west, banks of the river to Schongau by which time the glorious spectacle of the Alps should be clearly visible ahead. Day 5. The route continues on the west bank past Burggen to the Litzauer Schleife, a spectacular horseshoe in the river and a natural monument; along the Lech 'lake' to Lechbruch. Day 6. From Lechbruch through Prem and between the two lakes Bannwaldsee and Forggensee to Füssen. Day 7. Disperse after breakfast in Füssen. The price of this holiday includes bed and breakfast in good hotels or inns (rooms mostly with private facilities), luggage transport from place to place, the bus journeys, the guided tours and the lunch at Zollhaus.

The Romantische Strasse continues from Landsberg as the B17 and soon becomes a picturesque route with glimpses of the River Lech on the left. For some way the route passes through a charming area known as Pfaffenwinkel — very loosely translated as 'Priestly

PLACES OF INTEREST IN LANDSBERG

Bavarian Gate
Fifteenth century.

Town Hall (1699–1702)
Fine external stucco and a lovely fountain in front.

Church of the Assumption of the Blessed Virgin
Rich baroque interior with huge high altar. Fifteenth century.

Church of St Johannes (1741)

Vorderanger. Fine altars and paintwork.

Former Jesuit Church of the Holy Cross (1752–4)
Pulpit, wrought-iron railings and carvings on confessional boxes should be noted.

Museum
Von-Kühlmann-Strasse 2. Bronze Age finds, sculpture, painting and town history.

Corner'. The strange name was introduced into German literature in 1756 when Franz Sales Gailler, the priest of nearby Raisting published his book *Vindelicia Sacra*; it told of a land of ecclesiastics and monks, the Latin term *Angulus Sacerdotum* being rendered in German as Pfaffenwinkel. The area concerned certainly had more than its fair share of religious establishments; it is roughly bounded on the west and east by the rivers Lech and Loisach and in the north and south by the Klöster Andechs on the Ammersee and Ettal near Oberammergau.

Leaving Landsberg, the jagged outline of the Alps will — weather permitting — be clearly visible on the southern skyline some 70km away. The giant Zugspitze (2963m, 9718ft) is almost directly ahead and the spectacular peaks extend east and west as far as the eye can see. There is no finer approach to the Alps than this, even Switzerland cannot quite equal the long-distance view that is obtained as one travels the closing stretches of the Romantische Strasse. Ever since the Danube was crossed far to the north the road has been climbing imperceptibly, each town lying just a little higher than the previous one. **Hohenfurch** (population 1200), 22km from Landsberg, is already well into the foothills of the Alps at an altitude of 700m (2296ft). This is an attractive rural holiday resort but the object of a visit here should be to visit the parish church of Maria Himmelfahrt (Assumption) (noted for its stucco in the pattern of the Wessobrunn school) and the late Gothic chapel of St Ursula.

In about 5km **Schongau** (population 10,600) is reached, an *Erholungsort* and a popular centre for the exploration of a beautiful area. A favourite pastime in Bavaria is *Eisstockschiessen*, a sort of curling played on a smooth asphalt rink or *Bahn* which is played in Schongau all year round. The old town wall is well preserved and there are a number of interesting and attractive buildings. Here again the parish church is named Maria Himmelfahrt. It was rebuilt in the eighteenth century following the collapse of one of the towers of the previous building in 1667. The interior decoration was the work of a number of renowned artists including D. Zimmermann who created the stucco in the choir(1748) and a craftsman from Wessobrunn who was responsible for the stucco in the triple naves. The so-called Ballenhaus in the Marienplatz was erected in 1515 to serve as a *Rathaus*. Both summer and winter visitors are catered for here; there is a ski-school and cross-country skiing trails are marked out.

An *Erholungsort* , as here in Schongau, is a general health resort, a place for recreation and recuperation; *Kurort* or *Luftkurort* refer to resorts where a *Kur* may be taken — a course of medical treatment, diet, etc. The latter are places where the air is considered specially beneficial for certain conditions. Spas are major health resorts with a wide range of medical treatment, often based on water therapy, and the names of such places are prefixed by the word *Bad* (bath). Many people prefer to stay in a health resort for the wide range of leisure facilities rather than for medical reasons. In Schongau, as well as the customary *Hallenbad* and heated *Freibad*, more informal bathing may be enjoyed at several places along the Schongauer See, an 8km-long fjord-like lake which also provides opportunities for sailing, canoeing and wind-surfing. Boats can be hired.

There are also many well marked footpaths and a fairy-tale wood with a deer enclosure. A pleasant walk of 2km goes to **Altenstadt** where the Catholic church of St Michael is remarkably large for a rural parish church. In an area where it is usually thought that baroque reigns supreme it is surprising to find that this is an ancient basilica very much in its original condition. It is thought to have been completed around 1200 and King Ludwig I had it fully restored in 1826. Standing on a hill, the church is surrounded by a defensive wall, indeed, with its stumpy towers it looks like a fortified structure. Inside, the meagre decoration is in keeping with the character of the building but in the south nave there is one of the remaining Romanesque decorated wooden crosses, still with the original paint. Instead of the usual crown of thorns, the Grosse Gott von Altenstadt is depicted wearing a royal crown 3.21m (10.5ft) high and 3.20m (10.4ft) wide, the

---

PLACES OF INTEREST IN HOHENFURCH, SCHONGAU AND PEITING

HOHENFURCH
Parish Church of the Assumption
Stucco in Wessobrunn pattern and late Gothic chapel of St Ursula.

SCHONGAU
Town Hall

Parish Church of the Assumption
Fine stucco of the Wessobrunn style. Eighteenth century.

Ballenhaus (1515)
At one time the town hall. Inside, fine carved wooden ceiling.

Town Museum
Local and folklore collection.

PEITING
Parish Church of St Michael
Tower of the twelfth century or earlier.

---

cross dominates the otherwise almost bare interior. At one time the figures of Mary and John were here too but they have long since been removed to the Bavarian National Museum in Munich.

A mere 3km separate Schongau and neighbouring **Peiting** which is a town of similar size. St Michael is again the patron saint of the parish church which is worth a visit. The exact date of its tower is not known but it is certainly not later than twelfth century. The Romantische Strasse (still B17) continues southwards but a short detour to the east enables one to see several more places of interest. Take the B472 from Peiting to the health resort of **Hohenpeissenberg** (population 3000) and either of two picturesque routes from there to Peissenberg (population 10,500), 14km from Peiting, involving a fairly rapid descent into the Ammer valley.The view from Hohenpeissenberg (988m, 3240ft) is thought by some to equal that from any of the Alpine peaks three times as high. In **Peissenberg** the church Maria Aich and St George's Chapel with rare Gothic frescos are both worth visiting. Informal bathing and sauna facilities are available at the Rigi-Rutsch'n leisure park.

Doubling back to the south-west a road with striking views climbs steadily to bring us to **Böbing** in about 10km. A village of 1300 inhabitants, this is another recognised *Erholungsort* with provision for summer and winter visitors. Cross-country skiing is popular and many footpaths are kept clear for winter walkers. It is only about 5km to **Rottenbuch** (population 1700) yet another health resort. The old

PLACES OF INTEREST TO VISIT FROM LANDSBERG OR SCHONGAU

VILGERTSHOFEN.
(12km S of Landsberg, E of B17 and R.Lech)
Baroque Pilgrimage Church
Wessobrunn-style stucco, unusual ceiling painting.

WESSOBRUNN
22km SE of Landsberg in direction of Weilheim. Home of many famous artists and craftsmen of the eighteenth century.

**Parish Church of
St Johannes** (1757–9)

ALTENSTADT
(2km W of Schongau)
Parish Church of St Michael
Romanesque vaulted basilica.
Built about 1200.

HOHENPEISSENBERG
9km E of Schongau on B472.
Splendid views.

PEISSENBERG
(17km E of Schongau on B472)
Leisure Park Rigi-Rutsch'n

Church of Maria Aich

St George's Chapel
Rare Gothic frescos.

ROTTENBUCH
(12km S of Schongau on B23)
Former Augustinian Collegiate Church (1345)
Typical Gothic building transformed by later baroque decor.

Echelsbach Bridge
Over River Ammer.

The Ammer Gorge
Lovely Waterfalls.

WIES
(20km S of Schongau via B17 or B23)
Pilgrimage Church (1754)
The best-known of all small baroque churches.

STEINGADEN
(16km S of Schongau on B17)
Welfenmünster (1147)
Interesting façade. Within, many art relics from different periods.

Echelsbach Bridge (recently rebuilt) over the River Ammer should be noted and the former Augustinian collegiate church deserves attention. It is a Gothic basilica built on Romanesque foundations of the eleventh and twelfth centuries. The present church was dedicated in 1345 and is an example of a typical Gothic building transformed by baroque decoration. Entertainment is provided by traditional folk evenings (*Heimatabende*) and the peasant theatre has productions from May to September. Horse-lovers would be interested in the thoroughbred foal market in September. This is one of many places where the custom of the *Leonhardiritt* is observed. St Leonhard is regarded (along with St Martin) as the patron saint of animals and on St Leonhard's day, 6 November, horses are ridden around the church and traditionally blessed. The custom has developed into a full-scale folk festival in many places with a procession which includes decorated carts accompanied by the noisy cracking of whips.

A little to the south of Rottenbuch along the B23 turn right towards **Wildsteig** (population 1000), yet another *Erholungsort* — a former mining community — and a peaceful but popular spot especially for those wishing to discover some rare flora and fauna. The Ammer gorge or ravine is very attractive with lacy, veil-like waterfalls. Here again are *Heimatabende* and a peasant theatre (June-September) together with a *Leonhardiritt* which for some odd reason takes place in October. After looking at the parish church continue westwards and after a few minutes turn off the main road again to visit the most famous of all the little baroque churches. This is the so-called Wieskirche or, to be more precise, the Wallfahrtskirche zum gegeisselten Heiland in der Wies.

The origin of this church at **Wies** lies in an apparent miracle which occurred in 1730. A farmer here in this meadowland had in his field a religious emblem in the form of the Saviour tied to the flogging post and he insisted that as he passed one day the figure suddenly shed tears. He took this as a sign and immediately built a little field chapel at the spot. The story spread quickly and in no time at all the chapel became a great place of pilgrimage. It became necessary to replace the chapel with a proper church and after the necessary permission had been obtained the foundation stone was laid in 1746. The church was consecrated in 1754 and the interior decoration was completed with the installation of the organ 3 years later. The pale yellow walls and red roof outside in no way prepare one for the splendour within. Every detail of the decoration is purest rococo and it comes as no surprise to find that the prime architect was none other than Dominikus Zimmermann. In this creation he reached the pinnacle of his life's work and, in fact, he died here in a nearby house in 1766. Dominikus was assisted by his elder brother Johann Baptist (1680–1758) and by many other famous artists of the period. Words just cannot convey any idea of the spectacle of 'Wies'. Take time to visit this church, preferably out of the main tourist season. If not, attendance at one or more of the concerts given each year in June-August with the theme *Festlicher Sommer in der Wies* (Festive

The rococo church at Wies

Summer in Wies) would provide an opportunity for feasting ear and eye at the same time.

Back on the main road a left turn leads to Steingaden in about 4km. **Steingaden** (population 2400) is another recognised *Erholungsort* catering for summer and winter visitors with a good range of facilities and entertainments. The so-called Welfenmünster, founded by Duke Welf VI in 1147 before his departure to the second crusade, has preserved in its façade an authentic reminder of that period. The interior has an assortment of decorations from different periods, indeed, somebody described it as an open book on the history of art.

The remaining 22km of the Romantische Strasse leaves Upper Bavaria and the Pfaffenwinkel and re-enters Swabia in the area known as Allgäu, passing through pretty countryside and a series of small resorts, along the east shore of the Bannwaldsee with the 10km-long Forggensee sometimes visible behind. Much of the holiday activity here is naturally associated with these attractive lakes with their colourful summer camp sites. Approaching Schwangau two of the famous castles associated with King Ludwig II can be seen and this Romantic Road finally comes to an end in the town of **Füssen**, 350km from its northern tip in Würzburg. Castles and town will be described in Chapter 2.

Allgäu

Visitors must travel northwards now in order to explore that country lying between the River Lech and the western boundary of Bavaria; in other words, the Allgäu. This most beautiful area lies in the south-west corner of Bavaria or rather straddles the border between Bavaria and Baden-Württemberg and, for that matter, in terms of history and ethnic origins trespasses into the Austrian Bregenzerwald and into the near corner of Switzerland. However, no Allgäu border is marked on any map because it is, in the words of one authority, only 'a geographical idea' and certainly has nothing to do with today's administrative boundaries. This book is concerned, of course, only with Bavarian Allgäu.

In the height of the tourist season Allgäu is a very popular goal and the further south one goes the more people there seem to be. This is a very good reason for visiting the area 'out-of-season' if possible. There can be few more beautiful places than Allgäu in May when the fruit trees are in blossom and winter slowly withdraws to the high mountains, leaving the pastures to be covered with a lush green carpet which never dries out even in the hottest summer. The velvety brown cows emerge from their winter quarters and in some areas follow the receding snows up to the higher pastures. Not without reason does Allgäu claim to be the dairy of Germany with an enormous output of milk, butter and cheese. A remarkable phenomenon in spring and early summer is the arrival of *Tettigonia viridissima,* the great green grasshopper. Nowhere else is this insect seen in such numbers and the more normal small species are hopelessly outnumbered. The quiet days of autumn are also most pleasant, with the fruit being gathered, harvest festivals in swing and the cows ambling down to the lower pastures once again. The many excellent country inns are quiet after the hassle of the summer tourist season and the winter sports patrons have not yet arrived. In all seasons though, this is fine holiday country with many places of interest and beauty, as well as ample facilities for leisure activities.

Allgäu offers a number of gastronomic specialities and the visitor would be wise to try some of these when given the opportunity. The 'national' dish is *Allgäuer Kässpatzen* — noodles layered with fried onions and much cheese, most often *Emmentaler,* and melted butter poured over the whole. Various dumpling soups are popular especially on festive occasions. Freshwater fish from the many lakes in the Alpine foothills are very tasty and for the evening meal a lightly smoked country sausage called *Schübling* is often eaten. In general the menu will be weighted towards venison and similar dishes, frequently enriched with cheese. Cakes are very popular with the locals who are sometimes known to eat them as a main meal.

Thirty kilometres west of Landsberg the attractive town of **Mindelheim** (population 12,200) is one of those pleasant medieval towns where little seems to have changed over the centuries. The parish church of St Stephan was built at the beginning of the eighteenth century and incorporates the bell-tower from an earlier building. As recently as 1933 the interior was improved by the import of baroque contributions from various other churches. The Jesuit church in Maximilianstrasse was the work of the architect of the order, J. Holl (not to be confused with Elias Holl of Augsburg) and was completed in 1625–6. Holl was, however, able to make use of parts of an earlier Augustinian church. There is fine stucco work in the interior which is light and airy. The Liebfrauenkirche dates from 1455 but the interior had to be largely renewed after a fire in the eighteenth century. A famous wood-carving *Die Mindelheimer Sippe* is to be found here. It dates from about 1510–20 but the craftsman is unknown. Parts of the town wall and three of the towers are still preserved; one of these, the Obere Tor suffers the indignity of being dressed up in a grotesque costume each year at *Fasnacht,* the period of carnival which precedes Lent. On a hill just south of the town the Mindelburg — a castle dating from 1370 — provides a goal for a modest excursion with splendid views over the surrounding countryside.

Ten kilometres along a pretty road south-east from Mindelheim is the famous spa resort of **Bad Wörishofen**. Famous because it was here that Sebastian Kneipp founded his first centre to practise his particular kind of physiotherapy. Kneipp was born in the little Allgäu village of Stephansried in 1821, the son of a weaver. Probably through working in the damp cellar of his weaver father, he contracted consumption and for a time it seemed that he might not live. Sebastian appears to have been convinced quite early in life of the healing properties of water and he took the radical step of bathing in November in an ice-cold river which seemed successful in ridding him of the disease. Against the wishes of his parents he became a priest and eventually monsignor and papal chamberlain. At the same time,

PLACES OF INTEREST IN MINDELHEIM AND BAD WÖRISHOFEN

MINDELHEIM
Town Walls and Towers

Parish Church of St Stephan
Various baroque appointments.
Eighteenth century.

Jesuit Church (1625–6)
Maximilianstrasse. Fine stucco
work inside.

Liebfrauenkirche (1455)
Memminger Strasse. Contents
include famous wood-carving *Die
Mindelheimer Sippe*.

Mindelburg Castle (1370)

South of town. Splendid views of
the countryside.

BAD WÖRISHOFEN
Kneipp-Heilbad
The first medical treatment centre
founded by Sebastian Kneipp.

Parish Church
Former monastery church of
Capuchin monks with Wesso-
brunn-style stucco.

Dominican Klosterkirche
Rococo altars and stucco by D.
Zimmermann. Eighteenth century.

and now with opposition from the medical profession, he continued to develop his healing methods in Wörishofen. The success of his methods brought world renown, and many famous personages were amongst his patients; members of royal and aristocratic families from all over Europe and Russia, the Rothschilds from Paris and Theodore Roosevelt, later to become twenty-fifth president of the United States all made their way to Wörishofen. Sebastian Kneipp died in 1897 but his work lived on and there are now many Kneipp establishments in Allgäu combining modern medical centres with fashionable holiday resorts.

Having been awarded the honourable prefix, Bad Wörishofen today (population 13,600) is one of the outstanding spas of Germany. The high season is from 1 May to 15 October but this is very much an all-year resort and especially attractive in the short days of autumn. The sixteenth-century former monastery church of the Capuchin monks is the present parish church (with stucco in the style of the Wessobrunn school) The early eighteenth-century church and *Klos-ter* of the Dominican order is noted for its rococo altars and stucco by Dominikus Zimmermann.

Memmingen, 27km west of Mindelheim is quite a different matter. A busy town of 38,000 inhabitants, it is steeped in history as the first glance at the medieval town centre will show. One of the finest market places in Swabia is surrounded by stately old patrician houses and the Renaissance *Rathaus* (1589) with its rococo ornamentation. The so-called Siebendächerhaus (House with Seven Roofs) really does have this number and is one of the most photographed buildings in Bavaria. The house was built in 1601 by tanners who would hang out the hides to dry under the overhanging roofs which were provided for just this purpose. A former patrician palace of 1766 decorated in the rococo style now houses the town museum and art gallery. In Martin Luther Square, St Martin's Church was the result of a bequest made in the eleventh century although the church did not actually materialise for another 400 years. The choir stalls are dated 1499. The Frauenkirche, also built in the fifteenth century, is famed for its beautiful frescos. They had been covered over and only came to light again during restoration work in 1891. There are also many good examples of upper Swabian art of the late Gothic period on all the walls of the church.

Memmingen makes two contributions to jollity in July, firstly with a traditional children's festival and on the following Saturday with the famous Memmingen *Fischerstecken*. This is the occasion on which the town chooses its fisher-king for the following year. At eight in the morning spectators line the banks of the town stream and the fishermen spring into the water with their nets to fish out trout. In short, at the end of the day he who has landed the heaviest fish becomes 'king' but it is not, of course, quite as simple as that. Under the cheers and jeers of the townsfolk the fishers go about their task. Should they not get sufficiently wet during this hectic activity, the onlookers come equipped with buckets and pails to empty yet more water on to the hapless victims in the stream. The battle over, the fish are weighed in front of the *Rathaus*, the old 'king' is chased from the throne and the new one installed in his place. Needless to say, the associated festivities go on deep into the night. More conventional entertainment is provided in the town theatre and in the Stadthalle, a concert and exhibition hall and not to be confused with the *Rathaus*.

Ottobeuren, 10km to the south-east, is a *Kneippkurort* with 7000 inhabitants. Much of what was written about Bad Wörishofen applies equally to Ottobeuren but a significantly different history lies in Ottobeuren's close connection with the famous Benedictine abbey as it has developed. Although the establishment was founded in 764, buildings of the eleventh, twelfth, thirteenth and sixteenth centuries were the victims of fire and in the end the present complex was begun

PLACES OF INTEREST IN MEMMINGEN AND OTTOBEUREN

MEMMINGEN

Market Place and Town Hall (1589)
One of the best medieval town centres in Swabia.

Siebendächerhaus (1601)
Astonishing house with seven roofs, originally built by tanners for drying hides.

Town Museum
Zangmeisterstrasse 9. Housed in exuberant rococo palace of 1766.

St Martin's Church
Martin-Luther-Platz. Fifteenth century. Fine vaulted ceiling, carved choir stalls (1499).

Frauenkirche
Fifteenth century. Famous frescos, late Gothic wall paintings.

OTTOBEUREN

Klosterkirche of the Holy Trinity
One of the largest and most impressive baroque churches.

at the beginning of the eighteenth century. The most celebrated craftsmen of the day were assembled for the work and it is not surprising to discover that the industrious D. Zimmermann was amongst them together with his brother Johann Baptist and J.M. Feuchtmayer. The *Klosterkirche* is dedicated to the Holy Trinity and is one of the most impressive baroque churches as well as being one of the largest. The two towers reach up to 82m (269ft) and the interior is 89m (292ft) long with a world famous organ by Karl Riepp. This is the church in which Sebastian Kneipp was baptised on 17 May 1821. Nearby **Stephansried** was his birthplace and there is a memorial where his father's house once stood.

In this north-western corner of Allgäu there is a group of little resorts which deserve brief mention. The area is bisected by the north-south motorway A7, west of which is **Kronburg**, a little summer resort near the gorge of the River Iller with Schloss Kronburg and the Allgäu farm museum in nearby **Illerbeuren**. **Grönenbach** is a *Kneippkurort* (population 4200) with all the usual trimmings; the pilgrimage church of Maria Steinbach; the parish church of St Philipp and St Jakob (1479) which was given the baroque treatment in the seventeenth century and renovated in neo-Gothic in the nineteenth and, of course, the inevitable ancient castle. Other resorts include **Altusried** (population 7500) an *Erholungsort* noted for spectacular performances in the open-air theatre (July-August); **Dietmannsried** (population 6000), an unsophisticated scattered community close to the motorway with many footpaths, skiing trails and cycle routes and, finally, **Wiggensbach** (population 3200), a good family resort with plenty of interest — grass skiing on the slopes of the Blender (1072m, 3516ft), fine baroque church (1770-1).

Before going on to Kempten, the capital of Bavarian Allgäu, the visitor should look at one or two places between the A7 and the Romantische Strasse. **Wildpoldsried** (population 1900) 10km north-east of Kempten lies in the Leubas basin and is surrounded on three sides by Alpine foothills up to 900m (2950ft) in height, another good family resort specially suited to rambling and similar activities with a fifteenth-century parish church. **Obergünzburg** (population 5200), *Erholungsort*, at the junction of several picturesque roads on the River Günz, has a late Gothic parish church, *Heimatmuseum* with a specialised collection from the former German South Seas colonies and a historic folk festival cum rifle-shooting competition on the last Sunday in August and the first in September.

Kaufbeuren is a former free imperial city on the River Wertach. Today it has some 43,000 inhabitants. The medieval old town has some fine baroque houses, especially in the Kaiser-Max-Strasse. St Blasius' church, the oldest parts of which date from 1319, contains a famed carved altar by Jörg Lederer (1518) and many other items of historic interest. Several other old churches invite inspection including St Martin (1438–43), sixteenth-century Trinity and St Dominicus, originally from the twelfth century but rebuilt in the fifteenth, eighteenth and twentieth centuries. Kaufbeuren was the birthplace of the author Ludwig Ganghofer (1855–1920), a successful German writer. There is a memorial tablet on his house in Kirchplatz and the *Heimatmuseum* has a collection of mementoes associated with him. There is also a remarkable collection of crucifixes here.

Every year on the third Sunday in July there is the *Tänzelfest*, the oldest historical children's festival in Bavaria. Some 1600 children in authentic costumes present the ancient history of the town. The origins of this festival are not entirely clear but the popular view is that it was instituted by Emperor Maximilian I on 25 May 1497 after he had seen a boys' shooting festival and decreed that it should become an annual event. It was soon complemented by processions of drummers, pipers and flag-throwers. 'Emperor Maximilian' still plays a central role in the festival with a triumphal entry into the town. The main feature today is a procession in which the history of the town

PLACES OF INTEREST IN KAUFBEUREN AND MARKTOBERDORF

KAUFBEUREN

Baroque Houses in Kaiser-Max-Strasse

St Blasius' Church (1319)
Blasiusberg 13. Carved altar by Jörg Lederer (1518).

St Martin's Church (1438–43)

Heimatmuseum
Kaisergässchen 12–14. Collection includes memorabilia of writer Ludwig Ganghofer.

MARKTOBERDORF

St Martin's Parish Church (1732)
Striking windows, fine stucco and high altar.

Former Hunting Lodge of Bishops of Augsburg (1722–5)
Near church. Now houses part of Bavarian Academy of Music.

Heimatmuseum
In the old town hall. Town history and religious and folk art of eastern Allgäu.

from its foundation until the mid-nineteenth century is depicted by groups representing the various periods, the wars, the trades, happy times and sad times. There is an evening tattoo by torchlight outside the *Rathaus* and a firework display to round things off. Altogether a moving spectacle.

Marktoberdorf is an *Erholungsort* of 15,500 inhabitants. A pleasant well kept town in glorious countryside, it is especially favoured by those who prefer a fairly active holiday for which every facility is at hand. The parish church of St Martin was started in 1732 to plans by the Füssen architect J.G. Fischer who was born here in 1673. The building incorporates parts of an earlier Gothic church and a tower from 1680 although this was given an additional storey and an onion-dome. Close by the church is the Jagdschloss (1722–5), the former hunting lodge of the bishops of Augsburg. This was also the design of J.G. Fischer but the building was enlarged to its present size only 40 years later. Marktoberdorf is in the centre of a network of cycle routes, most of which are designed to be on traffic-free roads. It also serves the walker well with many well kept footpaths and is at one end of the long-distance path called Prälatenweg (Prelates' Way) which runs eastwards from here to Kochel in Upper Bavaria. Thus, starting in Allgäu, it crosses the Lech-Höhenweg already mentioned, crosses the Romantic Road and penetrates into the lake country described in Chapter 3. Space does not permit a detailed description of the whole route but the western section is varied and interesting and could make a good ramble in its own right.

The starting point is at the *Schloss* in Marktoberdorf where an inn, the Sailerkeller, supplies refreshments. Look out for the distinctive waymark of two bishop's crooks and start through the kilometre-long Lindenallee towards **Bertoldshofen**, 4km from the *Schloss*. Here, one must go past the church and the Königswirt inn (*Ruhetag* Monday), over the Geltnach bridge and follow the waymarks until the last house and follow a grassy track with a barrier, through a clearing with seats and into the undergrowth above the valley. Continuing uphill on the Schlossberg note a cross erected for Pfarrer (priest) Josef Izlinger who was killed here in 1481. The path leads into pastureland and here there is a broad view to the peaks of the Allgäu and Ammergau Alps. Reaching the hamlet of **Burk**, continue past the church, pass or call at Café Brugger (*Ruhetag* Tuesday) and leave via Stöttener Strasse, eventually coming down to a stream by a row of trees. Straight on past a parking place and in 700m at **Geldloch** go to the right over the bridge and up into the meadows, with a hill on the left and a small lake down on the right. Continue to climb and upon reaching a little road turn left into **Echt** (altitude 842m, 2761ft and 4.5km from Bertoldshofen) where drinks may be obtained from the Schneider family at house No 2. Past the wooden chapel, fork right down into a wooded ravine, cross the stream and resume climbing to **Settele** $^1/_2$km from Echt. Now there is a view of the Auerberg (1055m, 3460ft) which is the immediate goal although the waymarked route does not always lead directly in that direction.

Continuing generally uphill, keep the Weidensee (lake) on the right and past the end of it turn right, away from the surfaced road down into the valley of a little stream then climb again to the hamlet of **Buchen**. Before the sign 'Geisenhofen', turn right down past the little church and into the *Landschaftschutzgebiet* (protected countryside). Before going further, look back for a rewarding view. Now the path goes steeply up into fenced pasture — heavy going here after rain. A second opening points the direction and soon turn left on the road leading to the Auerberg with its *Gasthof* and church, 6.5km from Echt. The inn has been in the possession of the Stechele family since 1601; thirteen beds are available. If intending to stay overnight it is advisable to reserve in advance (☎ 08860-235). The inn is open continuously from April to mid-September, *Ruhetag* Thursday rest of year. The pilgrimage church is of interest, as is the fact that in the Ice Age the

summit of the Auerberg remained above the ice-cap. Take an
alternative route back to Marktoberdorf (doubling the distance of
course) or the 'bus which runs from nearby Bernbeuren. Check
details of the service before setting out.

Lechbruck is an *Erholungsort* with 2200 inhabitants and was
originally a *Flösserdorf* — that is to say it was engaged in the trade of
floating timber down the river as huge rafts, replicas of which are
sometimes made today as a tourist attraction. Lechbruck has all the
usual amenities of a holiday resort in this area and claims that it is a
familienfreundlich place. Families are welcomed and there is a lot of
accommodation suitable for them at the lower end of the price range.

Oy and Mittelberg are the principal constituents of a group of half
a dozen or so villages which cluster around the southern end of the
A7. Given the blanket name of **Oy-Mittelberg** this is a *Kneipp-* and
Luftkurort of nearly 4000 inhabitants. It lies between 900m (2952ft)
and 1100m (3608ft) above sea level and the big mountains are very
close. There are thirty ski-lifts and other mountain 'railways' within
15km and winter activities here are no less important than summer
ones. Not too much is made of historic buildings but in Oy the Zollhaus
(1448), a customs house formerly connected with the international
salt trade, is of interest while in **Petersthal**, a few kilometres from the
centre, the rococo parish church should be seen.

Kempten (population 60,000) is the capital of Bavarian Allgäu
and is one of the oldest towns in Germany. Many fine historic buildings
remain and each Saturday from May to October there is a free
conducted tour to the most important of them. Music, theatre and
folklore are offered regularly but particularly during the Allgäu Festival
weeks during the second half of August. This was once a Roman town
(Cambodunum) and there are still remains of walls etc of that period,
but the principal relics are to be found in the Roman collection in the
Zumsteinhaus. The collegiate church of St Lorenz (1651–3) was the
first big German church built after the Thirty Years' War; the style is
Italian baroque. The richly ornamented interior should be studied at
leisure. The old town church of St Mary (1427) nearby is a late Gothic
brick building which was given the rococo treatment in 1767–8. The
Gothic *Rathaus* with its onion-dome and double stairway graces the
Marktplatz. The bronze Rathausbrunnen (fountain) of 1601 is consid-
ered to be one of the finest Renaissance fountains in Germany. The
Residenz (1651–74) was the former seat of the prince-abbots. The
Fürstensaal (Princes' Hall) on the first floor has rich ornamentation in

PLACES OF INTEREST IN KEMPTEN

Remains of Roman Walls, etc

Zumsteinhaus
Residenzplatz 31. Museum with collection of Roman relics.

Collegiate Church of St Lorenz (1651–3)
Stiftplatz. Rich interior in Italian baroque.

Town Hall (1474)
Fine Gothic building.

Town Hall Fountain (1601)
One of the finest Renaissance fountains.

Residenz (1651–74)
Former seat of the prince-bishops.

stucco and the arrangements in and around a number of rooms were enlivened in south German rococo style between 1734 and 1742. In charge was J.G. Üblherr but he borrowed from the ideas of other artists including J.B. and D. Zimmermann.

South-west from Kempten, **Niedersonthofen** with its large lake is popular with campers and water-sports enthusiasts but is otherwise not noteworthy. Another twin set-up is that of **Missen-Wilhams**, a little to the south and less than 3km apart at the foot of the Hauchen-berg (1242m, 4073ft). Only 1290 inhabitants occupy this delightful area; summer and winter activities are arranged and skiing tuition is

Winter in the Bavarian Alps

an important feature with a special course for children who are even provided with a midday meal under supervision. The caravan park is open all year and the *Ferienwohnpark* 'Oberallgäu' has 131 apartments with 350 beds at the time of writing but is to be extended. This is splendid walking country. The Hauchenberg is a long, lean mountain running roughly north-east–south-west and a ramble along the ridge provides spectacular views all round.

From the car park in Missen village climb fairly steeply north-east — waymark 1 — for about 600m to the settlement of **Berg** where route 1 turns sharply back to the left. (The last 300m have been beside the main road which continues forward to Börlas.) From the turning, fork right almost immediately up the minor road serving the few houses of Berg and after passing the last of these, route 1 continues as a track climbing steadily through meadows and trees until the crest is reached about 1.5km from the main road. Route 2 from Wilhams comes in on the left here. Those starting the ramble in Wilhams may park near the church and take path 2 to the west of it to go towards Missen. After 650m turn left, noting that waymark 2 applies both ways and climb steeply, mostly through open pastureland for rather more than 1km to join route 1.

M
↦
ΔΔ
12-
14km

The worst of the climb is now over and the path continues in a north-easterly direction on the ridge with a variety of woodland and pasture. After 1km path 14 comes up the hillside on the right and about 800m later 19 comes up steeply from the left (from Wilhams) and 13 from Börlas on the right. No 1 continues straight forward and in another kilometre reaches the highest point of the walk at 1242m (4074ft). Now begin the gentle descent, still keeping to the ridge. Pass path 3 on the right from Diepholz and about 2km later are the Stations of the Cross which lead to the Lohweg-Kapelle, a remote chapel set amongst steep craggy rocks. Care is needed here; so confined is the space that photography is almost impossible. Return to the path and in another 100m or so leave path 1 and turn right into No 6 which in about 400m reaches the main road at **Freundpolz**. A little before this, however, path No 4 to the right runs parallel with the road back as far as **Diepholz**, about 2km. Diepholz is the watershed, for the streams to the north/north-east run down to the lake at Niedersonthofen, while those ahead go down to the valley at Missen and the waters eventually reach Lake Constance. From Diepholz follow the road — not a very busy one — for rather less than 4km back to the turning at Berg. Those returning to Wilhams go in here but then fork

Diepholz church in the Allgäu

left to join path 2 back to their starting point. Stout footwear is desirable for this walk.

The *Wanderkarte Erholungsgebiet Grosser Alpsee* is a local map and guide published in Immenstadt. Although the text of the guide is in German, the clear summaries of the fifty-three numbered routes in this area should be useful and the map itself (1:20,000) is extremely clear and has the legend in French and English as well as German.

The route has now reached the quite narrow corridor through which Bavarian Allgäu reaches its meagre section of the coastline of Lake Constance. The Deutsche Alpenstrasse (German Alpine Road) passes through here and provides the theme for the next chapter.

2 THE ALPINE ROAD

The German Alpine Road (Deutsche Alpenstrasse) runs between the extreme south-western and south-eastern corners of Bavaria, from Lindau on Lake Constance (Bodensee) to the Austrian border on the outskirts of Salzburg. The straight line distance is about 260km but the Alpine Road stretches some 350km. This must surely be one of Europe's longest routes of continuous scenic interest, with almost the whole road in, or very close to, the often snow-capped mountains.

The Bodensee is some 60km long and up to 15km wide but Bavaria can only claim about 12km of the shore line. It is a warm and sunny area with vineyards and orchards. The main Bavarian resort is **Lindau**, a town of 24,000 inhabitants with a delightful atmosphere reminiscent of more southerly lands. The historic centre is mainly a pedestrian zone and access for vehicles is severely restricted. There is a good reason for this for Lindau is, in fact, an island connected to the mainland only by road and railway bridges. There is a splendid traffic-free harbour promenade where visitors and locals alike gather to watch the coming and going of the lake steamers. A quite restful time may be had by using the frequent services to visit and explore the various towns around the lake in Germany, Austria or Switzerland.

The old *Rathaus* built 1422–36 in the Gothic style has been rebuilt and restored many times over the years. Cavazzen, built in 1729, has been described as the most beautiful citizen's house on the lake and today houses the town museum and a valuable art collection. The historic lighthouse at the harbour entrance dates from the thirteenth century. The oldest church on the island is that of St Peter (built about AD1000) in which the remarkable fresco, the Lindau Passion by Hans Holbein the Elder was only uncovered in 1967. The Protestant parish church of St Stephan was founded in the twelfth century but radical alterations in 1506 and 1781–3 mean that little of the original remains.

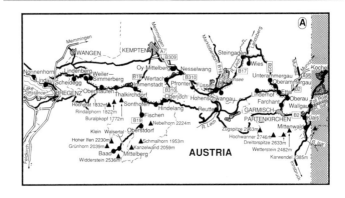

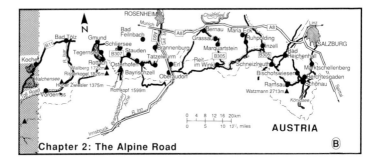

Chapter 2: The Alpine Road

Outside, the building is predominantly baroque, and the stucco and most of the rest of the decoration is from the late eighteenth century. The Catholic parish church also originated in the twelfth century but the present building was erected 1748–51 after the previous one had been burned down.

Lindau has belonged to Bavaria only since 1805. Before that, as a 'free' imperial city, it was tossed to and fro repeatedly as first the Austrians then the French took possession of it. Some of this history comes out in Geissler's delightful story of *Der Liebe Augustin*, that charming but entirely fictional philanderer born in Mittenwald in 1777 who made his home here in Lindau. Those who have enjoyed the story may well be tempted to discover for themselves the haunts described in the book. They will not be disappointed for Lindau has

PLACES OF INTEREST AND THINGS TO DO IN LINDAU

Old Town Hall (1422–36)
Gothic building with interesting stepped gable.

Town Museum
Marktplatz 4. Housed in beautiful citizen's house Cavazzen (1729).

St Peter's Church (about AD 1000)
Fresco *The Lindau Passion* by Hans Holbein the Elder.

St Stephan's Parish Church
Marktplatz. Predominantly baroque exterior.

Catholic Parish Church of St Maria (1748–51)
Marktplatz.

Dammgasse No 4
Legendary home of 'Der Liebe Augustin'

Harbour Promenade
Visit the historic thirteenth-century lighthouse.

Steamer Excursions
To lakeside resorts in Germany, Austria and Switzerland.

taken care to see that the myth is preserved to delight its visitors. The locals point out Dammgasse No 4 where Augustin lived and the visitor can climb the narrow stair to see the famous four-poster bed which featured in some of his exploits. Not only here but elsewhere in the town are memories of his stay; replicas of the musical boxes which he is supposed to have made may even be bought. All this is pure fantasy, but many come just to revel in a little harmless make-believe.

West of Lindau are the resorts of **Bad Schachen**, a pleasant lake-side spa, **Wasserburg** and **Nonnenhorn**, both of which enjoy the designation *Luftkurort* and are essentially summer places with much activity on the waterfront. Nonnenhorn is noted for its cherries and the enterprising local wine *Elbling*, drunk young and most refreshing. Note the *Weintorkel*, an enormous old grape press dating from 1591. A short ramble from the village centre following signs 'St Anton' leads up through vineyards and orchards to the tiny village of that name. The way up to the chapel, also called St Anton, can be seen and here at 460m (1508ft) (although only about 65m (213ft) above the lake level) there is a grand panoramic view southwards over the lake to the Swiss Alps and eastwards towards the Austrian and Allgäu Alps and the Bavarian hinterland. There are several alternative routes back to the starting point. Lindau and the places on the lakeside can all be reached by train, making this an ideal area for the visitor without his own transport.

L
↔
ΔΔ
4km

PLACES OF INTEREST IN LINDENBERG, WEILER-SIMMERBERG AND IMMENSTADT

LINDENBERG
**Baroque Church of St Peter
and St Paul** (1912–14)
Its twin towers are the emblem of
the town.

Museum
History of straw and felt hat-
making.

WEILER-SIMMERBERG
Weiler Parish Church (1745)

Weiler Town Hall (1681)

IMMENSTADT
Church of St Nikolaus (1707)
Late baroque.

Town Hall
Seventeenth century.

Königsegg Palace (1620)
Marienplatz.

Heimatmuseum
Linen weaving and old cheese
kitchen.

Laubenberg Castle Ruin
1.5km N of town.

**Pilgrimage Churches of St
Loretto** (1632) **and St
Stephan**
In Bühl 2km W of town.
(Thirteenth century.)

The Alpenstrasse leaves Lindau as B308 and runs northwards for a few kilometres before turning east to continue right across this southern fringe of Bavaria. After 20km the *Heilklimatische-* and *Kneippkurort* of **Scheidegg** (population 4000) is reached. The new resort designation refers to the benevolent climate. A wide variety of medical treatments is available here including those pioneered by Kneipp and another famed practitioner, Schroth. Children and young people have special pastimes and activities arranged for them in the resort. Summer and winter visitors are welcomed and there are some good value packages outside the high season. The resort includes the village of **Scheffau** about 5km to the south. Both places are within 3km of crossing points on the Austrian border, providing an opportunity for a round tour through the famous Bregenzerwald (Forest of Bregenz). In this remote corner of the state, one is much nearer to northern Italy than to the Bavarian capital!

Lindenberg (population 11,000) just a few kilometres along, a *Hohenluftkurort* since 1923, is in the centre of the west Allgäu Alpine foothills and enjoys an ideal climate with freedom from fog. Thus it is a good place for people with any sort of respiratory problem. The main attraction is the little lake called Waldsee where there is angling and bathing although there is also a *Hallenbad* with sauna. There is a good and varied entertainments programme and an excellent range of facilities for other leisure pursuits. Many footpaths attract summer ramblers and in the winter there is a ski-school and a ski-lift. Many of the tracks are kept clear for cross-country skiing or winter walking. The town has a history of straw and felt hat-making and there is an unusual museum devoted to the subject. The parish church of 1696 was rebuilt in the nineteenth century using the old tower. The new 'baroque' parish church (1912–14) of St Peter and St Paul with its twin towers graces the skyline and has become the emblem of the town.

Weiler-Simmerberg with **Ellhofen** are three neighbouring villages which constitute a *Luftkurort* with 4600 inhabitants and a mineral spring. Several different medical treatments are available here and the waters are said to be beneficial to sufferers of rheumatism. In Weiler the parish church dates from 1745 and the pretty *Rathaus* from 1681. The west Allgäu *Heimatmuseum* is to be found here and is well thought of. Incidentally, all the places mentioned can be reached by public transport, train to Röthenbach and thence by 'bus.

From the Alpenstrasse some of the majestic peaks of the Allgäu Alps can be seen ahead. The most prominent summits include Buralpkopf (1772m, 5812ft), Rindalphorn (1822m, 5976ft) and Hochgrat (1832m, 6008ft). In about 12km, **Oberstaufen** is reached. This is a *Kurort* of 6800 inhabitants and home of the original medical establishment of Johann Schroth. Regardless of the *Kur*, this is a delightful town in every way. Up to date in a refined sort of way and with every possible means of entertaining the visitor, Oberstaufen, home town of the female Olympic champions Heidi Biebl and Christl Cranz-Borchers, is ideal for an extended stay in the area. Many people visit Oberstaufen in order to take a *Schrothkur*. The name comes from the Bohemian Johann Schroth who discovered that controlled fasting could be helpful in the treatment of certain ailments. Fasting may come hard in an area with so many fine hostelries but the *Kur* is a fairly light-hearted affair with some emphasis on *Glühwein* (mulled wine) which 'improves the circulation and encourages regularity in the normal bodily functions'! The principle is that if the body is cleansed of all impurities many symptoms will disappear. If for a few days the pangs of hunger assail, there are many ways of forgetting this — perhaps a visit to a cheese factory or a walk to the little churches in Zell or Genhofen; or just to sit and contemplate the mountain scenery. Thursday is a 'big drink day' for those taking the

A fine morning in the Bavarian Alps

Kur. Breakfast is an eighth of a litre of *Glühwein* or herb tea, at midday there is vegetable soup, semolina and raspberry juice. At three o'clock another eighth of *Glühwein* is permitted and between then and midnight up to a litre of wine may be consumed. The evening meal is of home baking specialities liberally garnished with parsley and chives. Some people certainly find the treatment beneficial and *Schrothkur* establishments have a good reputation. New centres are still being opened to provide for the traditional inclination of Germans to take a *Kur*, an inclination reflected in the provision made for this in the German medical insurance system.

From Oberstaufen many excursions into the mountains are possible and maps and guides are readily available. One which can be recommended requires the use of car or 'bus from the town along the road to the south past Steibis and in about 8km arrives at the lower station of the *Kabinenseilbahn* (cable railway with four-seat cabins). From here, given sufficient time, the very fit could climb the steep path about 4km to the summit cross on the Hochgrat (1832m, 6008ft). More pleasant, especially for a family excursion, is to take the cable-car to the upper station (refreshments available) and walk the remaining short distance to the summit in about 20 minutes. If this

Feuchtwangen

The church at Wies

The village of Missen, in Allgäu

Allgäu pastures above Missen

lovely vantage point is chosen for a picnic, look out for the antics of the alpine choughs, cheekily demanding a share of the food.

The journey back to the valley can be accomplished on foot following the clear path which zig-zags to and fro across the cable-car route. A hut part way down provides much-needed refreshment, for even downhill the walk is quite a strenuous one. Do not be misled by the short distance; at least 2 hours should be allowed for the descent and good boots are really essential, even in dry weather. Experienced mountain walkers could follow the splendid, easily identified and gradually descending high-level walk eastwards from the summit towards Immenstadt. This takes in the summits Rindalphorn (1822m, 5976ft), Buralpkopf (1772m, 5812ft) and Stuiben (1749m, 5736ft). From the latter, the path, now waymarked 41, continues to descend until, about 2km short of the town, the upper station of a chair-lift is reached (1451m, 4759ft) which will take one down to the town if required. From Immenstadt the train may be used for the return to Oberstaufen. This is a magnificent walk in good weather with wonderful views on every side. Walking boots are essential and waterproofs, warm clothing and some rations should be carried. Not suitable for small children.

H
↔
△△△
5km

H
↔
△△△
14
or
15km

Eastwards from Oberstaufen, road and railway follow each other along the valley of the Konstanzer Ach, a little river. **Thalkirchdorf,** about 6km away, is enclosed in a rather narrow valley. It is a good rambling centre and a popular winter resort with several ski-lifts nearby. In this area, look out in the summer months for notices announcing a *Bergmesse*. This is a simple religious service conducted on a hill top with an improvised altar — a moving experience with the mountains all around. After the service, secular activities take over and a band arrives. Beer and other beverages are on sale and a huge vat of sausages is heated for the mid-day snack. The oom-pah music echoes over the hills and meadows and sometimes there is dancing and singing as well. An unusual experience, but one which should not be missed if the opportunity arises.

After Thalkirchdorf, road and railway pass either side of the Grosser Alpsee, re-uniting in **Bühl** at the east end to continue together into Immenstadt. This lake, 3km long and 1km wide, is very popular for water activities and is in surroundings of great beauty in the centre of the area covered by the *Wanderkarte Erholungsgebiet Grosser Alpsee* . Bühl, the only resort actually on the lake is a popular walking and skiing centre, the nearby Gschwender Horn (1450m,

4756ft) being served by two ski-lifts. The pilgrimage churches of St Loretto and St Stephan (thirteenth century) may be visited.

Immenstadt (population 14,000) has some historic buildings worthy of attention; the late baroque church of St Nikolaus (1707), the *Rathaus* (seventeenth century), the ruined castle Laubenberg just north of the town and Schloss Königsegg (1620) in the Marienplatz. Once again this is a place for active holidays the year round and there are well marked paths and cross-country ski-routes as well as downhill skiing.

The Alpenstrasse turns south-east to **Sonthofen**, reached in 7km. A *Luftkurort* of 21,000 inhabitants, this is not such an immediately attractive town as some. Nevertheless it is a popular holiday centre summer and winter as well as being an important business town. Guests are catered for with all the usual amenities and there are some attractions not found elsewhere. For example, the second Sunday in December sees the start of the 'Nikolaus' balloon race. There could hardly be a better centre for those wishing to explore the mountains, with more than a 100 mountain railways, ski-lifts and chair-lifts within a short distance. The camp site is open all year.

Fischen im Allgäu is a delightful resort, 7km south of Sonthofen on the often busy B19, which has retained much of the traditional charm of earlier years. Should there be cool days in summer, the visitor may still lounge comfortably on the terrace of the heated swimming pool enjoying the artificial sunshine of infra-red lamps. After a summer visit many people like to return in winter. Indeed, it seems that summer merges almost imperceptibly into winter for it is said that one can bathe in the open air on the nearby Sonnenalp until well into December. The secret is that the pool contains water heated in the depths of the earth so that on cool days the rising steam presents a vision almost like that seen in Iceland. So popular is this resort that it is as busy in November as other places are in the high season. Fischen has 3300 inhabitants and many different entertainments are laid on for visitors when they are not skiing or climbing mountains. Of interest is the early baroque Liebfrauenkirche in the cemetery with its high eight-sided domed tower.

Four or five kilometres further on is **Oberstdorf** at the foot of the 2224m (7294ft) Nebelhorn which can be ascended by one of the three mountain railways: there are also nineteen ski-lifts in the immediate vicinity for Oberstdorf (population 12,000), Germany's most southerly market town, is the most important winter sports centre in Allgäu.

PLACES OF INTEREST NEAR SONTHOFEN AND OBERSTDORF

FISCHEN
The Liebfrauenkirche
In the cemetery. Early baroque with eight-sided domed tower.

Swimming Pool heated by thermal springs

OBERSTDORF
The Lorettokapellen
Three little chapels.

Breitachklamm
Spectacular ravine with river and waterfalls.

KLEINWALSERTAL
Austrian enclave only accessible from Bavaria. Alpine scenery and good walking.

BAD OBERDORF
Parish Church
Fine altar and famous painting by Hans Holbein the Elder.

Town Hall (1660)
Former hunting-lodge of prince-bishops of Augsburg.

Nevertheless, it is equally a summer resort and visitors are offered a great variety of things to do all year round. Specially fine in autumn with, perhaps, a walk to the Lorettokapellen, three chapels one after another as if the next had been built because the previous one had become too small.

Before leaving Oberstdorf a short but rewarding walk could be undertaken starting at the Gasthaus Breitachklamm where there is a good car park. The Breitachklamm (ravine) was made accessible to the public in 1905 and has become one of the tourist highlights of the area. Over 1.5km long, the ravine is also one of the most spectacular in all the Alpine regions. Especially impressive on a rainy autumn day when the thousands of summer tourists have departed. The *Klamm* starts innocently enough but a short climb reveals the power of the water, rushing and plunging through the 100m-high (328ft) rocky walls which constantly drip and steam and create miniature waterfalls on all sides. Just after leaving the car park there is a kiosk beyond which there is a memorial to Pfarrer Johannes Schiebel from nearby Tiefenbach who discovered the *Klamm* just after the turn of the century. The well defined tourist track needs no map-reading but time should be allowed to admire this natural entertainment as the little river tosses itself from rock to rock. At the end of the ravine proper, past a picture postcard hut, keep to the left and climb steeply to the Walserschanz (991m, 3250ft) where the B19 crosses the frontier into Austria. There is a *Gasthof* here. Turn left along the road towards

M
↔
△△△
4km

Oberstdorf for about 200m then left again following the signs down to the Zwingsteg (bridge) which takes one across the ravine at a dizzy height of about 80m (262ft). It is possible to get down into the ravine here but to complete the round walk continue up the opposite slope on a zig-zag path and stroll northwards through little woods, across fields and eventually down through a wood to the starting place.

Oberstaufen and all the places mentioned since then are accessible by train but Oberstdorf is the end of the line.

The crossing of the B19 into Austria at Walserschanz is about 4km from Oberstdorf. Nobody here is likely to show any interest in passports or inquire about dutiable goods and an excursion into the Kleinwalsertal, which is now entered, is something of a novelty. The road and the River Breitach are hemmed in by imposing mountains such as the Hoher Ifen (2230m, 7314ft) and Grünhorn (2039m, 6687ft) to the west and the Kanzelwand (2059m, 6753ft) and Widderstein (2536m, 8318ft) to the east. The picturesque route leads through the resorts of **Riezlern**, **Hirschegg** and **Mittelberg** to come to an abrupt stop at **Baad**, 19km from Oberstdorf, with the mountains barring further progress except on foot. There is ample parking here and good tracks for a few kilometres leading to fine

mountain views. Given the time and the necessary stamina an all-day mountain walk to the summit of the Widderstein can start from here.

Go south from Baad across the River Breitach; after about 15 minutes enter the solitude of the Bärgundtal. Note the many wild flowers in the fields through which the Bärgundbach (stream) flows down the valley. All the time, the Dolomite-like summit of the Grosse

H
↔ ↔
ΔΔΔ
13km

Widderstein is seen ahead as the path is followed through the valley to the Unteren Bärgundalp, reached in $^3/_4$ hour from Baad. A little later the real climb begins and before a noticeably steep incline the path goes upwards to the right to the Oberen Hochalphütte (1889m, 6195ft) 2 hours from Baad. From here, keeping to the left and going roughly due east, the south slope of the Seekopf is crossed and the main track is then allowed to go away left while the walker takes the smaller path past the lonely Hochalpsee (a little lake) up to the beginning of the gorge-like gulley on the south side of the Widderstein. Go up the gulley, first over scree and then over short rocky

steps, and up to the left to the ridge over which the cross on the Grosse Widderstein (2533m, 8308ft) is reached in about $4^1/_4$ hours from Baad.

Retracing steps down the gulley but keeping left, reach the Obere

Widdersteinalp (2010m, 6593ft) and descend slightly to the Gemstelpass (1971m, 6465ft) in about 1¹/₄ hours from the summit. From here climb north-east through the Hochtal and in half an hour down to the Obere Gemstelalp (1692m, 5549ft); in another 10 minutes the Gsprengten Weg leads down over the ravine of the foaming Gemstelbach. After that, a long left and then a right hand curve brings the route to a good track at the Untere Gemstelalp, which leads due north to reach the settlement of **Bödmen** in 20 minutes. Here turn left into the good small road to reach Baad in half an hour, a total of 3¹/₂ hours from the summit. Refreshments may be available at the huts at the several 'alps' mentioned and overnight accommodation is possible at the Obere Widdersteinalp. Check on this before setting out from Baad but, in any case, remember emergency rations, warm clothing and stout boots. The map for this route is the 1:50,000 *Allgäuer Alpen*. Do not be misled by the modest distance; it is the total climb of 1300m (4264ft) which counts on this walk.

Splendid mountain scenery, rushing streams, wild flowers and perhaps animals, all this the Kleinwalsertal has in common with many other Alpine valleys. The novelty lies in its peculiar political and geographical situation. It is Austrian without doubt but there is access to it only from Bavaria. An agreement made in 1891 allies it economically with Germany but politically with Austria. If a resident wishes to avoid paying duty on his new car he must buy it in Germany but it will have to carry Austrian number plates. He will buy Austrian stamps for his mail, paying for them in German Marks while the Austrian Revenue Office in Bregenz calculates his taxes in Schillings and uses a strange exchange rate to render the tax bill in Marks. If the Austrian police have a warrant for the arrest of a criminal here they have to lift him out by helicopter to avoid passing through a foreign country. A German visitor is covered here by his own health insurance but should he decide he would like to buy a plot of land and build a house he promptly becomes a 'foreigner'. On the other hand, a man from Vienna could buy the plot without difficulty but would then have to comply with all the German customs formalities. And so on. One suspects that the inhabitants derive quite a lot of amusement from this remarkable situation.

Back on the Alpenstrasse (B308) **Hindelang** is reached (population 5000) about 8km after leaving Sonthofen. It is well known because of its winter sports associations but is a splendid centre for every season of the year and especially fine in the late autumn just before the snow arrives. When the snow does come, Hindelang is immediately invaded by skiers from near and far. At any season there are two things to attract the visitor regardless of weather. Both are to be found in the tiny church of **Bad Oberdorf** just 1km away. The first is a remarkably fine altar by Jörg Lederer and the other is the famous Holbein Madonna, more correctly the 500-year-old painting *Picture of the Mother of God* by Hans Holbein the Elder. The *Rathaus* is a

former hunting lodge (1660) of the prince-bishops of Augsburg. Continuing eastwards climb steadily along a section said to be the most twisty road in Germany. Motorists should exercise the greatest caution.

In 7km **Oberjoch**, at an altitude of about 1130m (3706ft), is reached. Rumour has it that babies born here are already wearing skis! At Oberjoch, the B308 goes ahead to cross the border and becomes Austrian road 199 leading to the heart of Tirol. B310 becomes the Alpine Road for a while, going north first to **Wertach** (population 2300), a *Luftkurort* only 10km south of Oy-Mittelberg visited in the previous chapter. Just before reaching Wertach a road on the right signed 'Jungholz' may be noticed. This is another Austrian enclave which can only be reached from the Bavarian side of the mountains. It is much smaller but otherwise, conditions are similar to those found in the Kleinwalsertal. In Wertach, as in all the other places mentioned in the last few pages, the autumn movement of cattle from the high pastures takes place around the third week in September, a factor to bear in mind, not only for the spectacle but also possible congestion on the roads. Wertach is a resort for summer and winter with reliable snow conditions for several months. Water activities are centred on the nearby Grüntensee, a small lake, along the south shore of which runs the Alpenstrasse, now turned eastwards again to pass through **Nesselwang** (population 3000) with its many excellent

facilities including the Alpspitz-Bade-Center, a swimming pool complex. There is a baroque/rococo parish church which is of interest. After Sonthofen the public transport user has to be reliant on 'bus connections from either Sonthofen or Oy-Mittelberg stations to reach the resorts, but at Nesselwang the main line railway is again at hand.

Pfronten is one of the foremost resorts in Allgäu and claims nearly 7000 inhabitants but this includes a dozen outlying villages. The town itself is not actually on the Alpine Road but on a loop to the south which crosses the frontier into Austria at the foot of the Breitenberg (1821m, 5973ft) and then continues through the Ty-

rolean resort of Vils to return to Bavaria after about 8km just outside
Füssen. Similarly, the railway which has reached Pfronten from
Kempten takes the more southerly route and only gets back into
Bavaria at the foot of the Zugspitze before running into Garmisch-
Partenkirchen. The skiing area served by Pfronten covers an altitude
of 900 to 1730m (2952 to 5674ft) so that good snow conditions are
virtually guaranteed for a very long season. The parish church of St
Nikolaus in Pfronten-Berg has baroque frescos and tower. Entertain-
ments are laid on in the summer and winter seasons and there are ski-
lifts, chair-lifts and *Kabinenbergbahnen* (cabin cable cars).

On the Bavarian side of the border the Alpenstrasse now continues past the pretty Weissensee into **Füssen**, an important centre of
13,000 inhabitants. (This is is also the finishing point of the Romantische Strasse route described in Chapter 1.)

Füssen is a *Kneippkurort* but it is by no means a place dedicated
solely or even mainly to those coming for medical treatment and its
claim is to cater for every taste. It has an art gallery, archaeological
collection, historic buildings, steamer excursions on the Forggensee
and, within walking distance, the first of the famous Königsschlösser,
the fantastic castles of King Ludwig II. The Forggensee is an artificial
lake nearly 10km long. It was formed by building a dam 323m (1059ft)
long and 41m (134ft) high across the valley of the Lech, the work being
completed in 1955 to provide a head of water for the hydro-electric
power station at Rosshaupten at the north end. The power station is
open to visitors. The lake takes its name from the village of Forggen
which now lies beneath the water. Walking is a favourite pastime and
there are 180km of footpaths including many in the fairly easy terrain
around the many small lakes and along the River Lech which tumbles
out of Austria just south of the town. The spray at the Lech Falls can
create delightful rainbows and here, in the rocky wall, is a bust of
Maximilian II, the father of Ludwig.

The nearby church marks the start of a modest but rather interesting walk. From the main road, path 17, yellow waymark, climbs
steadily through the woods and soon comes to the first of the 'Stations
of the Cross'. These take various forms as the path climbs, some   M
found in a small chapel. By the time the last Station is passed, the   ↔
summit (953m, 3126ft) is in view with three wooden crosses on the   ΔΔΔ
skyline, for this is the Kalvarienberg (Hill of Calvary), one of several   8km
so named in Bavaria. The crosses are on a platform from which there
is an extensive panoramic view of the countryside with the large

'Parken und Wandern'

Forggensee prominently below. Beneath the summit crosses there is a cavern containing a tomb with a stone figure representing Christ.

The path continues in an easterly direction until it joins a small road. Turn left here for a very short distance and then take path 14 to the right. This turning is about 1.5km from the start of the walk but something like 150m (492ft) has been climbed in this short distance. Path 14 continues in a left-hand curve above, but fairly close to, the south shore of the little Schwan-See (Swan Lake). After passing the lake, several paths continue in a generally easterly direction, keep towards the right and there are soon charming views down through the trees to the much larger Alpsee. The dominating Schloss Hohenschwangau is passed as the path drops down to the village of the same name. This is an opportunity to visit the castle from which there is a fine view of the newer Schloss Neuschwanstein across the valley as well as the steep mountains towards the Austrian border to the south. To return to Füssen, leave Hohenschwangau along the main road but soon fork to the left to follow a track away from the traffic for the level walk back to the starting point, about 3.5km.

PLACES OF INTEREST IN AND AROUND FÜSSEN

Former Benedictine Kloster Church of St Mang (1701)
Strong Venetian influence.

Heimatmuseum
In the former *Kloster* buildings.

Spitalkirche (1747–9)
Baroque with painted façade.

Hohes Schloss (1490–1503)
Palace which now houses part of Bavarian State Art Collection.

Forggensee
10km-long reservoir serving hydro-electric station. Boat trips.

Lech Falls
1km S of town centre.

Hohenschwangau Castle (1832)
3km SE of Füssen. Palace in the English Tudor style.

Neuschwanstein Castle (1869)
4km E of Füssen. Most famous of the palaces of 'mad' King Ludwig II.

Pilgrimage Church of St Koloman (1673)
4km NE of Füssen. Stucco by J. Schmuzer.

Another pleasant ramble is westwards from Füssen through the suburb of **Bad Faulenbach** and along the straight and virtually traffic-free minor road (path 24) to the Alat-See, an idyllic little lake amongst the trees reached in just over 4km. The hotel here is open all year and is a delightful spot for the afternoon *Kaffeepause* or a more substantial meal. Boats can be hired or walks can be taken right round the lake (about 1.5km). A slightly more strenuous route begins by turning right in Bad Faulenbach and continues via the Neuer-Kobel-Weg (path 25) through the woods. The distance is about the same. For the return to Füssen take either of the routes already mentioned (they merge about 600m (1968ft) from the lake) or take a track (27) from the north shore over the ridge to the Weissensee, turning right on reaching path 26 along the south shore and back to the town. This adds about 2km. Yet another possibility is to take path 28 from the south shore of the Alat-See and cross the border into Austria immediately after leaving the lake. Then, almost immediately, turn left through fields to a farm called Ländehof, about 1.5km from the border. From here path 21 follows the River Lech directly towards Füssen. In another 1.5km just before crossing back into Bavaria there is a fork where path 21 goes to the right and 22 to the left. Path 21 closely follows the river to pass the Lech Falls while 22 takes a slightly more direct route away from the river. The route back via Austria only adds about 1km to the total distance.

L
↔
△
8-
10km

There are many notable buildings in Füssen. The former Benedic-tine *Kloster* church of St Mang (1701) shows a strong Venetian influence, no doubt due to the fact that the architect, J.J. Herkomer, studied in Venice. The *Kloster* building itself was the work of the same architect and today houses the *Heimatmuseum*. The little baroque Spitalkirche (1748–9) has a completely painted façade and is a beautiful example of Bavarian outdoor painting. A thirteenth- to fourteenth-century castle was converted in 1490–1503 into a residential *Schloss*, the north wing of which now houses part of the Bavarian art collection.

Much written about Füssen is equally applicable to **Hohen-schwangau** for both resorts share many of the same sights and surroundings. The difference is that life here is dominated more by the two famous castles than by the excellent facilities. The 'old' castle is Hohenschwangau, standing on the site of a thirteenth-century build-ing, the ruins of which were cleared to enable the theatrical architect D. Quaglio to build the present palace in the English Tudor style in 1832 as summer seat for Crown Prince Maximilian of Bavaria, later King Maximilian II. The salons and drawing rooms are decorated with large murals depicting old German sagas and knightly exploits. These include scenes from some of the legends later used by Wagner in his music-dramas. Wagner was a frequent visitor here as guest of Max-imilian's son Ludwig who was his great admirer. Wagner's piano is still here and kept in working order.

There are splendid views from the terraces around the castle but the eye is drawn as by a magnet, to the imposing outline of what must certainly be the most well known and most photographed German castle, Schloss Neuschwanstein. King Ludwig II laid the foundation stone of his 'holy' and historically artificial palace in 1869. Neu-schwanstein was conceived as a coherent whole inspired by the opera world of Richard Wagner but the king adapted it to his own ideas. For example, the paintings from *Tannhäuser* and *Lohengrin* were not as Wagner had described the scenes for his operas but portrayed the old sagas on which the operas were based. Ludwig went into some detail in his criticism of one of the sketches for a painting: 'His Majesty wishes that in this new sketch the boat be further from the shore, then that Lohengrin's head shall not be so sharply inclined, also the chain from the boat to the swan is not to be of roses but of gold and the castle is to be in the medieval style.'

There have been many Bavarian idols over the centuries but none

Neuschwanstein

is dearer to the hearts of the people than Ludwig II. His great grandfather was the first king of Bavaria, Maximilian I, who died in 1825 and was succeeded by his eldest son, Ludwig I. His son in turn later became Maximilian II to whom a son was also born in 1845 and was given, naturally, the name of Ludwig, especially as he was born on 25 August, St Ludwig's Day. Ludwig I stood down in 1848 following the 'scandal' of his affair with the dancer Lola Montez. Maximilian II came to the throne and when he died on 10 March 1864 young Ludwig was not yet nineteen. Europe was in turmoil; Austria and Prussia were at loggerheads, the latest Polish rising against the Russians was being put down, the French had occupied Rome and Garibaldi was trying to dislodge them. This then was the world of the young king, handsome, mysterious and already a trifle sad. It is said that he loved his cousin Elisabeth who had married the Austrian emperor and that Ludwig was never able to forget her.

In 1871 Europe entered a period of peace which lasted almost half a century until 1914. Ludwig II spent the next 15 years in flight from reality; he created the world of Louis XIV in Schloss Herrenchiemsee and in Schloss Linderhof. The private productions of theatrical works from the courts of Louis XIV and XV were as numerous as those of the Wagner operas. The world of *Tannhäuser* and *Lohengrin* he built at Neuschwanstein; in Hundings Hütte near Linderhof he imagined himself as Siegmund; in the Moorish kiosk, an Arabian sultan and in the Wintergarden Residence in Munich, an Indian mogul. Not satisfied with all this fantasy he had plans drawn up for a Byzantine castle and a Chinese summer palace. Neuschwanstein was an anti-Bavarian demonstration on his part. The Bavarian lion was banished from the decorations to be replaced by the peacock and the swan. When he discovered the blue and white diamond of Bavaria in the pattern for a carpet he went into a frenzy. In the end, Ludwig shunned the light of day and would only travel by night in a splendid coach accompanied by faithful servants and torch-bearing outriders.

Finally, the most mysterious episode of all; he drowned in the Starnberger See on 13 June 1886. The only witness seems to have been his physician Von Gudden who died with him. The deaths have never been satisfactorily explained. No doubt the disappearance of Ludwig was something of a relief to the government and the possibility of foul play cannot be ruled out. A hundred years on, just as in England there is a Richard III Society, there is in Bavaria a Ludwig II Federation which keeps his memory alive. Whatever the government of the day thought about it, Bavarians today have much to be grateful to Ludwig for, as has the foreign visitor. No single individual has had a greater influence on the development of Bavarian tourism in the twentieth century than Ludwig. Those who visit the famous palaces every year are numbered in millions. Music-lovers throng to Bayreuth every summer for the annual Wagner Festival; would it ever have been founded — indeed, would Wagner's major works ever have seen the light of day, but for Ludwig's patronage and financial backing?

Neuschwanstein alone attracts over a million visitors each year so it makes good sense to visit outside the main tourist season if possible. Tours of the castle are conducted in many languages so a knowledge of German is not necessary to be able follow the guide's comments. In addition to the rooms provided as living quarters for the king and his court, the throne room and the music hall with its minstrel gallery are particularly worth seeing. The amateur photographer may be disappointed to discover that he cannot find a location from which to reproduce the spectacular picture of the castle which appears in so many books and on numerous posters. All the same, there are many

The Ammersattel Pass, west of Linderhof

good shots to be had, probably the best general view is that from the dizzy heights of the Marienbrücke, a footbridge over the gorge of the River Pöllat.

Before leaving the area visit the pilgrimage church of St Koloman, about 3km north of Hohenschwangau close to the main road. It was built in 1673 and has stucco by J. Schmuzer. Koloman appears to have been involved in some political intrigue and he was hanged in Austria as a spy. Many typically Bavarian festivals take place in the district, including the *Wurmfeiertag* on 26 May. It has its origins in a plague of cockchafers which played havoc with farming activities in 1754. The farmers made a pilgrimage to St Koloman to pray for relief, promising that if their prayers were answered they would repeat the pilgrimage annually, a promise which has been kept to this day.

Now there is a short break in the Alpenstrasse: it starts again at **Linderhof** 16km due east of Hohenschwangau but the way is barred by mountains such as the Hochblasse (1988m, 6520ft), the Scheinberg (1926m 6317ft) and the Klammspitz (1925m, 6314ft). The motorist must, therefore, make a considerable detour either to north or south. The north route involves returning along the Romantic Road as far as Steingaden, there to turn east and then south to Oberammergau, turning west to reach Linderhof. A shorter and quicker route goes south from Füssen to join the Austrian road 314 towards Reutte in Tirol. Before reaching Reutte a modern dual carriageway starts near Unterletzen and after about 6km connects with a road going east past the Plansee and back across the border at Ammersattel, a pass at 1118m (3667ft). The picturesque road now enters the German nature conservation area Ammergebirge and in about 7km arrives from the west at Linderhof and the re-start of the Alpenstrasse.

Ludwig II had Schloss Linderhof built to re-create the world of Louis XIV (Ludwig is the German form of Louis) and the rococo palace was designed by G. Dollman and built 1874–8. Highlights of the interior are the first floor rooms containing pictures of French celebrities of the reigns of Louis XIV and XV. In particular, the gold-covered bedroom, although relatively small, is quite breathtaking in its splendour. Behind the *Schloss* is a grandiosely laid-out park with many places of interest including a grotto with a tiny lake and a Moorish kiosk. The waterfalls lead to a Neptune fountain which can send a 32m-high (104ft) spout of water into the air. The fountains play daily each hour from 9am until 5pm in the summer months.

Leaving Swabia and entering Upper Bavaria continue eastwards along the Alpenstrasse which is flanked on either side by high peaks. After about 10km is **Oberammergau** (population 5000), a charming large village 850m (2788ft) above sea level. Here, there is a wide variety of leisure activities for the visitor's year-round enjoyment. In addition to many ski-lifts there are a chair-lift and a *Kabinenseilbahn.*

In 1632 the dreaded plague was brought to this valley by the Swedish mercenaries. In many parishes the whole population either died or fled to safety. Oberammergau sealed itself off and forbade anyone to enter or leave. A man of the village named Schisler was working meanwhile in nearby Eschenlohe and he took the risk of stealing into Oberammergau to see his family; he brought the Black Death with him and his own and many families were completely wiped out. In despair, the village council made a vow; if God would stop the plague they and their descendants would present a 'Passion of Our Lord' play every 10 years for all time. From that moment, it is recorded, no further deaths occurred and in 1634 the Passion Play was performed for the first time. It was repeated in 1640 and from that time the 10-year cycle has been broken only by twentieth-century wars. In 1984 an additional performance celebrated the 350th anniversary of that first production.

'Trompe l'œil' *painted doorway in Oberammergau, typical of this area of Bavaria*

Each play year the performance is repeated many times over between mid-May and the end of September. All the performers are residents of the village and the women who take part must be unmarried. The allocation of roles takes place at public auditions. Children leave school at the appropriate time to take part in the crowd scenes and return to their desks afterwards. In the crowd scenes there can be as many as 700 players on the stage at one time. The stage is in the open air but in the present theatre, built in 1930, the audience is under cover. The play goes on regardless of the weather and a duplicate set of costumes is kept so that one day's performance in the rain does not interfere with the following presentation.

The play is by no means a commercial venture and it is not staged for the enjoyment of the audience but to the glory of God in accordance with the ancient promise. Nevertheless, it must be admitted that the 10-yearly influx of visitors is of immense value to the economy of the village. Most people coming from a distance buy tickets which

---

PLACES OF INTEREST IN AND AROUND OBERAMMERGAU

Passion Play Theatre (1930)
In village. Used only for the 10-yearly play cycle but may be visited. Costumes etc on view.

Catholic Church (1736–42)
In village. Pretty, with charming rococo frescos and stucco.

Heimatmuseum
Dorfstrasse 8. Strong in wood-carving, also cribs.

Schloss Linderhof (1874–8)
10km W of Oberammergau. King Ludwig's rococo palace in the French style.

Kloster Ettal (1370)
4km SE of Oberammergau. Monastery church re-modelled in baroque in 1710.

---

include accommodation locally for the nights before and after the play which starts at about 8.15am and finishes in the late afternoon with a couple of hours' break at lunchtime. It might be thought that such a lengthy dramatic production is tiring or boring for the spectator, but this is not the case. The play is in German, but translations of the full text are available in almost every language so it is easy to follow the action. While there has been criticism in the past of certain features of the play, it is performed with such sensitivity that no Christian of whatever denomination could take exception.

Many of the 1400 or so people involved in every performance start the day with prayer in the Catholic parish church which was built 1736–42, another example of the work of J. Schmuzer of the Wessobrunn school. This pretty little church is well worth visiting, as is the *Heimatmuseum* with its examples of fourteenth- to eighteenth-century folk art and local wood-carving. Oberammergau is the home of the Bavarian School of Wood-carving and there are many souvenirs in the shops displaying the work of local craftsmen. A leisurely walk through the village reveals many houses with painted façades. Two of the best are the Geroldhaus and the Pilatushaus, painted at the end of the eighteenth century.

Oberammergau is one of many destinations in a programme of excursions by Deutsche Bundesbahn (Federal Railway) designed to allow the Munich city-dweller to walk in the mountains without needing to bother with transport. The train journey from Munich takes about $1^3/_4$ hours and upon arriving at Oberammergau the walkers are met by the leader — usually a member of the local Alpine club — who

Kloster Ettal

takes them for a $4^1/_2$ hour ramble to Linderhof from where they leave by 'bus to Oberammergau for the return train. Many of the excursions, however, return via a different route. These excursions are ideal for the visitor staying in Munich who wishes to see something of the mountains without changing his base.

Five kilometres south of Oberammergau is **Ettal** (population 1000) which is an attractive village in its own right but is principally of interest because of Kloster Ettal, one of the best-known monasteries in southern Germany. The first religious institution was founded here in 1320 and after the installation of a Madonna brought from Italy by the emperor of the day, it quickly became an important centre of pilgrimage. In 1370 the monastery church was completed as a twelve-sided Gothic building based on the Church of the Holy Sepulchre in Jerusalem. In 1710 it was remodelled in the baroque style, retaining the twelve-sided design. The architects responsible were E. Zuccalli and F.X. Schmuzer and in 1745–52 a baroque dome was added by the latter following fire damage. The lavishly decorated façade and another choir were added in the eighteenth century. The twelve-sided section is more than 25m (82ft) across and is dominated by the gigantic dome fresco of J.J. Zeiller (1746). J.B. Zimmermann was responsible for the organ loft and the stucco work.

The picturesque B23 from Oberammergau continues another 5km

Garmisch, with the Zugspitze in the background

to **Oberau**, a small resort in the Loisachtal, where the B2 is joined for the 8km south to Garmisch-Partenkirchen. In between is **Farchant** (population 3400), a resort with a good selection of holiday accommodation including many holiday flats. Unfortunately the main road is very busy and this rather detracts from the undoubted assets of Oberau and Farchant. At the time of writing the A95 from Munich disgorges its traffic on to the B2 just north of Oberau. No doubt in time the motorway will extend to the outskirts of Garmisch-Partenkirchen but there do not appear to be any immediate plans for this.

Garmisch-Partenkirchen (population 27,000), another example of the double name of which the Germans are rather fond (the towns were united in 1935), is one of the major Alpine resorts and is the starting point for excursions to Germany's highest mountain, the Zugspitze (2963m, 9718ft) which towers above the town. Garmisch-Partenkirchen has many dramatic and musical traditions; the composer Richard Strauss lived here in the street named after him until his death in 1949. In Garmisch the sights include the old church of St Martin although little remains of the original building of about 1280. When the church was extended in 1446, a spire and fine net vaulting in the nave were added. The Gothic wall paintings include a larger-than-life St Christopher (thirteenth century) and scenes from the Passion (fifteenth century). The new parish church of St Martin was built by J. Schmuzer (1730–4) and he was one of the craftsmen responsible for the stucco. King Ludwig II spent time here too and his Schachen hunting lodge just to the north was built as a picturesque retreat and now houses a museum of local history. The Moorish room is specially notable. The Werdenfels Museum at 47 Ludwigstrasse was founded in 1895 to demonstrate the work of the technical school of wood-carvers and cabinet-makers. The exhibits include folk culture, costume, ceramics and sixteenth- to eighteenth-century sculpture. At 45 Ludwigstrasse is the Gasthof Zum Rasen where folk dramas are performed by the Peasant Theatre between mid-July and mid-September.

In Partenkirchen the pilgrimage church of St Anton (1705–39) has an older octagonal part and later building is probably by J. Schmuzer. Unremarkable externally, the two parts merge harmoniously within. The most striking feature is the ceiling painting by J.E. Holzer (1739). The parish church of the Ascension of Our Lady (1865–71) has paintings by the Venetian B. Letterini (1731).

There is a great deal to do in Garmisch-Partenkirchen but the outstanding excursion is to the summit of the Zugspitze. The modern cog-wheel train which goes the greater part of the journey starts from beside the main station and climbs steadily for about half an hour when it calls at Eibsee, a dark mountain lake surrounded by trees. One can change here and go direct to the summit by cable car, a massive altitude change of about 2000m (6560ft) in 10 minutes or so. By staying in the train, the Schneefernerhaus Hotel, at an altitude of 2650m (8692ft), is reached in another $^3/_4$ hour. The actual summit is then reached by means of a cable car in just 4 minutes. Here at the top is the permanent glacier skiing area with a series of ski-lifts having a total capacity of over 3000 persons per hour. It is possible to do the round trip from Eibsee, one way by train and the other way by cable car, and descent from the summit into Austria is another option. The Schneefernerhaus is a modern hotel built right into the side of the mountain and it looks out over a fantastic range of snow-covered peaks as far as the eye can see. A night here — albeit a rather expensive one — is a memorable experience especially if there is a sunset or sunrise.

The Zugspitze excursion by no means exhausts the activities in

PLACES OF INTEREST IN AND AROUND GARMISCH-PARTENKIRCHEN

Old Church of St Martin
(1280–1446)In Garmisch.
Fine net vaulting in nave. Wall
paintings (thirteenth and fifteenth
centuries).

Parish Church of St Martin
(1730–4) In Garmisch.

Schachen Hunting Lodge
Just N of Garmisch. Picturesque
retreat of King Ludwig II.
Museum of local history.

Werdenfels Museum
Ludwigstrasse 47. Wood-carving
and cabinet-making.

**Pilgrimage Church of
St Anton** (1705–39)
In Partenkirchen. Striking ceiling
painting.

**Parish Church of the
Assumption** (1865–71)
In Partenkirchen. Venetian
paintings.

Zugspitze
Germany's highest mountain
(2963m, 9718ft). Cogwheel
railway and cable cars. Summit
hotel.

the Garmisch-Partenkirchen area for there are no less than eight other cable railways as well as numerous ski-lifts. Details of many Alpine 'railways' are given in 'Further Information'.

The Alpenstrasse B2 continues eastwards out of Partenkirchen with the peaks of the Wettersteingebirge prominent on the right, marking the border with Austria — Hochwanner (2764m, 9065ft), Dreitorspitze (2633m, 8636ft) and Wettersteinwand (2482m, 8140ft). After about 12km fork right in Klais leaving theAlpenstrasses for a little while, to visit nearby **Mittenwald**. A town of 8300 inhabitants tightly squeezed in between the mountains, this is another of the outstanding Alpine resorts of Bavaria and the supposed birthplace in 1777 of that fictional character Augustin Sumser encountered at the beginning of this chapter.

Towering over the town to the east is the sheer wall of the Karwendel with its west summit (2385m, 7822ft) sitting astride the border and today easily reached in 10 minutes from the lower station beside the River Isar by the Karwendelbahn cable car. This is the latest and most spectacular addition at Mittenwald and makes it possible for the average tourist to enjoy views previously only seen by energetic climbers who spend many hours on the ascent from the valley. A deservedly popular summer resort but with plenty of winter facilities also. There are many kilometres of well kept and marked footpaths radiating from the town for walks of every length and degree

L-M
↔
ΔΔ
18
or
24km

of difficulty. Many of the paths are kept clear in winter so rambling does not have to be regarded as a purely summer activity.

From the *Kurpark* near the lower station of the Kranzberg chair-lift take the easy nature trail (*Naturlehrpfad*) following the little River Lainbach until the Lautersee is reached at 1010m (3312ft). There is a café here and a pleasant natural bathing place. The nature trail goes along the east lake shore and crosses a minor road. Turn right here and continue to the end of this road at the Ferchensee (1059m, 3473ft — café) and continue straight ahead on an easy path along the north bank of the Ferchenbach — a stream fed by the lake just passed — eventually crossing the stream and following the other bank for a short distance, then crossing back and dropping down to Schloss Elmau, now a hotel. Turn east here, choosing the minor road beyond the *Schloss* or the rather more difficult hill path going off to the right just before reaching it. After about 4km the two routes cross so there is an opportunity for a change of mind. The path soon crosses the Kreidenbach and the road does so a little later near Schloss Kranzbach. They combine again shortly before the hamlet of Klais about 8km from Elmau and from here it is possible to get a 'bus or train back into Mittenwald.

There are several possible walking routes back, none of them very direct, if one wishes to avoid the main road traffic. Easy walking is possible by following the Rossgraben (a little river) south from Klais to the Wildensee (1136m, 3726ft — café) then dropping down past the Korbinianhütte (café) to the starting point. The last 2km could be avoided by using the Kranzberg chair-lift from near the Wildensee. The distance from Klais to Mittenwald is around 6km. This walk has the advantage of getting away from the crowds in and around Mittenwald, especially at summer weekends. Choose a quieter time for sight-seeing there.

The parish church of St Peter and St Paul was built 1738–40 to the plans of J. Schmuzer of Wessobrunn and incorporates the Gothic choir of an earlier building. Schmuzer's decoration is unique, the vaults and friezes are covered in tendrils and blossoms, some of the finest stucco work in Germany. The paintings on the ceiling and high altar (1740) are by M. Günther who also painted the tower when it was completed in 1746. Most people know that Mittenwald is famous as a centre of violin-making and credit for this is given to one Matthias Klotz (1653–1743) who probably studied under Amati in Cremona and returned to found the Mittenwald industry. There is a memorial to

A Mittenwald pension *with the Karwendel*

him in the church. The history of violin-making here is graphically portrayed in the Geigenbau-Museum (Violin-making Museum) and there are collections of other instruments as well as a section devoted to peasant culture.

The carving skills of the inhabitants are nowhere better seen than in the fantastic wooden masks they make for men to wear at the time of the pre-Lenten celebrations called *Fasching* or *Fastnacht*. The colourful activities come to a climax on the Thursday before Lent and the opportunity is taken, not only to prepare for the period of fasting, but to drive out winter and welcome spring. There are processions which are accompanied by much bell-ringing as a mountaineer arrives dressed in the traditional *Lederhosen* (leather shorts) and a decorated belt to which sixteen bells are attached and he leads a group of similarly equipped bell-ringers. The wooden masks are donned by many of the male participants before the procession and there is a great deal of jollity and leg-pulling as the groups go from hostelry to hostelry. The masks are not removed, even for drinking, until the day comes to an end. Later on there is dancing and by tradition no woman may refuse a masked man's invitation to dance.

On leaving Mittenwald return to the Alpenstrasse and in 10km reach the pleasant resort of **Wallgau**. The route follows the Rivar Isar eastwards along a picturesque private toll-road — it cannot officially be called the Alpenstrasse — for about 12km to **Vorderriss** where the road becomes the B307 and can re-assume the name. Vorderriss was the childhood home of Ludwig Thoma, the writer. For another 11km the route continues to follow the river, sweeping across the beautiful Sylvenstein-Stausee on a modern viaduct, but at the foot of the Hoher Zwiesler (1375m, 4510ft) it divides and the left fork becomes the B13 to follow the Isar north towards Bad Tölz.The B307 continues to the Achen Pass (941m, 3086ft) where a hairpin bend takes it briefly into and out of Austria to follow the Grosser Weissach river down to the Tegernsee which is reached at the resort of **Rottach-Egern**. There is another break in the Alpenstrasse and from Rottach-Egern, for about 12km to the south-east, follow another toll-road through impressive scenery with Wallberg (1722m, 5648ft) and Risserkogel (1826m, 5990ft) to the right and Brecherspitz (1685m, 5526ft) and Rothkopf (1599m, 5244ft) on the left. After passing the Rothkopf, the road turns back on itself to go due north up the valley of a stream called the Brandenberger Ache. This Austrian stream with its source in Bavaria runs south to empty into the Inn.

PLACES OF INTEREST IN AND AROUND MITTENWALD AND BAYRISCHZELL

MITTENWALD
Parish Church of St Peter and St Paul (1738–40)
Outstanding stucco decoration and paintings.

Museum of Violin-making
History of violin-making; collection of other instruments; peasant culture.

Karwendel
Dizzy ascent by cable car to the 2385m (7822ft) summit.

BAYRISCHZELL
Parish Church
Gothic tower; eighteenth-century stucco and frescos.

FISCHBACHAU (8km NE of Bayrischzell).

Parish Church of St Martin (1110)
Romanesque building with stucco of the seventeenth and eighteenth centuries.

Old Parish Church
Even older than the present St Martin. Good stucco and rococo organ.

OSTERHOFEN (5km NE of Bayrischzell)
Wendelstein Cable Railway
Summit (1830m, 6000ft) with church, observatory and hotel.

TATZELWURM (10km E of Bayrischzell)
Home of the fiery Tatzelwurm, a mythical monster.

The road climbs up to the Spitzingsattel Pass at 1127m (3696ft) and then descends steeply for 2 or 3km to rejoin the B307. Another 2 or 3km and a road goes off left to both **Stauden** nearby and **Fischbachau** about 3km away. Benedictine monks founded a cell at Fischbachau in the eleventh century but they did not remain long. They had already decided that the climate at Bayrischzell further south did not suit them and they wandered off northwards to locations beyond Munich. The capricious behaviour of the monks did not commend itself to the farming community hereabouts but they did inherit a fine church which was consecrated in 1110, long after the monks had disappeared. The Romanesque building owed something to the spirit of Hirsau in the Black Forest where the monks originated but was considerably altered in the seventeenth and eighteenth centuries when abundant stucco was introduced. The frescos in the nave show scenes from the life of St Martin to whom the church is dedicated and date from 1737–8. However, Fischbachau has an even older church, used before the monks descended upon them, and known as the Alte Pfarrkirche (Old Parish Church). Externally the main building is still pure Romanesque but the interior was given stucco treatment around 1630. Of particular interest is the charming rococo organ of 1750.

H
↔ ↔
△△△
13km

Back on the B307, the cable railway up the west side of the Wendelstein (1838m, 6028ft) can soon be seen. A strenuous ramble taking in the Wendelstein summit starts at the **Osterhofen** station of the cable railway (5 minutes from the DB station) where there is parking space. Set off in an easterly direction on a gently rising track to the settlement of **Hochkreut**. At the second farmhouse from there — house No 16 — join the Wendelsteinweg from Bayrischzell and follow its red markings through the wooded west slopes of the Legerwaldgraben. In $^3/_4$ hour the little Siegel-Alm (1325m, 4346ft) is reached, not far from a stream which has to be crossed. After $^1/_4$ hour arrive at the basin of the Wendelstein *Almen* (Alpine meadows). Now walk up to the right for half an hour to the gap between the Kesselwand and the Wendelstein and then to the left to reach the saddle at the foot of the Wendelstein summit in about $2^1/_2$ hours from Osterhofen. (Save time by using the cable car for the ascent.) Up to the left is the little Wendelstein church, the highest place of worship in Germany, while to the right there is the upper terminus of the cog-wheel railway up from Brannenburg. It takes about 20 minutes more to reach the summit at 1830m (6002ft) and there is a small fee to use the good path, for the actual summit is private property. The stupendous view makes it money well spent. To the east, below the highest point, are the domes of the sun observatory and the mast of Bavarian Radio.

With cable car and railway to bring the tourists it is not surprising to find a hotel up here as well. From the hotel terrace go down stone steps and then follow the curves through scree beneath the cableway and follow the sign 'Breitenstein, Feilbach'. After $^1/_4$ hour fork left (Breitenstein) to reach an *Alm* hut (Quellbrunnentrog) in about the same time. Just before the hut keep left at the sign for Geitau and Breitenstein. Parts of the path (red waymarks) across the *Alm* basin are narrow but in an hour from the summit a climb up to a broad meadow saddle reveals splendid views to the south. A waymark points to the Koth-Alm. Turn half-right after 10 minutes and then at a wooden cross, turn right down to the Koth-Alm at 1448m (4750ft). A track leads to the Kesselalm (refreshments) and later down a zig-zag path to reach the first houses of **Birkenstein** after half an hour. Go right here to a surfaced road; 100m to the right is the Gasthaus Oberwirt. The route now turns south to the end of the surfaced road at a cattle grid. About a 150m further at a second cattle grid follow the sign for Geitau and the clear path straight ahead; shortly before reaching the railway at **Geitau** join a surfaced road until, in front of a house near the embankment, a sign to the left indicates 'Bayrischzell' (there is a *Gasthaus* 50m to the right, *Ruhetag* Thursday) and this eastbound path between a wood and the railway reaches the starting point at **Osterhofen** in $1/_4$ hour. The whole circuit takes about $5^1/_2$ hours or about 3 hours if the ascent is made by cable car. There is overnight accommodation at the Wendelstein Hotel and at the Koth-Alm.

Five kilometres on from Osterhofen, **Bayrischzell** (population 1600) is where the Benedictine monks first came to in 1075 to found their short-lived cell, and the *–zell* in the name has survived. This is regarded by some as the ideal Alpine village and it is indeed a place for superlatives. Upper Bavaria is certainly not short of attractive villages but Bayrischzell stands supreme. Those early monks complained about the transport problems and for most of its existence Bayrischzell lay off the beaten track and was little visited, for the railway south from Schliersee only reached here in 1911. Today a fast train comes from Munich in 90 minutes. The Alpenstrasse between here and the next resort — Sudelfeld — provides the ideal jumping-off place for a wonderful rambling and skiing area going up to 1450m (4756ft). In the ravine of the Tatzelwurm it is easy to conjure up a vision of the Bavarian fantasy-dragon of that name. Around 1930, hoaxers persuaded some newspapers of the existence of this creature but — like the Loch Ness Monster — it has never been seen since. However — like its Scottish counterpart — it has been good for the tourist trade and souvenirs include a marzipan version.

 Well worthwhile are visits to the outlying mountain *Gasthäuser* in locations selected for the splendour of their outlook. In Bayrischzell, the late Gothic tower of the church stands out from quite a distance and it is surprising to find on closer investigation that the main part of the building is eighteenth century and was decorated in 1736 with stucco and frescos. This is one of the few places where Sunday church-going is still an occasion for wearing the attractive traditional costumes of the district.

The curvaceous final section of the B307 is a spectacular road between the mountains so do not hurry and miss the views that constantly open up. **Sudelfeld**, reached after about 7km is an outlying part of Bayrischzell. The road ends at **Tatzelwurm** — yes, there really is a place with that unlikely name. Once again, further progress can only be made on a private toll-road; to the right this leads

---

PLACES OF INTEREST IN BRANNENBURG, DEGERNDORF, BERNAU AND GRASSAU

BRANNENBURG
Wendelstein Cog-wheel Railway

Church of the Assumption
Rebuilt in rococo style at the end of the eighteenth century.

DEGERNDORF
Church of St Aegidias
Romanesque nave, late Gothic tower, baroque ornamentation of 1741.

Klosterkirche Reisach
12km S. Fine wooden reliefs.

BERNAU
Gasthof zum Alten Wirt (1697)
Distinguished old inn surrounded by fine houses.

GRASSAU
Parish Church (1491)
Historic frescos and painting (1700).

---

to Oberaudorf and into Austria. A short distance from the junction is the Berggasthof Feuriger (fiery) Tatzelwurm, evidence that the monster is doing its bit for tourism. The *Gasthof* is closed from 5 November until 15 December and on Tuesdays, January to May.

To the left the private road leads to **Flintsbach** (population 2500) and **Brannenburg** (population 5000) both of which are health resorts in the *Luftkurort* category. They, together with **Degerndorf**, are within a stone's throw of each other. This is the Inn Valley shared by the river, the railway, the motorway A93 and several other roads. Brannenburg is the lower terminal of the cog-wheel railway which goes up to the Wendelstein (upper station 1723m, 5650ft) in 55 minutes. Several places of interest in the vicinity are often overlooked. Brannenburg's late Gothic church Mariae Himmelfahrt was rebuilt in the rococo style at the end of the eighteenth century while Degerndorf's St Aegidias has a nave which is still Romanesque, a late Gothic tower and baroque ornamentation of 1741.

There are many worthwhile short excursions to be made in this area — the *Klosterkirche* at **Reisach**, and **Oberaudorf** with its colourfully painted houses and a church noted for its rococo decoration and a late Gothic Madonna. At **Bad Feilnbach**, about 8km northwest of Brannenburg, is one of the largest camp sites in Upper Bavaria and many self-catering apartments.

After Tatzelwurm, the road heads north as the Alpenstrasse. Leaving Brannenburg and crossing the *Autobahn*, join B15 and con-

Reit im Winkl

tinue through Rieschenhart and Raubling until in about 6km the junction with the Munich-Salzburg motorway A8 is reached. This now becomes the Alpenstrasse for 19km, travelling east to **Bernau** (population 5000), a *Luftkurort* near the south-west corner of the Chiemsee (explored in a later chapter).

Bernau is a distinguished village at the north foot of the Kampenwand (1669m, 5475ft). The finest house is the Gasthof zum Alten Wirt which was erected in 1697 although its origins go back as far as 1477. Today it is a listed building and noted for the comfort of its accommodation. Leaving Bernau, the B305 is the road to follow to the end of this chapter. **Rottau** and **Grassau** comprise a *Luftkurort* with a population of 5300. The church in Grassau (8km from Bernau) dates from 1491, it was extended in 1696 and its Romanesque tower was capped with an onion-dome in 1737. Inside, a fresco from the fifteenth century has been laid bare and restored. Even more noteworthy, over the entrance door is a detailed portrayal of a Corpus Christi procession dating from 1700.

Three kilometres on, **Marquartstein** (population 2900), a *Luftkurort* at the foot of the Hochgern (1743m, 5717ft) on the River Tiroler Ache, is an unsophisticated village overlooked by a medieval fortress which was restored in the last century. Music lovers may be interested to know that Richard Strauss was very fond of this village and it was here that he composed his *Salome* at the beginning of this century. Much of the 17km from Marquartstein to Reit im Winkl is in a narrow gorge with sheer cliffs rising on either side of the road. In between are the villages of **Unterwössen** and **Oberwössen**, the latter of interest for the three little lakes accessible from here. Two of them, the Eglsee and Wössener See are quite near but the Taubensee is high above at an altitude of 1138m (3732ft) and demands a long and strenuous ramble to reach it. The Austrian border actually passes through the centre of the lake.

Reit im Winkl (population 2800) is an entrancing Alpine village where the houses are outstandingly decorated with colour and flowers. It has grown from a tiny frontier hamlet into a popular resort and yet has retained its rural charm. Admittedly, it is even more charming outside the main tourist season but that is something it shares with most other places in these Bavarian mountains. There are two chair-lifts and twenty-one ski-lifts. For the walker there are rambles of all grades starting from the village centre. A modest stroll could start from the church and follow the road to the end of the village and then climb gently to the Grünbühel where the ditches are the remains of earthworks dug during the Tirolean war of liberation in 1809. Although this little climb takes only a few minutes, the whole valley lies below and, to the south-west, are wonderful views to the 'Emperor' mountains including the so-called Zahmer (peaceable) Kaiser and the Wilder (ferocious) Kaiser, all in Austria and with the highest peaks well over 2000m (6560ft).

L
↔
ΔΔ
2km

The path continues to climb fairly gently (10 minutes) to the war memorial chapel (1924) visible on the Pankrazhügel. Here there is a fine view in every direction. Behind the chapel the path now climbs rather steeply in a northerly direction towards the Hausberg and after many twists and turns reaches the Hausbachfall (waterfall) at 835m (2738ft) in another 10 minutes. From here a path leads directly — and rather steeply — back down to the village. The whole walk should be accomplished within an hour. It is as well to remember that the Austrian border is only about 2km to the west of the village and it is obviously prudent to carry a passport when rambling in this area.

Once more between mountains and through a fairly sparsely populated but remarkably pretty countryside, the B305 passes a string of lovely little lakes — Weitsee, Mittersee, Lodensee and Forchensee in that order. Several villages offer refreshment or

PLACES OF INTEREST IN RUHPOLDING AND INZELL

RUHPOLDING
Parish Church of St Georg
(1738–57)
Fine pulpit, choir stalls and altars.
Famous Madonna.

Heimatmuseum
Schlossstrasse 2. Housed in
former hunting lodge of 1587.

**Museum of Rural and
Religious Art**
Roman-Freisinger-Strasse 1.
Gorgeous cupboards, glass,
crockery, etc.

Fairy-tale Park
3km SW. Models of fairy-tale
characters, miniature railway,
adventure playground, café.

INZELL
Gasthof Zur Post
In village centre. Beautiful old
sixteenth-century inn.

Parish Church of St Michael
(1727)
In village centre.

unsophisticated accommodation but there is no holiday resort as such until, just after passing Weich, the road goes northwards to reach **Ruhpolding** (population 6800) about 30km from Reit im Winkl. Ruhpolding has both a very large *Freibad* and a *Wellen-hallenbad* — an indoor pool with artificial waves. The village itself is not too hemmed in by high mountains for four Alpine valleys converge here making it an open, airy place. There is a cable railway to the Rauschberg (1645m, 5395ft), three chair-lifts and ski-lifts, so once again there is ready access to the slopes in summer and winter. If Ruhpolding is visited when it is not thronged with tourists so much the better.

The parish church of St Georg is reckoned to be one of the finest village churches in Upper Bavaria. Its size is the first surprise for it is no less than 40m long (130ft) with a width of 14m (46ft) and a height of 19m (62ft). Built between 1738 and 1757, this is a fine church. There is a richly decorated pulpit, beautiful choir stalls and several interesting altars. The baroque decoration is a veritable feast for the eye. But the artistic highlight of the church is the Romanesque Madonna, the creator of which is unknown, only re-discovered in 1955 and which now graces the right side-altar. Despite its age, this carving with its out-of-proportion baby Jesus in his mother's lap could well have been the work of a modern artist. It is something not to be

missed. The *Heimatmuseum* is highly acclaimed and is housed in a former hunting lodge dating from 1587. The Museum für Bäuerliche

Ramsau church

und Sakrale Kunst (rural and religious art) is also very fine and complements the *Heimatmuseum*.

A popular ramble is to the pilgrimage church of Maria Eck. Leave the village at the north end and, past the hospital, turn left and take the right hand of two roads to **Obergschwendt**. By the first house on the right (bear in mind possible new building) take the path to the right and follow this as it runs fairly level, mostly in the wood. If the hospital turning is missed this same path may be reached by walking about 5 minutes more along the road in the direction of **Eisenärzt** (the next village) and turning left — look for the sign. The path runs roughly parallel with the road and the last part before Eisenärzt climbs continuously — not really to be recommended after rain. The road is rejoined and just before entering the village a little road goes off to the left; an alternative good track goes up between the station and the church. Both routes climb steadily to reach Maria Eck (823m, 2700ft) in about 40 minutes.

M

ΔΔ

13km

In addition to the church itself there is a Minorite *Kloster* and a *Gasthaus*. There are splendid views to the high mountain ranges, to the Chiemsee and even to the Bayerischer Wald (Bavarian Forest) far to the north, given good visibility. From Maria Eck, south-westwards past the *Gasthaus*, a ramble leads to the Scheichenberg (1256m, 4120ft) in about 3km, a steady climb. Keep right here and drop down to the Hocherbalm and then to the Steinberger Alm (refreshments) and continue downhill following a little stream until Ruhpolding is reached.

If there are children in the party, visit the Ruhpolding Märchenfamilienpark (Fairy-tale Park) with its many models of fairy-tale characters — Snow White and the Seven Dwarfs, Hansel and Gretel, the Sleeping Beauty and many more as well as a miniature railway, adventure playground, mini-dodgem-cars and a café.

Back to the Alpenstrasse and in less than 8km reach **Inzell**, the third of these charming Upper Bavarian villages which, with Reit im Winkl and Ruhpolding make up the so-called Chiemgauer Feriendreieck (Chiemgau Holiday Triangle). Inzell with 3500 inhabitants has many holiday flats. The Gasthof Zur Post dates from the first half of the sixteenth century and its artistic corner towers and courtyard entrance beautify the village centre. Opposite, the parish church of St Michael dates from 1727 and has a double onion-domed tower; it is not overloaded with decoration within, the principal sight being the cross at the triumphal arch.

At Inzell, the Deutsche Ferienstrasse, nearly at the end of its long journey from the Baltic, loses its separate identity and joins the Alpenstrasse. On the left, just after Inzell, is the tiny Zwingsee and the end of the valley of the same name, a relic of a glacial gorge from the Ice Age. At **Weissbach** the rocky walls and cliffs climb steeply up out of the valley to over 1000m (3280ft). The small village of **Schneizlreuth** (population 650) is a good centre for exploring many little lakes and two typical Alpine gorges, the Aschauerklamm and the Weissbachschlucht. If one wishes to stay in a more sophisticated resort, however, the prosperous spa town of **Bad Reichenhall** (population 20,000) is less than 8km to the east and offers every conceivable diversion for the holidaymaker.

The Alpenstrasse drops down into the Saalachtal and after Unterjettenberg where the main road to Bad Reichenhall goes off, climbs to the Schwarzbachwachtsattel Pass at 868m (2847ft). Now there is a view down into the Ramsau valley, one of the most delightful in the Berchtesgaden area which is by no means short of fine views. The pilgrimage church of St Fabian and St Sebastian must be one of the most photographed churches in Upper Bavaria because of its beau-

Plansee

Lautersee and the Karwendel Mountains

Schloss Linderhof

In the garden, Schloss Linderhof

Schönau with mountains of the Watzmann group in the background

tiful setting and no calendar is complete without at least one picture of it. The church itself is not without merit either; it was founded in the early sixteenth century and the seventeenth-century groined vault, the baroque high reliefs and medieval wood-carvings ensure a continuing pilgrimage, now of art lovers rather than the pious.

A pleasant short ramble goes through the Zauberwald (Magic Forest) to the Hintersee. Take the Hintersee road west from Ramsau and after about 2km, at the Gasthof Datzmann, go right at a sign marking the entrance to the Zauberwald. Walk downhill to start with, then over a stream, after which turn to the left and a little later to the right over a bridge into the wilderness of the forest. Follow the rushing stream, the Ramsauer Ache, and arrive at a well made track through this near-primeval landscape. Huge rocks overgrown with moss are scattered through the wood, witnesses of a time when these great mountains were less stable than they are today. Twenty minutes from the main road is the point where the boggy bank of the Hintersee reaches almost to the side of the track. Turn right along the lake (note the reflections of the mountains) and after a good 10 minutes reach the old Hinterseestrasse. Now walk up to the right on this little road, then downhill again. Mountains dominate the scene ahead with a

L
↔
ΔΔ
7.5km

distant view of the permanent snowfield of the Blaueisgletscher (Blue Ice Glacier) up to the right. After a bridge, turn right into the dark pines of the Zauberwald and see on the left a miniature cable railway and other Alpine scenarios operated by a water-wheel. At the next fork go left and reach the Gasthof Datzmann again after a short climb.The total time for the circuit is about $1^1/_2$ hours. Return along the road to Ramsau or wait for the occasional post-bus. This is also suitable as a winter walk.

The Alpenstrasse now enters one of the outstanding mountain holiday areas on the whole route, the so-called Berchtesgadener Land. This mountain-ringed area comprises the almost adjoining resorts of **Berchtesgaden**, **Bischofswiesen** and **Schönau** together with the surrounding countryside and settlements along the B305 from Ramsau to Marktschellenberg where the road disappears over the border into Austria on the outskirts of Salzburg. The total population is around 20,000 but is, of course, well scattered. Two mountain railways, two chair-lifts and over two dozen ski-lifts are here to serve the visitor as well as all the more usual leisure facilities. Berchtesgaden even boasts a golf course, a rather rare thing in Bavaria. But as with all the other resorts along the Alpine Road, it is the scenery which stands supreme and in this furthest corner of Bavaria it hardly matters which way one turns for exploration for there are delights on every side.

To the south-west, the mighty Watzmann (2713m, 8898ft) towers over the land, second only to the Zugspitze in height. To the south, the village of **Königssee** stands at the north end of the tranquil lake of the same name which nestles between the peaks. One of the most beautiful lakes in Bavaria, it is a favourite excursion and somewhat overburdened with tourists during the peak summer holiday season. From the northern tip — the lake is 8km long, 2km wide and up to 188m (616ft) deep — one can see the tiny church of St Bartholomä across the water. Built in 1700 in the shape of a clover leaf with attractive cupolas, the church, occupying space between the lake and the east wall of the Watzmann, can only be reached by motor-boat from the pier at the north end. At St Bartholomä one can disembark to enjoy the peace. This excursion is one which no visitor should forego. The quietness is occasionally enhanced rather than broken by the demonstration of the remarkable seven-fold echo when a trumpet call is flung back and forth from the Falkenstein precipice. The motor-boat trips operate throughout the year except when the lake is frozen.

The Königssee near Berchtesgaden

The Alpenpark is an area of about 460sq km surrounding the resorts. The southern part of the area is given over to the Nationalpark Berchtesgaden, a conservation area. The last native bear was killed in 1835 but there is no lack of wildlife here including chamois, deer, ibex and — above 1200m (3936ft)— marmots. A climb through the nature reserve south of the Königssee to the Funtensee (1601m, 5251ft) provides a good chance of seeing some of these creatures in their natural habitats. The picturesque autumn ceremony of bringing the cattle down from the high pastures is always of interest but has a particular attraction here for the animals have to be ferried across the Königssee. The possibilities for climbing, walking, motoring or cycling excursions are endless. Mountain weather being what it is, there is always the chance of a wet day when the natural attractions are less than enticing. This need not be an unmitigated disaster for there are many ways of putting the day to good use.

In **Berchtesgaden** the *Heimatmuseum* can be recommended; its exhibits are largely from the College of Wood-carving and include 400 hand-carved coats of arms. The former Augustinian canonry church of St Peter and St Johannes is on a site first dedicated to these

PLACES OF INTEREST IN AND AROUND BERCHTESGADEN

Heimatmuseum
Many exhibits from College of Wood-carving.

Schloss Museum
Housed in the Residenz (former canonry from about 1410). Art collection.

Salzmuseum
Bergstrasse 83. The story of salt-mining.

Salt Mines
First opened in 1517. Exciting underground tours.

Augustinian Canonry Church of St Peter and Johannes
Tombs of the prince-priors; interesting choir stalls. Thirteenth century.

Frauenkirche am Anger
Sixteenth century.

Baroque Market Place and Fountain

Pilgrimage Church Maria Gern (1709) (3km N)

Pilgrimage Church of Fabian and Sebastian
In Ramsau 10km W. Charming sixteenth-century baroque church in splendid alpine setting.

Königssee
5-13km S. Beautiful Alpine lake with church of St Bartholomä (1700). Motor boat trips.

Nationalpark
To the south around and beyond the Königssee. Huge unspoiled area rich in wildlife.

saints in 1122. In the thirteenth century the second building (from which the west part and the cloisters have survived) was erected. Prior Johannes added the slender early Gothic choir in 1283–1303 and around 1470 the Romanesque nave was pulled down and replaced by a pillared hall. The choir slopes upwards at the end of the nave, a unique example of early Gothic in Bavaria. There are striking tombs of the prince-priors in red Untersberg marble, in particular the high tomb of Prior P. Peinzenauer (1432) by the Romanesque west entrance. The notable choir stalls (1436–43) have intertwining animal designs on the side pieces. The residential building of the canonry later became the Residenz and is now owned by the Wittelsbachs. The building has been much altered over the years but the Romanesque cloisters are among the best of their kind. The Residenz now houses the Schlossmuseum, mainly concerned with the princes' excellent art collection which includes works by such famous names as Veit Stoss, Tilman Riemenschneider, Erasmus Grasser and Lucas Cranach.

The Salzmuseum is a specialist museum dealing with salt-mining and the lives of salt miners. It works in cooperation with the Berchtesgaden salt mines opened in 1517 and still operating today. In earlier years only members of royal families, church dignitaries and the like were allowed to visit the mines but today they are open to all as a major tourist attraction with about half a million visitors each year. Today's thousands, like the distinguished visitors of the past, must don the clothing worn by the miners of old and start the tour horseback fashion by riding astride the old mining train through a 600m-long (1968ft) tunnel to the Emperor Franz pit, an enormous cavern with a ceiling area of 3000sq m. At a lower level is a grotto, bright with many-coloured salt rocks, reached by a sedate walk downstairs or, more excitingly, down a 34m-long (111ft) chute polished over the years by the seats of miners' (and tourists') trousers. Here there are a film theatre and displays of the various equipment and activities associated with the mine. A second chute takes one down to the illuminated underground salt lake crossed on a raft. After passing through another sparkling grotto, an inclined elevator returns the visitor to a higher level to rejoin the 'train' for an exhilarating dash back to the open air. The visit, including time for changing clothes, takes approximately $1\frac{1}{2}$ hours.

Other wet weather sights include the Frauenkirche am Anger (sixteenth century), the much-photographed pilgrimage church of Maria Gern (1709) north of Berchtesgaden and the pilgrimage church of Kunterweg (1731–3) west of the town. The baroque market place is amongst the finest in Upper Bavaria but the fountain crowned by the Bavarian heraldic lion was only installed in 1860 to celebrate the 50th anniversary of Berchtesgaden's allegiance to the blue and white kingdom; there are memorial tablets listing all the Wittelsbach monarchs. During Advent the houses round the square are illuminated and the fountain carries an enormous *Adventskranz* (Advent wreath). Winter visitors can enjoy the added attractions of the various festivities which go to make up the Advent-Christmas-New Year seasons. A nice custom here in Berchtesgaden on Christmas Eve is the placing of a lighted candle on every grave in the cemetery.

For many older people the name of Berchtesgaden may be synonymous with the dark days before World War II and Neville Chamberlain's abortive visits to Bavaria to secure 'peace in our time'. He was entertained high above Berchtesgaden by Adolf Hitler who had bought a house called Wachenfeld with a marvellous view of the mountains. When Hitler was released from Landsberg prison in 1925, he rented from a Frau Winter this fine country home with its completely encircling balcony and a roof of shingles secured by heavy stones as seen so often in Alpine regions. When Frau Winter sold Hitler the house in 1929 she could hardly have guessed that a few years later it would be the scene of such dramatic events, events which coloured the world's view of Berchtesgaden for many years. Hitler's later additions to his accommodation up here were destroyed shortly before the end of the war but the Teehaus, the so-called Adlerhorst (eagle's nest) at 1834m (6015ft) survived and today (as the Kehlsteinhaus) is run by the Alpine Club as a mountain *Gaststätte*.

Fifteen kilometres north of Berchtesgaden the Alpenstrasse crosses into Austria and the city of Mozart, Salzburg. The music-lover could easily enjoy the world-famous Salzburg Festival from a base on the Bavarian side of the border. Salzburg and Berchtesgaden together with Bad Reichenhall, although separated by the present national boundary, have a common political and economic history and today form the Austro-Bavarian Holiday Triangle.

3 THE LAKES

An area of some 900sq km south-west of Munich has been named Fünf-Seen-Land by the tourist authorities — Five Lakes District — although there are really many more lakes than that. Five of them, however, are readily accessible from Munich using the excellent suburban railway system (S-bahn) and it is better to explore these first before going further afield to visit others right up to the Alpenstrasse. From the city centre the S-bahn journey takes 30–50 minutes according to destination. Trains are at least every 40 minutes, often more frequent. For the tourist wishing to use the S-bahn the very economical 24-hour tickets are to be recommended. The cost for an adult is little more than the price of an ordinary single journey ticket from Munich to, say, Starnberg and the 24-hour ticket can be used for the return journey and for any other journey on the MVV (Münchner Verkehrs- und Tarifverband) whether by S-bahn, U-bahn (underground), 'bus or tram within 24 hours. Children pay one-third of the adult price.

The whole of the 'Five Lakes' area is excellent rambling and cycling country and there are many package arrangements for exploring the countryside without carrying luggage. Rewarding day walks can be started from any of the S-bahn stations or from any other point round the lakes. The Starnberger See is the biggest Bavarian lake after Chiemsee and its northern tip is only 20km from the centre of Munich. The lake is about 20km north to south and up to 5km wide. It is served by S-bahn line 6 and four stations are adjacent to the lake; Starnberg is at the north end and Possenhofen, Feldafing and Tutzing are on the western shore.

The MVV has been responsible with other organisations for waymarking a comprehensive network of footpaths, and a map showing those in the vicinity can be found at each station. The 48km of the route right round the Starnberger See are more than could be

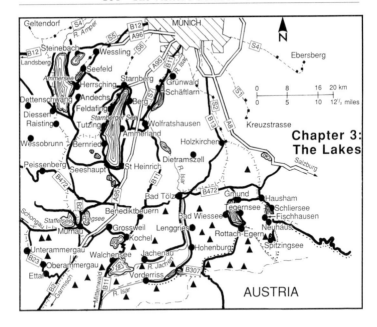

accomplished in one day but there are plenty of places for overnight stops along the way. For the rambler there is a special map, *Wanderkarte-Fünfseenland* (l:50,000), and an accompanying pocket guide giving a description of ten selected one-day walks. These publications are also useful for the cyclist planning his own route. Cycles may be hired at railway stations and elsewhere — see 'Further Information' for details.

From around the end of March until the end of September there are regular steamer services on the Starnberger See. There are also dance cruises on Saturday evenings from July to September. **Starnberg** with its surrounding villages has some 18,000 inhabitants and is a busy and attractive small town right on the lake shore. The excellent transport facilities between here and Munich have made it a popular residential town for city workers as well as an excellent holiday centre. Water activities feature strongly, of course, with much boating, wind-surfing, diving, etc. The old parish church of St Josef (1764–6) is regarded as Starnberg's trade mark. It is a rococo building and the high altar is considered a fine example of the work of Ignaz Günther. The picture gallery in the *Heimatmuseum* has works by

Starnberg

several artists who were active here, including Lenbach, Schwindt and Uhde. Starnberg is the base of the organisation LEO Aktiv Reisen which looks after 3–10-day cycle tours, mainly in the Fünf-Seen-Land and Pfaffenwinkel.

All the principal sights and resorts mentioned in the next few pages are in the itinerary of one or other of these tours. The 'packages' include hire of cycles suitable for the terrain, pre-booked overnight accommodation, maps and literature, transfer of luggage from place to place and so on. The north-east corner of the lake provides for an easy ramble with fine views across the water.

Start on the Seepromenade near the landing stage opposite Starnberg station and go eastwards following waymarks '1'. Still following the shore turn into Nepomukweg and pass the Hallenbad and then the lake bathing area to reach the recreation area of **Kempfenhausen** in about 2km. Now turn south, continue to follow the shore through some wooded plots and past numerous attractive houses until **Berg** is reached in another 2km. The *Schloss* here has less to offer the sightseer than the rather fine surrounding park. Ludwig II had a neo-Gothic chapel erected in 1876 — he spent happy youthful days here and here it was, in 1886, that he met his death. A cross in the reeds at the water's edge marks the spot where his body was found on the morning of 13 July. A chapel was built here in 1900 in neo-

L
↔
ΔΔ
11km

*Ludwig II Memorial
Chapel beside the
Starnberg Lake*

Romanesque style in memory of the unhappy monarch.

From Berg, Ludwig could look across the lake to Possenhofen, the home of his cousin Elisabeth (Sissy) who was later to become empress of Austria and who was one of the few relatives with whom he was always on good terms. As empress, Elisabeth had her summer seat at nearby Feldafing on the west shore for 24 years and thought that the views to the east and south across the lake were the finest in the world.

The walk continues through the Berg Schlosspark past the memorial chapel, more or less following the shore line. There is a good viewpoint at a Bismarck monument (1899) before reaching **Ammerland** where, during the summer months, there is the opportunity of crossing the lake by steamer to for the train back to Starnberg or Munich. The walk from Berg represents the first section of the long-distance path called the König-Ludwig-Weg which was opened in 1977 and can be walked as a *Wandern ohne Gepäck* (walking without luggage) holiday which includes six overnight stops. The route is designed to embrace as many places of interest as possible, amongst them Kloster Andechs, the Ammersee (steamer crossing), Wessobrunn, Hohenpeissenberg, Rottenbuch, Wies, Neuschwanstein, Hohenschwangau and Füssen. A detailed description of the route is not given here as those participating in the 'package' are provided with all necessary maps and guides. For those wishing to make their own arrangements there is no problem either, for maps and guides are readily available in Starnberg and Füssen.

If there are children in the party an alternative to the lake crossing after arriving at Ammerland is to visit the beautiful Märchenwald Fairytale Park in **Wolfratshausen** about 7km to the east. First walk about 2km to **Münsing** where there is a 'bus service to Wolfratshausen. Here, all the favourite fairy tales are brought to life with the press of a button which sets the characters in motion. There are also a large play area, a miniature railway and old-timer cars to travel in and a racing track with miniature cars and motor-cycles for budding juvenile drivers. There is a 'bus service back to Starnberg or those returning to Munich can do so direct from Wolfratshausen by S-bahn.

Further south on the east shore is **St Heinrich** with its Marienkirche of 1324. At the southern tip **Seeshaupt** is another important resort but as it is beyond reach of the S-bahn it is less likely to get completely overrun at summer weekends. This is the starting point for an excursion into the Osterseen, a group of no less than twenty-one tiny lakes (so much for five lakes!) the origins of which go back to the Ice Age and there is much to interest geologists here. The largest of these lakes is called Ostara after the heathen goddess. This is a landscape conservation area and even if the summer months are not short of sun-soaking bodies in and around the lakes, there is plenty left for the nature-lover who is prepared to park the car and walk.

Continuing round the Starnberger See, the route leads to **Bernried** where a splendid Nationalpark with many fine old trees was the gift in 1913 of the appropriately named German-American Mrs Busch-Woods. The old *Kloster* was founded in 1121 by the Augustinians; of their buildings erected in 1653 only one wing remains. The parish church was originally a Romanesque building but was given decorative treatment in the early baroque period. The tower, which stands on original foundations, was the work of Caspar Feichtmayr who came from this area and was a successful architect.

Johannes Brahms lived in **Tutzing** in 1873 and there is a memorial to him on the Brahmspromenade. The sixteenth-century *Schloss*

PLACES OF INTEREST AROUND THE STARNBERGER SEE

STARNBERG
Parish Church of St Josef
(1764–6)
Rococo with fine altar by
I. Günther.

Heimatmuseum
Includes a gallery with pictures by artists active locally.

BERG
Schloss and Schlosspark
Neo-Gothic chapel (1876), Ludwig II memorial chapel (1900), site of Ludwig II's death in lake. Bismarck Monument (1899) (viewpoint) before reaching Ammerland.

WOLFRATSHAUSEN
Fairy-tale Wood
All the favourite fairy-tale characters brought to life; miniature railway; junior race track.

ST HEINRICH
Marienkirche (1324)

OSTERSEEN
Many tiny lakes in conservation area. Geological interest.

BERNRIED
Nationalpark with fine trees

Remains of Augustinian Kloster (1653)

Parish Church
Romanesque with baroque overtones.

TUTZING
Schloss (sixteenth century)
Two Parish Churches

FELDAFING
Kalvarienberg

Roseninsel with Schloss and Teehaus
Boats to the island leave from Feldafing.

POSSENHOFEN
Schloss
Former home of Elisabeth, Empress of Austria and cousin of King Ludwig II.

has been, since 1957, the home of a Protestant academy. Of Tutzing's two parish churches the oldest, a late Gothic building which was transformed 200 years ago, is the most attractive. Already mentioned for its views **Feldafing** has a golf course and a well known Kalvarienberg. In the park of the rather pricey Kaiserin Elisabeth Hotel there is a statue of the one-time empress. This is the embarkation point for the very short trip to the Roseninsel with its *Schloss* and the Teehaus Maximilian II. Ludwig II came here often but unfortunately the fine rose borders which gave the island its name have disap- peared. The former home of Elisabeth in **Possenhofen** has been in private ownership since 1950. In 1958 the city of Munich purchased land on the shore here which is now the popular bathing place, Paradies, which will accommodate 10,000 bathers.

The other big lake is the Ammersee lying a little to the west of Starnberg. The road between the two goes past Kloster Andechs where the visitor should stop for one of the most rewarding sights in this area. Heiliger Berg (Holy Mountain), is the local name for the 711m-high (2332ft) hill on which the *Kloster* and its church stand; at a slightly lower level is the beer hall where the famous Andechs brew is dispensed. Less than 100m from the church, food and drink are available and souvenirs abound. A castle here in the twelfth century was the seat of the counts of Diessen-Andechs but in 1209 it was destroyed by the Wittelsbachs and the last count (Otto) died in exile in 1248. To prevent the treasures of the castle chapel falling into Wittelsbach hands, these were buried under the chapel together with three consecrated communion wafers and the building was razed to the ground. The treasures were rediscovered in 1388 and this resulted in the hill becoming a place of pilgrimage and led, at the beginning of the fifteenth century to the building of the present church and later the *Kloster* which was occupied by Benedictine monks from the Tegernsee.

The church was rebuilt over the years and finally, in the middle of the eighteenth century, Johann Baptist Zimmermann, the stucco artist, converted the building to a baroque masterpiece. Time is needed to absorb every aspect of the church which, in truth, is neither Gothic nor quite baroque but a harmonious blend of styles. The Klostergasthof (*Ruhetag* Thursday) stems from the fifteenth century but was tastefully modernised in 1969 to make it a most pleasant and well cared for hostelry. The visitor, exhausted perhaps by the sightseeing, should retire down to the spacious Bräustüberl (open daily) or its terrace with a fine view towards the Alps. Here there is no waiter or waitress service. One has to collect one's own beer and food — including famous Andechs *Kloster* cheese — from the counter and sit down at one of the bare wooden tables.

Down on the east shore of the Ammersee, **Herrsching** is an attractive resort of about 6000 inhabitants. It is the terminal of line 5 from Munich, the only S-bahn station on the lake. Steamers (April–October) are timed to fit in with the trains. Herrsching claims to have the longest lakeside promenade in West Germany — 10km without a break. Here again, recreational activity tends to centre on the lake but there is a variety of entertainments and leisure pursuits for all tastes.

In the south-west corner of the lake, **Diessen** is of similar size and is served by the Federal Railway. The outstanding sight in this popular holiday resort is the church of St Maria, formerly a collegiate church of Augustinian canons. The present building was begun in 1720 and the shell was almost complete when it was torn down and started afresh to plans by Johann Michael Fischer, the noted baroque architect from Munich who later went on to work at Ottobeuren. The church in Diessen is one of the most important baroque buildings in Bavaria. The leading artists of the day worked on the interior with stucco work by the brothers F.X. and J.M. Feuchtmayr, also J.G. Üblherr from Wessobrunn. Some of the sculptures were designed by François de Cuvilliés the Elder, creator of the Munich Residenztheater. The outstanding feature is the high altar up a flight of steps. Behind the altarpiece is a platform which can be fitted with different pictures to suit the various holy days. While in Diessen, the church of St Georgen at the west of the town is worth seeing. Originally a fifteenth-century building, it was enlarged in 1750 when such famous craftsmen as F.X. Feuchtmayr and M. Günther were involved. Diessen provides for a comprehensive range of water sports and other activities. A regular annual event is the south German *Töpfermarkt* (pot market) which takes place on Ascension Day. The König-Ludwig-Weg passes through here and there is a 280km network of marked paths for which a *Wanderkarte* is available.

Four kilometres to the south at **Raisting** is one of the technological wonders of today, the Deutsche Bundespost (Post Office) satellite tracking station. The tiny idyllic village hosts one of the most modern bridgeheads in the intercontinental telecommunications service. Huge parabolic antennae are directed to the skies and automatically follow the paths of the satellites. For most people the astonishing view of the installation is sufficient but those with a technical inclination may be allowed to visit it. The enormous 'dishes' tend to overshadow the historic environment but the parish church of St Remigius (1692–6) with a rococo interior is worth a pause. Two kilometres to the south, the former pilgrimage church of St John the Baptist near an old Roman road in an open field is actually adjacent to the satellite-tracking station and it is possible to take rather bizarre photographs of 'ancient' and 'modern'.

A modest motor tour (35–40km) from Diessen covers two more important churches. Due west via Dettenschwang and Issing is the

PLACES OF INTEREST NEAR THE AMMERSEE

ANDECHS
Kloster Church (1420–48)
Gothic with later baroque reconstruction and rococo decoration.
Restaurant and beer hall.

DIESSEN
Church of St Maria (1730)
One of the most important baroque buildings in Bavaria.

Church of St Georgen
Enlarged 1750 by famous baroque craftsmen. Fifteenth century.

RAISTING
Satellite Tracking Station of German Post Office

Parish Church of St Remigius (1692–6)
Rococo interior.

Pilgrimage Church of St John the Baptist
Bizarre background of the tracking station.

VILGERTSHOFEN (16km W of Diessen)
Pilgrimage Church
Outstanding stucco by famous craftsmen.

WESSOBRUNN (10km SW of Diessen)

(Home of Wessobrunn school of painters and stucco workers.)
Parish Church of St John (1757–9)

Former Benedictine Kloster Church

700-year-old Lime Tree

SEEFELD
(6km NE of Herrsching)
Schloss and Schlosspark near Pilsensee

WIDDERSBERG
(SE of Pilsensee)
Second-century Roman Gravestone

STEINEBACH
(At N end of Wörthsee)
Church of St Martin
Frescos from 1730.

Church of St Martin
In Walchstadt. Seventeenth century.

WESSLING
(5km E of Steinebach)
Old Parish Church of the Assumption (1778)

Parish Church of St Georg
Modern but with spectacular dome and ancient relics within.

pilgrimage church of **Vilgertshofen**. It was one of those listed for destruction in 1803 but fortunately was reprieved. The history of the pilgrimage goes back to 1670 when the local priest was miraculously healed and attributed this to his veneration for a certain old religious picture. As usual, the story got around and he was soon leading pilgrimage processions which brought up to 20,000 people a year to his church. Today's church was the work of Johannes Schmuzer who was also responsible for the stucco carried out in the Wessobrunn style by artists like J.B. Zimmermann, F.X. Schmuzer and Johannes Baader. The latter was also responsible for three unusual ceiling paintings in the nearby inn which show biblical characters in the garb of Lech valley farmers.

South-eastwards from Vilgertshofen a pretty road soon reaches **Wessobrunn**, a village mentioned before. It is hard to understand today, how this village could have been the eighteenth-century cradle of so many fine craftsmen. Whole families were involved, the Schmuzers, the Zimmermanns, the Feuchtmayrs and others. In those days, Wessobrunn was the hallmark of good workmanship, artistic genius and even fantasy. These workers were certainly encouraged by the Benedictine monks in the nearby abbey but this does not account for the artistic heights they reached.

The Benedictine *Kloster* founded by Duke Tassilo II developed quickly so that already in the ninth century a monk was able to write the *Wessobrunn Prayer*, the oldest text in the German language, the original manuscript of which is now in the State Library in Munich. When secularisation brought an end to the *Kloster* the superb church was saved to become the parish church of St John. Originally a Romanesque building, it received lavish baroque treatment (1757–9), largely the work of F.X. Schmuzer with ceiling frescos by J. Baader. A valuable relic is the wooden crucifix from about 1250 which had been in the earlier Romanesque church. Behind the old *Kloster* walls can be seen the so-called Tassilolinde, a reputedly 700-year-old lime tree with a circumference of 13m (42ft).

Before passing on to some of the smaller lakes in this first group, here are details of a pleasant walk linking the Starnberger See and the Ammersee. This is a good outing for the Munich-based visitor who should take the S-bahn train to Starnberg.

After leaving Starnberg station turn right on the promenade and following waymark '3' cross back under the railway at the first subway to go more or less ahead into Söckinger Strasse and shortly turn left into a street called Maisinger Schlucht. This leads into the actual *Schlucht* (glen) but care is needed not to miss the signs. Once in the glen it is only a matter of going forward on the shady path (notice the picturesque caves) until **Maising** is reached in about 4.5km. Walk on almost to the end of the village street and shortly before the road makes a pronounced turn to the right, keep left and go along a beautiful path to the Gasthaus Seehof (*Ruhetag* Monday) on the Maisinger See. There are several paths here and the route goes up on to the embankment to continue in a south-west direction with the lake on the right through a *Naturschutzgebiet* (nature reserve) to **Aschering**. About 50m past the 'bus stop in this village the route bears to the left and there is a sign for Andechs. Following this woodland path the tiny Ess-see with the renowned Max-Planck-Institut is shortly passed on the left and soon after this the main road just before **Rothenfeld** has to be crossed. Pass through the car park opposite and take care not to miss the small path on through the wood; emerging from this a few minutes later Kloster Andechs is seen on its hill ahead. Follow the path with the Stations of the Cross up to the *Kloster*. From here, clear footpaths go down either side of the little River Kienbach to **Herrsching** and the stream is followed through the town to the S–bahn station for the return train to Munich if desired.

A short distance north of Herrsching is the Pilsensee with the S–bahn station of Seefeld-Hechendorf at its north end. **Seefeld** has its *Schloss* and *Schlosspark*, Burg Seefeld, which is privately owned. **Widdersberg,** a short distance to the south-east of the lake, was already settled in Roman times and there is a Roman gravestone from the second century. A mere stone's throw to the north is the Wörthsee (S-bahn station Steinebach, line 5) which surprisingly lies 27m (88ft) higher than either the Pilsensee or Ammersee.

Wanderweg No 4 starts at the station and makes a complete circuit of the lake, almost exclusively on the water's edge. The route is so obvious that no description of it is needed here. The lake is 3.5km long and 1.7km wide and takes its name from the tiny island near the west shore, known to the locals as Mausinsel (Mouse Island). **Steine-bach** was once a sleepy farming village but is now a popular bathing place, busy at weekends. The modern church Zum heiligen Abend-mahl (The Lord's Supper) was only built in 1964. The old church of St Martin was re-organised in 1735; worth seeing are the frescos dating from 1738 which were only uncovered after World War II. In adjoining **Walchstadt**, St Martin's church from the second half of the seven-teenth century was restored in 1969 and contains a number of important relics. Neither Pilsensee nor Wörthsee are big enough to have a steamer service but both have boats for hire and plenty of space for water activities.

L

↔

ΔΔ
13km

Finally in this area, the miniscule Wesslinger See — only 600m by

PLACES OF INTEREST IN AND AROUND MURNAU

MURNAU
Parish Church of St Nikolaus (1717–27)
Fine fresco and stucco. High altar from Ettal monastery. Church of Mariahilf and the village churches in Seehausen and Froschausen are also worth seeing.

GROSSWEIL
Open-air Museum von Glentleiten
8km E of Murnau. Old Bavarian farmhouses; craft demonstrations; animals.

500m — is fine for a refreshing dip and this is regarded as one of the 'Five Lakes'; it is the nearest one to Munich (S-bahn station Wessling, line 5). For a small place **Wessling** has many churches. The church of Christ König is near the station. The original parish church of Maria Himmelfahrt close to the lake was built in 1778 but the walls are part Gothic; the interior was completely refurbished in 1860. The new parish church to the east — St Georg — was consecrated in 1939; it has a spectacular high onion-dome with a built-in clock and several much older relics have been installed within — a larger-than-life Christ figure (sixteenth century), a statue of St Georg (seventeenth century) and a Madonna from the fifteenth century on the left side-altar. Then on the way back to the station there is the church of the Holy Cross and beyond the railway along Grünsinker Strasse there is an old pilgrimage church.

South-west from, and within 20km of the south end of the Starnberger See, are two lakes close together, the Riegsee and the Staffelsee with the resort of **Murnau** between them. Staffelsee is the larger, some 4km from north to south and east to west but they share the same very picturesque countryside and have access to similar facilities. Both lakes have camp sites and good natural bathing places. The Riegsee is one of the warmest lakes in Upper Bavaria. The Staffelsee has motor-boat trips in summer. There is a DB station at Murnau but the S-bahn is beyond reach. This is a *Luftkurort* with a population of 10,500 and a good range of visitor facilities. The Alpenhof Motel Murnau has been awarded a coveted Michelin star for its local specialities such as *Grillierter Staffelsee-Hecht*, grilled pike from the Staffelsee. There is good walking here but cyclists will notice that it is steeper here than around the 'Five Lakes'. Murnau itself is at an altitude of 700m (2296ft).

Traditional farm building at the von Glentleiten Open-air Museum

There is an annual spectacle on the Staffelsee the second Thursday after Whitsun when Fronleichnam (Corpus Christi) is celebrated at the village of **Seehausen** with a procession of about 100 boats and barges all colourfully decorated following a vessel carrying the Monstrance, making stops at the lake islands of St Jacob and Wörth. The village churches in Seehausen and the one in **Froschhausen** are worth seeing. In Murnau the parish church of St Nikolaus was built 1717–27 on the site of a former twelfth-century building. The architect is unknown although it was once thought that J.M. Fischer was responsible. The powerful vault fresco in the dome was a nineteenth-century addition. There is good stucco and the high altar has excellent sculpture. It was first erected in the monastery at Ettal in 1730 and brought to Murnau in 1771. The church of Mariahilf also justifies a visit.

Ten kilometres south of Murnau is **Eschenlohe** where the unfortunate Schisler was working before he returned to Oberammergau, taking the plague with him. About the same distance east is another of Bavaria's beautiful lakes, the Kochelsee. Before Kochelsee, however, visit the outstanding Freilichtmuseum (open-air museum) von Glentleiten on the slopes above Grossweil. Typical old farmhouses from all over Upper Bavaria have been carefully dismantled and re-erected here to provide a unique historical record of rural life. Some forty buildings from the sixteenth century onwards, but mostly from the eighteenth century, are here. There are regular displays of traditional craftsmanship and other special events such as the erection of the *Maibaum* (maypole) on 1 May, a children's week in August (advance booking advisable) and a *Christkindlmarkt* at the end of November.

Roughly the same size as the Staffelsee, the Kochelsee lies at an altitude of 600m (1968ft). Its north end leads out to a flattish moorland — a protected area — but if one looks south the spectacular backdrop of the Alps gives the lake a gloriously romantic appearance. This is one of the most pleasant bathing places in Upper Bavaria and is also a popular camping area. The resort of **Kochel** (population 4700) is at the north-east corner of the lake and provides well for summer and winter visitors. Kochel is the eastern terminus of the long-distance path, the Prälatenweg from Marktoberdorf mentioned in Chapter 1. The main road south (B11) starts to climb as soon as it leaves the Kochelsee and ascends by a series of somewhat alarming hairpin bends to the Kesselberg (858m, 2814ft) before dropping to the north end of the Walchensee at 802m (2630ft). With an area of 16.4sq km this is by far Germany's biggest mountain lake; it has a depth of 196m (642ft) and is well stocked with fish but the water is on the cool side for bathing. Walchensee is the starting point for an excursion to the Herzogstand (1600m, 5250ft). A chair-lift takes just 11 minutes to reach it with outstanding views of the lakes and mountains.

Two more major lakes should be visited, the Tegernsee and the Schliersee, mentioned briefly in Chapter 2. From Walchensee the motorist must go round the south end of the lake, the road round the north end being barred to motor vehicles. The route is a very pretty one and follows the valley of the little River Jachen between a series of imposing peaks with the Benediktenwand (1801m, 5907ft) on the left and the Zweiterköpfl (1432m, 4697ft) on the right with the higher Alpine summits of the Karwendelgebirge behind.

This is a toll road running more or less parallel with the Alpenstrasse route. Indeed, that route through the beautiful Isar valley (also a toll road) provides an alternative to the Jachen valley and is an opportunity to pass the man-made lake, the Sylvenstein-Stausee, a remarkably beautiful fjord-like stretch of water used to regulate the flow of the Isar waters and prevent flooding further down the valley. The road which follows the River Jachen, however, allows a stop in

Walchensee

the scattered village of **Jachenau** to see the church, not only because of its stunning situation — a bonus for photographers — but because its history goes back to 1291. It was renovated in the eighteenth century and dedicated to St Nikolaus.

A new name from Wessobrunn, Franz Doll, came here to create the stucco decoration. A few years later he went on to work with other famous craftsmen in the church at Benediktbeuern between Kochel and Bad Tölz. The Rivers Isar and Jachen join forces near **Hohenburg** with its medieval castle, the present form of which was only achieved in 1710 following a fire. The nearby chapel of 1722 has a copy of the Altötting *Gnadenbild*, the so-called Black Madonna (see Chapter 5).

Continuing northwards through the Isar valley, the resort of **Lenggries** (population 10,000) is a *Luftkurort*; the wide range of facilities for guests includes the Brauneck (1530m, 5018ft) cable car and two chair-lifts. In winter these are supplemented by no less than eighteen ski-tows. From the lower station of the Brauneck cable-way a splendid mountain walk to the summit starts with an immediate stiffish climb keeping to the right (north) of, and at first, roughly parallel with the cables. The route continues westwards climbing all the time and in about 1¹/₂ hours the Reiseralm (refreshments) is reached at 900m

(2952ft). More than half of the climb is now over and the clearly defined route soon turns south-west towards the upper cable car station. For the moment the path continues in the wood but coming out into the Garland basin the goal is clearly visible. Across the basin there is a stiff climb to a small saddle a few metres before the station and in another 10 minutes the summit cross is reached at 1555m (5100ft). A little below the summit at the Brauneck-Hütte (refreshments and overnight lodgings) there is a first-rate viewing platform. On a clear day the greater part of the Alpine chain can be seen, far to the south perhaps a glimpse of the sparkling glaciers in the central Alps and to the north-west, the Upper Bavarian lakes.

The descent is on the south side of the cables and soon after passing the station near two *Alm* huts there is a sign 'Kot-Alm'. In fact, from here the Kot-Alm hut (refreshments) can be seen below but it takes another 20 minutes or so to reach it across an area which is sometimes boggy. At the east end of this *Alm* basin a little road is reached and the descent is continued until shortly after the lower edge of the woods the path goes left, leaving the road. Close the cattle gate here and continue down along a meadow track along a fence, through a short, rather overgrown cleft to reach a much more obvious track going roughly due north. Pass a quarry on the left and the hamlet **Gildenhöfe** can be seen ahead. Go through this, climb briefly and pass — or call at — the Café Bergbahn and in a few minutes arrive back at the starting point. This walk entails a total climb of 900m (2952ft) and good stout footwear is essential. A total of 5 hours should be allowed for the whole circuit but the time can be halved by using the cable railway for the outward leg. The *Wanderkarte* sheet L8334 Bad Tölz (1:50,000) is useful.

The Isar follows the route for another 10km to the spa of **Bad Tölz**. With some 13,000 inhabitants this is the most important centre in this area and a wide range of medical treatment is available here but there is plenty for the fit and healthy to do. The Blombergbahn chair-lift takes one from the valley to a height of 1237m (4057ft) in two stages which can be used separately for access to some excellent mountain walking. A golf course is at hand but summer and winter seasons are equally popular here. The original settlement owed its existence to a crossing place of one of the old salt roads over the Isar. It became the home of boatmen and fishermen and developed slowly over the centuries. In 1846 an iodine spring was discovered and led to the founding of a health resort. Out of the main holiday season one may

---

PLACES OF INTEREST IN AND AROUND BAD TÖLZ

Parish Church of the Assumption (1513) **with Winzererkapelle**

Pilgrimage Church Mariahilf (1735–7)
Frescos by M. Günther.

Heimatmuseum
In the former town hall.

Leonhardikapelle
On the Kalvarienberg N of town. Goal of the annual 'ride'. Fifteen little chapels on the way.

Church of St Benedikt (1680–6)
In Benediktbeuern 14km W of Bad Tölz. Outstanding baroque with Italian influence. Much to see.

Historic Glassworks Museum
In former *Kloster* buildings at Benediktbeuern. Glass technology and development of optical industry.

Collegiate Church of Augustinian Canons (1729–41)
In Dietramzell 14km NE of Bad Tölz. Fine stucco and paintings.

Parish Church of St Martin (1722)
Adjoining next above.

Pilgrimage Churches of St Maria im Elend (1690) **and St Leonhard** (1774)
To be found respectively S of the *Kloster* and N of village at Dietramzell.

---

stroll in a leisurely fashion through the old town — as distinct from the more modern spa area — and enjoy the colourful façades of the old gabled houses. In summer, and especially on Sundays, the place appears to be a permanent traffic jam although a southern bypass under construction may help to relieve the situation.

The town parish church Maria Himmelfahrt was developed from a late Gothic building damaged in a fifteenth-century fire and altered many times since. The tower was only added about 100 years ago and seems to stand a little uncomfortably beside the rest of the building. Belonging to this church too, is the Winzererkapelle of 1513, named after a distinguished citizen Kaspar Winzerer to whom there is also a memorial in front of the former *Rathaus*, now the *Heimatmuseum*. Another significant religious house is the pilgrimage church Mariahilf built 1735–7 to plans by Josef Schmuzer. Matthias Günther painted the frescos of the Tölz plague procession of 1634.

A modern procession is the *Tölzer Leonhardifahrt* which takes place annually on 6 November. St Leonhard is the patron saint of animals (he shares the honour with St Martin) and in many Bavarian towns and villages it is the custom for horses to be ridden round the church and blessed in the *Leonhardiritt* (Leonhard Ride) on the saint's day (*Leonharditag*). In Bad Tölz the ride has developed into a full-scale folk festival with a procession of decorated carts accompanied by whip-cracking and other festive noises. The church associated with the event is the Leonhardikapelle which occupies a fine vantage point on the Kalvarienberg (708m, 2322ft) north of the town. This was the gift of a town official Friedrich Nockher in 1718 and originally there were seven little chapels marking the way to the Cross but over the years they have been replaced and added to so that there are now no less than fifteen of them. This makes a fine and interesting walk at any time of the year. After the traditional procession there is a display of whip-cracking in the Marktstrasse using old-time coachmen's whips.

If **Benediktbeuern** was not visited from Kochel it is a rewarding excursion to make from Bad Tölz. It lies about 14km westwards along the B472. The Benedictine *Kloster* was founded in the middle of the eighth century, was destroyed by the invading Hungarians in 955 and re-established in the eleventh century. The monks here were much occupied with cultural activities including painting and literature. This is where, in the thirteenth century, the *Carmina Burana* was written, well known today through the exciting musical setting of the work by Carl Orff. The *Kloster* was burned down in the fifteenth century, and rebuilt only to be dismembered in the 1803 secularisation. For a time, the buildings became a glassworks and research establishment until in 1930 they were once more taken over by a religious order and since then, have been a Salesian monastery and college. Some of the lavishly decorated rooms are the work of J.B. Zimmermann.

The buildings are haunted by the spirit of baroque but it is the church of St Benedikt which stands out as the remarkable architectural achievement. Construction took place between 1680 and 1686 on the site of the late Gothic building. The nave is a broad pilastered hall with a shallow barrel-vaulted roof and deep side-chapels with low galleries above them. The Italian influence is obvious, especially in the lavish stucco decoration on the pilasters, arches and vaulting. H.G. Asam, father of the famous brothers was responsible for the ceiling frescos and son Cosmas Damian painted the picture on the Antonius altar. J.M. Fischer's Anastasia chapel north of the sanctuary (1750–8) is a jewel of baroque. Two stucco marble piers joined by cornices give the small room a monumental look. The silver gilt bust reliquary of St Anastasia is by E.Q. Asam, the other son.

The cultural and secular history of the *Kloster* buildings is recorded

Benediktbeuern

in a museum in which the old glassworks with its ovens has been reincarnated and is a reminder that while the Fraunhofer firm had the premises they developed optical instruments and lenses of exceptional quality. The name Fraunhofer continues to be associated with glass technology and in 1986, York Glazier's Trust, the body responsible for the medieval glass in England's famous York Minster and other city churches, collaborated with the Fraunhofer Institute in experiments designed to protect the valuable old glass throughout Europe from the effects of 'acid rain'.

Tegernsee

Before going on to the remaining two lakes call at **Dietramzell** 14km north-east of Bad Tölz, a modest resort with apparently little in the way of organised leisure activities for visitors. Nevertheless it is a picturesque location and the churches are a good reason for coming here. Pride of place goes to the former collegiate church of the Augustinian canons built 1729–41. The architect is unknown and the exterior gives no hint of the visual feast within. J.B. Zimmermann was largely responsible for the decoration including fine stucco work and pastel-coloured frescos together with a painting of the Assumption of the Virgin Mary which is the centrepiece of the massive high altar. This splendid church came within a hair's breadth of destruction in the 1803 secularisation purge. Adjoining the collegiate church is the parish church of St Martin consecrated in 1722. Again there are stucco and paintings by J.B. Zimmermann which were seriously damaged after 1803 but were restored in 1966. There are two pilgrimage churches nearby; south of the *Kloster* is Maria Im Elend (1690) with an onion-dome, interior fitments from 1791 and a rich assortment of memorial tablets.

North, on the road towards Munich, is the rococo building conse-crated in 1774 and dedicated to St Leonhard. It is finely decorated and has a dome fresco dating from 1769. This church is another to which

PLACES OF INTEREST AROUND THE TEGERNSEE

GMUND
Church of St Aegidius (1693)
Marks the significant influence of Italian baroque on Upper Bavarian churches.

TEGERNSEE
Parish Church of St Quirin (1684–9)
The former Benedictine *Kloster* church. Contains the bones of the saint and fine art work.

Historic Steam Railway

Heimatmuseum
In Schloss Tegernsee. Includes memorabilia of artists and writers who worked in the vicinity.

EGERN
Parish Church of St Laurentius (1466)
Stucco treatment 1671–2. Famous Madonna.

Old Cemetery
Graves of Ludwig Thoma, Ludwig Ganghofer and Leo Slezak.

New Cemetery
Graves of Heinrich Spoerl and Olaf Gulbransson.

pilgrims and horses come for blessing although in this case, on the third Saturday in July. Dietramzell had a period of some fame in the years 1922 to 1932 for it was here that German President Hindenburg chose to spend his summer holidays, a fact recorded by a relief on the wall between the parish church and the *Kloster*. However, in the presidential elections of 1932 most of the residents gave their vote not to Hindenburg but to Hitler.

South now to the Tegernsee and the four main resorts on its shore, Gmund (population 4000) at the north end, Bad Wiessee (population 5000) on the west bank, Tegernsee (population 4700) on the east bank and Rottach-Egern (population 6500) in the south-east corner. The lake is 7.5km north to south and 2.5km east to west. The most popular resort on the lake is **Bad Wiessee**. Originally a farming village, Wiessee climbed quickly to spa status with the discovery of iodine and sulphur springs in the first decades of this century. Here and there one can still find reminders of its rural origin but it is as a health and holiday centre that it is known today. Bad Wiessee offers a comprehensive programme of activities for its guests including conducted rambles in the valley or mountains according to season, coach or sleigh rides and there is a golf course. Five ski-tows are available for the winter visitor and concerts and theatrical productions take place from time to time throughout the year.

The yacht harbour at Tegernsee

Gmund, the smallest of the four main settlements around the lake, shares in the visitor facilities of the larger places. St Aegidius parish church is one of the most significant buildings on the lake. The present structure was consecrated in 1693, the work of the architect Lorenzo Sciasca. A high altar from the Tegernsee *Kloster* church was obtained, which was then enriched with a painting by H.G. Asam. The pulpit is also worth seeing. St Aegidius, through its architect, helped to put the stamp of Italian baroque on Upper Bavarian church building.

It was about 746 that Benedictine monks from St Gallen in Switzerland founded a *Kloster* in **Tegernsee**. Its status had something of a boost in 804 when the bones of St Quirin were left to it and this is the origin of the name borne by the church today. At the height of its fame, Tegernsee was one of the most important cultural centres in Europe; the illumination of manuscripts and calligraphy reached its peak here. One of the distinguished guests at the monastery in those early days was the minnesinger Walther von der Vogelweide. But the

area has always attracted artists and writers and the *Heimatmuseum* housed in Schloss Tegernsee recalls the satirical humorist Ludwig Thoma, whose living and working quarters are displayed, and the

PLACES OF INTEREST IN SCHLIERSEE

Parish Church (1715)
Many famous artists contributed to the decoration. Numerous priceless relics.

St Georg's Chapel
High altar with St George and dragon. Many other treasures. Fourteenth century.

Pilgrimage Church of St Leonhard (1670)
In Fischhausen 3km S. Abundant stucco and fine altars.

work of artist and caricaturist, Olaf Gulbransson. Both died here, as did the Alpine novelist Ludwig Ganghofer. Incidentally, many of the historic rooms of the *Schloss* are included in the museum. The former *Kloster* church, now the parish church of St Quirin, dates from a radical re-building in 1684–9, most of the previous building having been destroyed by fire. H.G. Asam was responsible for the stucco and frescos. The façade with two towers, the oldest in Bavaria was remodelled by Leo von Klenze in 1817. Altogether a fine building, especially the Quirinus and Benediktus side-chapels with their ornate rococo decoration although, unfortunately, only a few of the altars in the three-aisled basilica have survived. As a resort, Tegernsee has plenty of visitor facilities and railway enthusiasts will find the historic steam railway between Tegernsee and Schaftlach of interest.

It is a pity that, in contrast with Tegernsee's much-visited church, the parish church of St Laurentius at **Egern** is often overlooked. It dates from 1466 and was stuccoed in 1671–2. From the fifteenth century until secularisation this was a goal of pilgrims coming to revere a Madonna known as the *Egerner Gnadenbild*. Egern is part of the health resort called Rottach-Egern; Ludwig Thoma had a house built here in 1908 where he wrote most of his works. He died in 1921 and his tomb is in the Alter Friedhof (old cemetery) together with those of Ludwig Ganghofer (died 1920) and the opera singer Leo Slezak (died 1946). Heinrich Spoerl, the writer, died nearby in 1955 and is buried in the new cemetery, as is Gulbransson (died 1958). In addition, all the usual facilities are on offer and there is access to the mountains by three chair-lifts and a *Gondelbahn* — a cable railway with four-passenger cabins. The latter takes 12 minutes to climb up to the Wallberghaus (refreshments) at 1620m (5313ft) from where the Wallberg summit (1722m, 5648ft) can be reached on foot in about 45 minutes. The motorist can use a toll road to reach Moosalm at 1113m

Schliersee

(3650ft) for splendid views, but to reach the Wallberg must then go on foot for about an hour to get to the Wallberghaus.

Less than 10km east of Tegernsee is the little Schliersee with the resort of the same name (population 6300) the only real centre on the lake and including the outlying villages of Fischhausen, Neuhaus and Spitzingsee. At the beginning of the present century **Schliersee** had only 700 inhabitants but the tourist influx following the construction of the railway soon changed this. Another factor in the village's rise to fame was the founding of the Schlierseer Bauerntheater (Peasant's Theatre) by the landlord and actor Xaver Terofal in 1892. The proud theatrical tradition is carried on today by the theatre group of the local *Trachtenverein* (Traditional Dress Club) and the idea has been adopted by many other villages in Upper Bavaria.

There are two *Gondelbahnen* and two chair-lifts, supplemented in winter by no less than fifteen ski-tows. The church, consecrated in 1715, retains the late Gothic tower of an earlier church but it only received the present pointed dome in 1873. The atmosphere of the bright, spacious interior is enhanced by Zimmermann's stucco and he was also responsible for the chancel ceiling picture. The church contains a number of priceless relics as well as examples of the creative work of the several important artists.

A little above the church on the way to the lower station of the Schliesbergbahn — a small-cabin cableway — there is a hill surmounted by the chapel of St Georg. The hill is called the Weinberg but this has nothing to do with grapes as one might expect, but is a term used in some parts of Upper Bavaria for a Kalvarienberg and means 'hill of weeping'. St Georg's chapel is from the fourteenth century and was renewed in the early part of the seventeenth. Understandably, the central feature of the high altar is a representation of a mounted St George despatching an angry dragon. Two late Gothic wooden figures portray St Sixtus and St Barbara.

It is possible to walk right round the lake in about 2 hours.From the parish church go southwards along the east shore, past boat moorings, the Kurpromenade and the Park-Strandbad. The walk is waymarked 'K1' but is pretty obvious. It continues along Seestrasse and later Neuhauserstrasse. After $^1/_2$ hour the road moves away from the shore and about 150m past a boat mooring place keep right along a little road past boathouses and the outlying dwellings of Fischhausen. Ten minutes later, join a wide road and follow it as it curves to the right round the south end of the lake and eventually join a surfaced road northwards along the west bank. In **Fischhausen** there is another pilgrimage church of St Leonhard (1670) situated at the roadside but with enough space round it for the traditional ride, celebrated here on the saint's day, 6 November. The charm of the interior lies in the abundant homely stucco decoration of the so-called Miesbach-Schlierseer-Schule and in the three colourful rural altars from 1671.

L
↔
ΔΔ
7.5km

Continuing northwards, the woods rise to the left upon the slopes of the Brunstkogel. When the track climbs a little to the left, cross the railway and turn right to walk parallel with the line, noting the tiny island of **Wörth** out in the lake , once the site of a gruesome prison with cells so small that the prisoner could either sit or stand but not both!

In **Krainsberg** cross back over the railway and immediately turn left to continue following the line northwards. Cross a road running down to the Freudenberg 'peninsula', go straight on for 100m then turn right into a woodland path to the Hotel Freudenberg. Keep left at the entrance, cross a little stream then keep right over a gangway to the Tegernseer Weg along the north shore back to the church. A good walk at all seasons; even in winter the paths are kept clear.

The list of Bavarian lakes is by no means exhausted and several more, are covered later, including Bavaria's 'ocean', the Chiemsee.

4 MUNICH

Neither the revolution after World War I, the collapse of the monarchy, the deluge of bombs in World War II, nor the confusion following that war, have left traces which make the Bavarian metropolis unworthy of admiration. Munich is sometimes called Germany's secret capital. After Berlin and Hamburg, Munich, with 1.3 million inhabitants, is the third biggest city in the whole Bundesrepublik. The population growth, especially since World War II, means that less than one-third of the population now consists of born *'Münchners'* Some 200,000 are foreigners, and there are some100,000 students at the university and other centres of learning. The general opinion of Germans from other parts seems to be that the quality of life in Munich is better than in any of the other big cities.

To a large extent, the history of Munich is that of Bavaria itself. Perhaps today's citizens, and the annual throng of tourists, should give a retrospective vote of thanks to Duke Heinrich of Bavaria and Saxony who, in 1158, knocked down the Isar bridge, belonging to the bishop of Freising, at Föhring and had it rebuilt further upstream to capture the lucrative salt trade from the Reichenhall district. The move brought in a rich reward in tolls and taxes and the village called Bei den Mönchen quickly became known as it grew in importance.

By 1175 the citizens decided to build their first town wall so that their bridge should not suffer the same fate as the Föhring bridge. However, as a result of negotiations in 1180 the town fell to the Wittelsbachs who remained dominant from that time on, although their rule was not entirely uninterrupted. Austria, which until this time had belonged to Bavaria, was now separated and elevated to an independent duchy. The size of the town increased five-fold under Emperor Ludwig dem Bayern; it had long since outgrown the original town wall and in 1319 he started the building of a new wall with four main gateways which, with the exception of some of the latter, was

Painted house in Oberammergau, showing the story of Red Riding Hood

Kurpark, Mittenwald

Alpine meadows near Mittenwald

Wessobrunn, the birthplace of Bavarian baroque

only removed around 1800.

The eighteenth century found Munich in an impoverished state and many of the citizens hungry. The currently ruling branch of the Wittelsbachs died out and into the breach sprang a member from another branch of the family who took over the princely throne with the title Maximilian IV Josef. So the *Münchners* had a ruling prince again but very little to fill their stomachs. Then Benjamin Thompson, who had fled from the American War of Independence, arrived in Munich. He was the originator of *Erbsensuppe* — pea soup made from dried peas, ham and herbs. Thus he was able to provide some nourishment for more than a thousand hungry citizens each day. By this time Thompson had been given the title of Graf Rumford and the people found the *Rumford-Suppe* an improvement on their previous diet of potatoes. The *Münchner's* aversion to potatoes has endured to this day. Graf Rumford went on to join the Bavarian civil service in 1784 where he re-organised the army and founded work-houses!

In 1806 Maximilian became king of Bavaria as Maximilian I Josef, with Munich as the seat of government. He died in 1825 and was followed by his son who became King Ludwig I. Under his rule, Munich blossomed into a glittering centre of art and partly from his private purse, the king financed many fine buildings including the Pinakothek, the Glyptothek and the Feldherrnhalle. His aim was to build a city which would have such a reputation that nobody could claim to know Germany without knowing Munich. The scandal of his association with the dancer Lola Montez — Maria de los Dolores Porris y Montez — finally resulted in his abdication in 1848 when his son Maximilian II took over the throne. The new ruler fostered learning and amongst other things built the Maximilianeum, today the home of both houses of the Bavarian parliament.

Maximilian II was succeeded in 1864 by his son Ludwig II. Although Ludwig supposedly hated Munich, the city continued to flourish during his reign, especially as a result of his patronage of Richard Wagner. This period too, saw the building of the Neues Rathaus in neo-Gothic style. After the death of Ludwig II in 1886 his brother Otto should have succeeded to the throne but he was in poor mental health and in consequence Prince Luitpold governed as regent for 25 years. Luitpold's son became King Ludwig III but World War I broke out 2 years after his accession. The end of the war also signalled the end of the Wittelsbach dynasty and Ludwig III died in exile in Hungary in 1921.

4a Munich City Centre

Every visitor to Munich can obtain information for exploration of the city from the city information office at the south-east exit from the *Hauptbahnhof* on Bayerstrasse opposite platform 11. The office is open from 8am to 11pm on weekdays and 1pm to 9.30pm on Sundays and holidays. Accommodation can also be obtained through this office. Munich makes special efforts to cater for young visitors and there is a special youth nformation centre at Paul-Heyse-Strasse 22, open Monday to Friday 11am to 7pm and Saturday 11am to 5pm. A booklet *München – Leitfaden für Jugendgruppen* (Guide for Young People) is available from the information office and contains a wealth of useful information. Addresses of several youth hostels, youth hotels etc in and around the city can be found in 'Further Information'.

The Münchner Verkehrs- und Tarifverband (MVV) is responsible for all urban transport in and around the city and has a special information centre in the S-bahn station beneath the *Hauptbahnhof*. The intensive train, 'bus and tram services make movement about the city quick and easy, and for the visitor making use of public transport the 24-hour tickets are a real bargain. They can be purchased at ticket offices and from vending machines, tourist information offices, many hotels and many small shops — tobacconists and kiosks — displaying a white 'K' on a green background. Enjoying Munich means seeing the sights: reminders of the royal Bavarian past, the Residenz, Schloss Nymphenburg, the baroque and rococo churches and the spacious parks. A shopping tour through the extensive pedestrian zone and across the big food and flower market together with a visit to the famous Hofbräuhaus and some museums or art galleries should be included. Inevitably, all this takes time but then, Munich is not a place to be rushed.

Most people have heard of the *Oktoberfest* and most have a vague idea of what the term means. For a festival known far and wide, not only in Germany but all over the world, the *Oktoberfest* has a remarkably short history. Surprisingly, it originated in horse-racing, long a popular sport in Bavaria. In 1810, a non-commissioned officer in the National Guard suggested that racing, which had been dropped as an economy measure, should be revived as a suitable way of celebrating the marriage of Crown Prince Ludwig (later King Ludwig I) to Princess Therese of Saxe-Hildburghausen. King Maximilian gave his consent and the races were run on 17 October of that year,

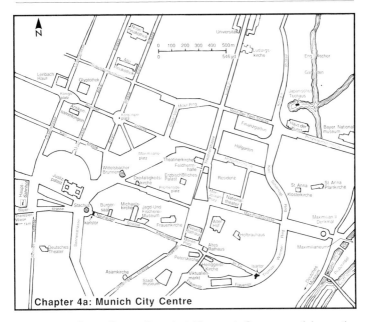

Chapter 4a: Munich City Centre

sixty horses from all over Bavaria taking part. So successful was the event that the fields where the races had taken place were named Theresienwiese in honour of the princess and they have kept the name ever since.

The king agreed to the races being held annually and until the beginning of this century they formed an essential element of the festivities. In 1811 they were accompanied by an agricultural show which still continues every 2 years. In 1818 booths and beer tents similar to those seen today made their appearance. The Silver Wedding of Ludwig and Therese in 1835 was marked by a procession which was the forerunner of today's splendid opening procession when decorated brewers' drays, carnival floats and tableaux, also Dirndl-clad waitresses and civic dignitaries parade from the Bavarian State Parliament building to the festival grounds. The *Oberbürger-meister* (Lord Mayor) taps the first barrel of beer and the festival is then officially open. It now lasts for 16 days, finishing on the first Sunday in October when there is another procession.

Some of today's beer tents can seat 5000 people but in addition to the serious business of beer drinking there is ample opportunity for eating and drinking in the numerous restaurants or from the many stalls selling meat and fish delicacies, sweetmeats, candy floss, ice cream and so on. There is an enormous fun-fair with hair-raising rides including an alarming roller-coaster. The visitor need not feel intimidated by the noisy crowds in the beer tents. If he finds an empty seat he will immediately be welcomed by his neighbours and even if he cannot speak a word of German will quickly become involved in the general conviviality and be introduced to the art of *Das Schunkeln*, the linking of arms and swaying back and forth in time — more or less in time, anyway — with the raucous beat of the brass band. Outside, the crowds seem to spend much time just promenading up and down the broad avenues, looking at the side-shows, stopping for the odd drink or snack or trying out the latest heart-stopping device in the fun-fair. The festivities go on well into the night — indeed, it is a wonder that any work is done at all during the *Oktoberfest* weeks — but eventually everybody wanders or staggers off home or back to hotels for a good sleep in preparation for the next evening's session.

The other principal time of merry-making in Munich is the pre-Lenten carnival period, 7 January until Ash Wednesday. Here it is called *Fasching* and it is celebrated a little differently. Balls always played a prominent part in the Munich scene and in 1893 a society was formed to inject some order into the various *Fasching* balls and parades. The first *Fasching* prince was chosen in 1894 and this is now an annual appointment; he is accompanied by a princess of his own choice and they reign supreme throughout the season, supported by suitable male and female retinues. The balls are splendid and varied with constant endeavours to find new themes.

But if the *Münchners* make the most of the secular festivities, they are no less positive in their approach to the various religious festivals. *Fronleichnam* (Corpus Christi) is celebrated with a colourful festive procession and the beautiful squares of the inner city are gaily decorated to match. Advent sees the beginning of Christmas music concerts in many of the churches and also the Christmas market which is held in the Marienplatz in front of the new town hall. It was previously called the *Münchner Kripperlmarkt* because only crib figures were sold but nowadays all the usual Christmas oddments are to be found there and the name *Christkindlmarkt* seems to have been adopted as in Nuremberg and several other towns. Traditionally, Sunday church-going is followed by the *Frühschoppen*, the morning or early lunch-time drink, sometimes with sausages and bread, so

*Munich from the Englischer Garten
with the Frauenkirche and Theatinerkirche*

that man's earthly needs are not forgotten after the spiritual ones have been taken care of. Even the priests sometimes take this opportunity to mingle informally with their parishioners.

The centre of Munich is dominated by the distinctive twin towers — one 99m and the other 100m (328ft) high — of the **Frauenkirche**, a late Gothic brick building which has become the city's symbol. The church in its present form was built in the fifteenth century and was consecrated in 1494 although the towers were not then complete and only received their onion-domes in 1524–5. First class restoration work after the damage done in World War II means that the building is now seen at its best and probably in better condition than at any time since its construction. It is a hall church with ten bays and unusually high side-chapels. The nave is separated from the side-aisles by twenty-two octagonal pillars. Much of the medieval content has been lost or destroyed but the fourteenth–sixteenth-century stained glass windows in the chancel have survived more or less intact. Most important is the Scharfzandt window (1473) in the middle, by the Strasburg master P. Hemmel. The numerous gravestones and memorials include the grave slab of the famous architect J.M. Fischer who was responsible for no less than thirty-two churches, twenty-three monasteries and numerous secular buildings.

Many churches in Munich contain works by the two Asam brothers (painters, stucco workers and master-builders) who belonged to the group of most significant artists of the seventeenth and eighteenth centuries. Father Hans Georg (1649–1711) was the teacher of his more celebrated sons. Cosmas Damian (1686–1739) and Egid Quirin (1692–1750) completed their education in Rome. Working closely together, the painting fell naturally to Cosmas and the sculptural work to Egid. The family traditions were carried into yet another generation by Franz, son of Cosmas Damian. Some of the most important works of the brothers are to be found in the frescos of the Trinity Church, the parish church of St Anna im Lehel, the little palace of Maria Einsiedel in Thalkirchen, the St Johann Nepomuk church and in the decoration of Freising cathedral.

The church of St Johann Nepomuk, in Sendlinger Strasse, is commonly referred to as the **Asamkirche**. It was built 1733–46 and shows how passionately the brothers pursued their work. In this case they were more than just decorators to the order of some patron for Egid bought the land with his own money and between them the young men financed the construction of the building. Here they were able to pursue their ideas to the ultimate; shape, colour and light work harmoniously together. The walls are covered with red stucco marble. The massive high altar is framed by four twisted columns and the lower part contains a glass sarcophagus with the wax figure of St Nepomuk. On the right and left of the altar are portrait medallions of the brothers themselves, painted in various shades of grey.

The Franciscan monastery church of **St Anna im Lehel** in St Anna-Strasse, not far from the Nationaltheater, was consecrated in 1737, one of J.M. Fischer's works in the city. It was badly damaged in World War II but afterwards was rebuilt in its original form with certain nineteenth-century modifications omitted. Most of the stucco and paintings were irretrievably lost but the ceiling paintings by C.D. Asam were restored in 1971–2. Altars by the Asam brothers and a pulpit survived in part and were also restored.

In Neuhauser Strasse the 1291–4-built core of the former Augustinian monastery church at No 53 has survived; it was extended in the fourteenth and fifteenth centuries and radically altered in 1618–21. Thereafter it was de-consecrated and served first as a toll hall, then as police headquarters and finally as the **Deutsches**

St Nepomuk, the
'Asam' church,
Munich

Interior of St
Nepomuk

Jagdmuseum (Hunting Museum) which is its present function. In the same street, part of the pedestrian precinct, is the **Bürgersaal,** built for the Marianist congregation in 1709 by G.A. Viscardi. Under glass above the baroque doorway is a Madonna on the Crescent Moon. It is a two-storey building and the walls of the lower have fifteen Stations of the Cross painted in bright colours on wood. Here too is the grave slab of the Jesuit Rupert Mayer (1876–1945), a well known priest and resistance worker. The baroque oratory in the upper storey has fourteen views of Bavarian places of pilgrimage painted around 1710. The guardian angel group under the organ gallery is by J. Günther (1762).

Still in Neuhauser Strasse, the Jesuit church of **St Michael** was built in 1583–9 as a spiritual centre of the sixteenth-century Catholic renewal movement. It is, to say the least, a spectacular building. The façade was only restored in 1972 after war-time bomb damage; there is a figure of Christ on the gable, below that Emperor Otto is shown as victor in the field at Lech in 955 and then follows a series of the emperors and dukes who established Christianity in Bavaria. There is a bronze statue of St Michael (1592) in a niche between the two doorways and the saint is also portrayed with the Devil on the massive high altar (1589). The interior is dominated by the huge barrel vault with a span of more than 20m (65ft). In the princes' vault under the choir are the graves of forty Wittelsbachs including Wilhelm V, Maximilian I and Ludwig II.

The Marienplatz in front of the **Neues Rathaus** is the city's main square. It is part of the pedestrian zone and provides a good and safe place for the crowds who gather at 11am each day (also at 5pm in summer) to see the *Glockenspiel* on the 85m-high (278ft) tower of the town hall. The mechanical display shows a procession of brightly painted figures representing Duke Wilhelm V on the occasion of his marriage to Renate von Lothringen. Beneath this is the *Schäfflertanz* (Coopers' Dance) first mentioned in 1463 and previously performed every 7 years at carnival time by members of the guild.

Across the square is the church of **St Peter**, the oldest parish church in Munich. Originally, a Romanesque building occupied the site and this was replaced 1278–94 by a Gothic one which had to be rebuilt after a fire in 1327. The unusual tower, completed in 1386, has become a Munich landmark. The balcony round the tower is open to the public and provides a good view of the city. It is, however, a little alarming if the enormous bells are struck while one is up aloft. The

SOME PLACES OF INTEREST IN CENTRAL MUNICH

Frauenkirche
Enormous late fifteenth-century Gothic church with distinctive twin towers.

Jesuit Church of St Michael (1583–4)
Princes' vault with graves of forty Wittelsbachs including Ludwig II. Many works of art. Significant contribution to Bavarian baroque.

Theatinerkirche-St Kajetan
Beautiful church with works by many masters. Begun 1663.

Parish Church of St Peter
The unusual tower is a Munich landmark and gives good views over city. Thirteenth century.

Church of St Johann Nepomuk (the Asam Church) (1733–46)
Outstanding creation by the Asam brothers.

Franciscan Monastery Church of St Anna im Lehel (1737)
Restored to its original form after World War II.

Bürgersaal (1709)
Baroque oratory with paintings of places of pilgrimage.

New Town Hall (1867–1908)
Imposing neo-Gothic with 85m (279ft) tower and colourful *Glockenspiel* (chimes and revolving figures).

Old Town Hall (1474)
Now houses a toy museum.

Residenz
Complex of interesting buildings linked by attractive courtyards. Sixteenth to nineteenth centuries.

Viktualienmarkt
Outdoor food and flower market. Interesting statues.

Hofbräuhaus
Munich's most famous beer dispensary.

Alte Pinakothek
Paintings of the fourteenth to eighteenth centuries.

Neue Pinakothek
Paintings and sculpture of the eighteenth to twentieth centuries.

Deutsches Museum
Largest technical and scientific museum in the world.

State Gallery of Modern Art
International painting and sculpture of twentieth century including Picasso and Moore.

Many other Museums and Galleries
See 'Further Information'.

pillared basilica is over 90m long (295ft) and nearly all the famous artists working in Munich in the fifteenth–eighteenth centuries contributed to the interior decoration. Most important is the high altar of 1730 by N. Stuber, restored to the original design after the last war.

The **Theatinerkirche** on Theatinerstrasse, the Catholic parish church of St Kajetan, was built by Elector Ferdinand Maria and his wife Henriette Adelaide in thanks for the long-awaited birth of an heir to the throne. The princess was of Italian origin and chose A. Barelli of Bologna as architect. Building started in 1663 but in 1674 Barelli was replaced by the Swiss E. Zucalli with the 71m (233ft) dome still incomplete. Zucalli added the towers and the façade was only provided in 1765–8 by François de Cuvilliés. Despite the long period of construction and decoration and the many different craftsmen involved, the end result is a remarkably unified whole and no visitor with even the slightest interest in architecture should fail to visit it.

The **Feldherrnhalle** just across the Odeonsplatz from the Theatinerkirche, is at the south end of Ludwigstrasse which King Ludwig I had built as a show street modelled on the Loggia dei Lanzi in Florence. The hall was built in 1840–4 and has statues representing the famous Bavarian generals Tilly (1559–1632) and Wrede (1767–1838) while the army memorial is in honour of the dead in the Franco-Prussian war. Facing the Theatinerkirche across Odeons-

platz is one corner of the **Residenz,** not a single building but a complex linked by a series of fine courtyards. It was intended to replace the Alter Hof which had been the court of the Wittelsbachs since 1253 when Duke Ludwig decided to move from Landshut following the division into Upper and Lower Bavaria. The Alter Hof was being rapidly hemmed in by the growing city but even after the new Residenz had been completed it was not abandoned. It survived until World War II when it was badly damaged but it was excellently restored in the years 1946–66 and today houses the finance department with the mint appropriately adjacent.

The Residenz is entered from Max Joseph-Platz and the present buildings include the Königsbau (King's Building), the Alte Residenz, the Festsaal , Cuvilliés Theatre, the ruined court church, the Residenz Theatre and the National Theatre. The courtyards are charming, the most important being the Königsbauhof which contains G. Petel's statue of Neptune (1641). The Grottenhof is surrounded by arcades with the Perseus fountain (1590) in the centre. Some of the Wittelsbachs were keen on building and most of the important stages were under their direction. The so-called Neuveste (New Fortress), started in 1385, stood in the north-east corner of the present Residenz and was burned down in 1750, although some remains can be seen in one of the courtyards, the Apothekenhof.

Do not leave the central area without seeing the **Altes Rathaus**

The old town hall, Munich

at the end of Marienplatz and the nearby **Viktualienmarkt** (open-air food and flower market) with its charming sculptures of the music hall figures Karl Valentin and Ida Schuhmacher. Then for interest or thirst, the **Hofbräuhaus** with its many rooms, cellars and terraces and its historical connection as an early meeting place of Hitler's

The Viktaulienmarkt

followers in the 1920s, justifies a little time. At most of the museums there is a modest admission charge but it is worth noting that at the art galleries, **Alte Pinakothek** and **Neue Pinakothek**, there is no charge on Sundays. The world famous **Deutsches Museum** occupies an island in the River Isar and provides many days of interest. Its numerous departments include mining, shipping, railways (with an extensive model layout), aircraft, musical instruments, chemistry, ceramics, printing, glass technology, photography and so on.

Munich is one of Europe's foremost cultural centres with music of all kinds featuring prominently. The summer season commences in June with a splendid concert series held in the gorgeous baroque palaces at Schleissheim and Nymphenburg. At the same time there are serenade concerts in the Residenz. All these lead up to the opera festival which usually runs from mid-July to the beginning of August. At other seasons, the Bavarian Radio Symphony Orchestra, the Munich Philharmonic, the Bavarian State Orchestra and the Munich Bach Chorus carry on the great musical tradition. Opera is not confined to the festival season either and the works of composers who had a special connection with Munich are often performed, including Mozart, Wagner, Richard Strauss and Carl Orff. The Bavarian State

Opera performs at the Nationaltheater but the Kammerspiele Playhouse and the Light Opera House on Gärtnerplatz are not to be overlooked. Nor is the rococo Cuvilliés Theatre in the Residenz where a Mozart opera is a rare delight.

Munich caters for every taste and lovers of modern music are not forgotton either. 'Pop' concerts take place frequently and the Munich *Jazz-Szene* has its own special programme. In August 1983, the first *Münchner Rocksommer* was held in the **Alabamahalle** (Schleissheimer Strasse) and this has become an annual event. **Das Theater der Jugend** (Youth Theatre) puts on shows in the Schauburg am Elisabeth-platz in Schwabing, catering for different age groups. For children, the **Münchner Marionettentheater** in Blumenstrasse has performances afternoons and evenings all year and there is also the **Münchner Märchenbühne** (Fairy-tale Stage) at Dachauer Strasse 46. Concert and theatre tickets can be quite expensive but there may be reductions for children, groups, students or pensioners with the appropriate identification. At the Nationaltheater and some others, standing places are offered at a very low charge, useful for hard-up youngsters.

4b Munich and the Surrounding Area

Munich has many parks and gardens, the largest and most well known being the **Englischer Garten** running down to the banks of the Isar. It is a favourite spot with the *Münchners* in summer and acres of flesh sizzle as the sun-worshippers bare all for maximum effect. The spectacular Chinese pagoda here stands at the centre of Munich's biggest beer-garden which has room for 6000. One of Europe's foremost zoos, the **Tierpark Hellabrunn** is easily reached by 31, 52 or 57 'bus or by S-bahn lines 7 or 27 to Mittersending station. The zoo is on the banks of the River Isar south of the city centre and covers an area of 360,000sq m to house some 5000 animals. It is regarded as one of the most advanced zoos in the world and is in beautifully landscaped surroundings. Another popular goal during the summer is **Grünwald** a short way to the south, reached from the city by tram or S-bahn and tram, where the Isar provides an attractive bathing and sunning place.

Equally attractive but more formal surroundings can be found at the several *Schlösser* within easy reach of the centre. Nearest is **Schloss Nymphenburg**, north-west of the *Hauptbahnhof* and not

Statue of Venus at the Nymphenburg Palace

too far to walk if one has time. Otherwise take U-bahn line 1 to the Rotkreuzplatz terminus and tram 12 from there or S-bahn lines 1–6 to Laim and change to a 41 or 68 'bus. Remember that with the 24-hour ticket you can change between the various means of transport without formality.

The central pavilion of the extensive Nymphenburg complex was built by the Italian A. Barelli from 1664–74 as a summer residence for Henriette Adelaide, mentioned earlier. The buildings were extended by subsequent Wittelsbachs; Max Emmanuel had the central section enlarged by A. Viscardi in 1702 with square three-storey pavilions linked to the main building by two-storey blocks. J. Effner built wings in 1715–16 showing French influence and he was responsible too for the Pagodenburg (1716–19), the Badenburg (1718–21) and the Magdalenenklause (1725–8). The Amalienburg in the extensive grounds was built (1734–9) to plans by Cuvilliés the Elder and the central section has remained the focal point of the *Schloss*. The *Festsaal* (banqueting hall) was refurbished in 1756–7 with frescos and stucco by the brothers J.B. and F. Zimmermann. The adjacent rooms are also lavishly decorated. The park was transformed into a picturesque garden in 1804–23 by the famous landscape gardener F.L. von Sckell in the strictly geometrical French style.

The *Schloss* complex incorporates two museums; the Mar- stallmuseum is a history of the electors' horses and stables with a display of many ornate state carriages. The Zoologische Staatsamm- lung is a museum of zoology. Adjoining the Nymphenburg park on the north side are the Botanic Gardens with extensive hothouses and outdoor beds featuring plants from all over the world. **Wasser- schloss Blutenberg** (1435) lies a little to the west of Nymphenburg and can be reached via S-bahn line 2 to Obermenzing. This is a former hunting lodge and is mainly of interest for its chapel which has a winged altar by Jan Pollack.

Schloss Schleissheim is 13km north of the city centre, the nearest S-bahn station being Oberschleissheim on line 1. There are really three separate palaces here. The Altes Schloss was built as a country retreat for Duke Wilhelm V in 1597 with completion in 1616. It is a simple gentleman's residence of the period. The Neues Schloss is the most important: the foundation stone was laid in 1701 and looking at this substantial building today it is difficult to believe that its early years were little short of disastrous. E Zucalli was responsible for the start of the work but seems to have been less than meticulous in checking the technical details, for no sooner had the entrance hall been built than it collapsed due to inadequate foundations. The *Schloss* was being built for Elector Max Emmanuel but when he was forced into exile after the War of Spanish Succession, only the shell was complete and work came to a halt. A plan to build a wing to connect the new and old buildings was dropped although this would have made it one of the largest palaces in Europe. Zucalli's idea of a tower in the centre of the main building was also abandoned. When work re-started in 1719 they concentrated on completing the existing building; J. Günther created the east portal, C.D. Asam painted the vault fresco above the extensive staircase and J.B. Zimmermann was engaged for the stucco and decoration of the banqueting hall. This is where the famous Schleissheim summer concerts take place so there is plenty for the eye as well as the ear on these occasions.

All in all, the central part of the Neues Schloss is one of the finest examples of German baroque. Under King Ludwig I in 1847–8, the staircase was completed to the original design and the façade was reworked by Leo von Klenze in the early nineteenth century. World War II was responsible for a certain amount of damage but this has since been made good. The Gartenschloss Lustheim was built by Zucalli in 1684–7 and was modelled on Italian baroque palaces. Central in the building is the great hall, the distinctive feature of which is a mirror vault. The interior of the palace is uniformly outstanding. Today it houses a significant collection of porcelain including much famous and priceless Meissen ware.

Two stops further out, Lohhof is the nearest S-bahn station to **Schloss Haimhausen**, once owned by a count of the same name and a purely private creation. The original seventeenth-century building was elegantly modernised by F. Cuvilliés the Elder starting in 1747. There is an exterior staircase similar to that at Nymphenburg. Today the *Schloss* makes a fine setting for a display of antiques in thirty rooms and occasional special exhibitions.

Dachau, a town of some 40,000 inhabitants on line 2 of the S-bahn suffers the drawback that its name will forever be associated with some of the worst atrocities committed by the Nazi regime before and during World War II. At Alte Römerstrasse 75, there is indeed a concentration camp memorial with exhibits relating to the history of the camp and of persecution under the Nazis. Nevertheless, the town is completely charming and has an air of stolidity with its old gabled houses, and one can understand why, from the middle of the nineteenth century, it attracted large numbers of artists — their association at one stage numbered some 300 members. The much-travelled Ludwig Thoma lived at Augsburger Strasse No 13 from 1893 until 1897. In his peasant stories he described the town as having a 'rough, old Bavarian zest'.

Schleissheim Palace

The parish church of St Jakob (1584–1629) was repaired after war damage in 1648. There were several later additions and the towers were increased in height. It contains a number of items of interest, including a chased silver figure of its patron saint dating from 1690. Dachau is proud of its cultural life which centres largely upon the *Schloss*. The original eleventh-century castle on the site was replaced by a new building in 1546–73. Rebuilding took place in 1715 but it fell into disrepair in the early nineteenth century and only the south-west section survived. The banqueting hall (*Festsaal*)is the most important element in the building today. It is approached by a noble staircase (J. Effner) and has a splendid coffered wooden ceiling, also a grisaille (shades of grey) frieze painted in 1567. Unfortunately the *Festsaal* can only be seen during exhibitions or concerts.

Places of interest encircle Munich like satellites. **Freising** (population 35,000), a bare 32km out, is one such place. It is the northern terminus of S-bahn line 1 and has more than enough sights to keep the visitor occupied for a day. It lies at the foot of the Domberg above the River Isar and developed as one of the spiritual and ecclesiastical centres of south Germany. It was a cathedral town from the eighth century until the see was moved to Munich in 1821. Churches, chapels, clerical residences and the buildings of the bishop's palace can be seen today. Watching over the town from the Domberg, the Romanesque cathedral of St Maria and St Korbinian was rebuilt in 1160 although it was altered in the seventeenth century by Renaissance rebuilding and additions. Then in 1723–4, the Asam brothers decorated the interior with extravagant rococo paintings and lavish stucco. The choir stalls and vaulted ceiling date from the 1480s. The high altar of 1625 now has only a copy of Rubens' painting *Woman of the Apocalypse*, the original of which was removed to the Alte Pinakothek in Munich after the 1803 secularisation. The crypt is known to have existed before 1205. It is a four-aisled room, the roof being supported by three rows of eight columns. Most interesting is the famous 'beasts column' on which dragon-like monsters are seen in battle with men. Experts have puzzled for years over the precise meaning of the carvings. There is a world of difference between the crypt with its stone coffin of St Korbinian and the Maximilians-Kapelle built on to the crypt in 1710. The stucco and frescos here were by the Asam father, Hans Georg. The cathedral is a building of contrasts and contains treasures which really should be examined item by item if time permits.

As well as the early Gothic Johanniskirche (1320) nearby, the path between the *Dom* and the bishop's *Residenz* has yet another rare attraction. This is the Diocesan Museum which has a collection of valuable works of art. The display of Christmas cribs is quite outstanding and if there are children in the party these will keep them happy for a long time. The former monastery church Neustift, built by Viscardi in 1710, is also well worth a visit. It is a strongly marked baroque building yet there is a distinct rococo orientation in the high altar. Everything is grandiose, colourful and bright. The ceiling frescos by F.X. Feuchtmayr are specially fine. The oldest brewery in the world (1040) is to be found nearby in the former Benedictine abbey of Weihenstephan. The Benedictine monks were making beer here before the town of Munich had even been founded and they continued to do so until 1803. Appropriately, the Technical University of Munich has taken over the premises and has here its departments for brewing and food technology as well as for agriculture and garden design. There is even a state school of flower art, not so surprising really in a land where flowers and plants feature prominently in almost every household. Freising is a pleasant and restful base for the exploration, not only of Munich, but of a very pleasant rural area as well.

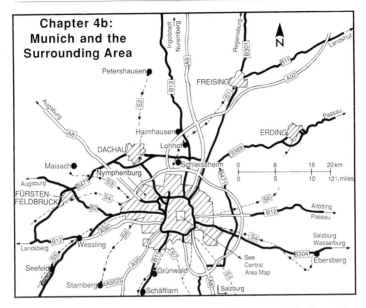

**Chapter 4b:
Munich and the
Surrounding Area**

To the north-east of Munich is the little town of **Erding**, the terminus of S-bahn line 6, 35km from the city. From the visitor's point of view it is rather like Freising although less than half the size. Cycles may be hired to explore the rather flat Erdinger Moos (moor) south and east of the River Isar. The eye is immediately attracted by the Landshuter Tor, also called the Schöner Turm (Beautiful Tower) built in 1400 as part of the encircling wall. In 1648 the town was almost completely destroyed by fire so the dignified houses with their balconies, gables and little towers nearly all stem from the eighteenth century. Happily, the monumental Gothic parish church of St Johannes (1450) survived. A distance of 5m separates the church from its bell-tower which was formerly the station of the town watchman. Despite the age of the church most of the furnishings are nineteenth century but the most valuable item is the so-called Leinberger Crucifix made by H. Leinberger in the 1520s, Gothic with the first hint of baroque. The pilgrimage church Heiliges Blut (Holy Blood) on the edge of the town was given its present form in 1675–7; the stucco is unusually imaginative and the delicate gallery is of particular note.

There are several other interesting churches in and around the town. The parish church Maria Verkündigung in the older village of

Altenerding is a rococo building from 1724 and is well worth seeing.

Even smaller is **Ebersberg** (population 8000), the terminus of S-bahn line 4 almost due east and 32km from the city. The former *Kloster* church of St Sebastian has an imposing dome-capped white tower. The building has suffered so many alterations over the years that no one architectural style is dominant but the foundations of the original building (1312) can be identified. It is said that the skull of St Sebastian was brought to Ebersberg from Rome in 931 thus giving the *Kloster* its name. The sacristy is decorated with carved figures from the workshop of I. Günther and the chapel of St Sebastian above it has fine stucco and a reliquary bust of the saint. The market place is graced by baroque and Biedermeier houses; the town hall (1529) has net vaulting and a carved wooden ceiling.

Round now to the south side of the city, the station of Ebenhausen-Schäftlarn on S-bahn line 7 gives access to one of the most significant *Kloster* complexes in the Munich area. Standing in open country with a backdrop of wooded hills, the *Kloster* at **Schäftlarn** looks most impressive. The earlier history of the site is one of many changes but the present buildings were erected at the beginning of the eighteenth century to plans by Viscardi. The tower (1712) was erected before the church (1735–51) following the collapse of an earlier tower. Consecration was in 1760 and both church and buildings escaped the ravages of secularisation in 1803 and were given back to the Benedictine order 50 years later. The church was excellently restored in 1954–9 and is regarded as a gem of Bavarian rococo architecture. Many famous artists contributed to the interior decoration and special mention must be made of J.B. Zimmermann who created some of his finest work in the stucco and frescos. It is hard to imagine that he was well into his seventies by the time the job was finished. A pleasant beer-garden nearby provides a place for a rest and a drink when the sight-seeing has been done.

To complete this outer circuit of Munich go west on S-bahn line 4 to **Fürstenfeldbruck**, two separate places with about 31,000 inhabitants. Bruck is the old settlement which grew up around a crossing place over the River Amper. Fürstenfeld is the place where a famous monastery was built in the thirteenth century. Do not neglect Bruck, a town of some charm with a Leonhardskirche containing the text 'God Bless the Horses'. The long market is enhanced by the old judges' house (1626) with ornamental balconies and the parish church of St Magdalena should not be missed.

SOME PLACES OF INTEREST IN THE MUNICH SUBURBS AND BEYOND

Schloss Nymphenburg
5km W of the *Hauptbahnhof.*
Complex of fine buildings
(1664–1739) set in classical
French gardens.

Schloss Blutenberg (1435)
4km W of Nymphenburg. Former
hunting lodge. Chapel with famous
winged altar.

Englischer Garten
1–9km NW of centre. Extensive
parkland on banks of Isar.
Beer gardens. Restaurant.

Hellabrunn Zoo
5km S of city centre on banks of
Isar. Outstanding large modern
zoo, beautifully landscaped.

Schloss Schleissheim
(1597–1848)
13km N of city centre. Really three
separate palaces.Several
architectural styles including fine
baroque. The Neues Schloss has
an art gallery and Schloss
Lustheim a porcelain collection.

DACHAU (22km NW of city)
Charming old town, earlier the
haunt of artists. *Schloss.*

FREISING (32km NE of city)
Picturesque town above R. Isar.

**Cathedral of St Maria and St
Korbinian** (1160)
Rococo paintings and lavish
stucco added 1723–4.

Diocesan Museum
Noted for its collection of
Christmas cribs.

ERDING (35km NE of city)
Dignified houses and several
interesting churches including the
Gothic St Johannes (1450)

EBERSBERG (32km E of city)
**Klosterkirche of
St Sebastian**

Town Hall (1529)
Set in graceful market place.

SCHÄFTLARN (25km S of city)
Kloster Rococo Church
(1760)
A significant religious building.
Beer garden.

FÜRSTENFELDBRUCK
(25km W of city)
**Former Cistercian
Monastery Church of the
Assumption** (1701–66)
Outstanding Italian/German
baroque. Fine organ.

However, the visitor should see the *Klosterkirche*, one of the most important sacred buildings in Upper Bavaria. The macabre origin of the *Kloster* in no way detracts from the beauty of the present church. Duke Ludwig the Strong suspected that his wife, Maria von Brabant, was being unfaithful and had her beheaded. When it was revealed that his suspicions were entirely without foundation Ludwig was filled with remorse and as a penance founded the *Kloster* on the *Fürstenfeld* (Duke's Holding) in 1263. The early Gothic brick church on the site was replaced in the eighteenth century by the present building. Work started in 1701 under G.A. Viscardi but was interrupted by the War of Spanish Succession and did not start again until after Viscardi's death. Although the Italian influence of Viscardi's design is clearly evident, the long delay meant that elements of German baroque crept in. Although the church was consecrated in 1741 it was not until 1766 that the interior was finally finished. By then, secularisation was not far off and when that time came it was threatened with destruction by cannon fire. Only by the spirited intervention of one Louis Philipp Weiss, a keeper of post-horses, was the deed prevented. Apart from the church, the *Kloster* buildings were removed from the control of the religious body and continue today in secular use.

The façade of the church is quite striking with figures of St Benedikt and St Bernard on the balustrade and a statue of Christ the Redeemer in a central niche. Inside, there is a rather bewildering mixture of colours and different styles: Italian, French, Bavarian and the individual contributions of the distinguished masters responsible. Suffice to say that the Italian artistic colony working at the Theatinerkirche in Munich provided craftsmen to do the stucco. The frescos in the choir and main aisle are by C.D. Asam and the side-altars of St Sebastian and St Peter and Paul are the work of his brother Egid Quirin. The master of the high altar is unknown although plans for this by Egid have been found. As in many other great churches, the problem here is to spare time to see all there is to see. Every corner holds something of interest; of particular value is the late Gothic gilded wooden statue of the enthroned Madonna with the child Jesus which was part of the high altar in the earlier building. The great organ is the only one in Bavaria still essentially the original two-manual instrument of the first half of the eighteenth century. It was built by Johann Georg Fux (1670–1738), 'Citizen and organ-maker of Donauwörth'.

Returning to Munich if time really presses, one of the city 'bus tours starting from the *Hauptbahnhof* could be interesting. Throughout the year there are daily round tours lasting about an hour and taking in all the principal sights. A slightly extended version includes the ascent of the Olympic Tower — a wonderful viewpoint — and lasts about $2^1/_2$ hours. Another variation is a tour taking about the same time and including some inside visits, for example, to the Nymphenburg Palace

Olympia Park and Stadium, Munich

or the Frauenkirche. More ambitious would be 'Munich by Night', starting at 7.30pm on certain evenings and lasting until midnight. This is a tour through the illuminated streets and buildings, with visits to three typical night-spots, including a restaurant. The price of the trip is fully inclusive — not cheap but certainly 'a night to remember'.

5 THE INN VALLEY AND THE CHIEMGAU

Ast of Munich, in the south-eastern corner of Bavaria, is an area of great charm. Numerous holiday and health resorts have grown up along the river banks and round the numerous lakes, and there are literally hundreds of villages in the rural countryside. The land is closely veined with small rivers and streams so that most villages have a water course of some sort. The area has many camping and caravan sites and is very favourable for caravan touring since there are few significant hills, a fact which makes it popular with cyclists too. The southern fringe of Chiemgau with the huge Chiemsee in the centre has already been touched upon in Chapter 2 so this chapter concentrates on the more low-lying part of the area which, nevertheless, lies generally at an altitude of 500m (1640ft) or more.

In the north-east of the area, not far from Passau, join the River Inn at Neuburg to travel upstream. The river forms the frontier with Austria. **Neuburg am Inn** (to distinguish it from Neuburg an der Donau visited later) with a population of 3300, is a holiday resort overlooked by the mighty Schloss Neuburg perched on a steep rock 100m (328ft) above the valley. It was built in the eleventh century and in the course of its long history has withstood attacks of all kinds. In 1908 Prinzregent Luitpold gave it to a Passau artists' association which, with similar organisations, has turned it into a hotel and recreation home for the artistic community. There are splendid views over the Inn valley and Austria from the *Schloss* which, with its fourteenth-century chapel, is well worth a visit. During the Passau *Europäischen Wochen* (European weeks), serenade concerts are given in the castle courtyard.

At **Neuhaus** (population 3000) where the River Rott flows into the Inn, a bridge connects with the Austrian town of Schärding. From the Inn-Promenade the Schloss Neuhaus can be seen on an island. Founded in the fourteenth century and rebuilt by J.M. Fischer in 1752,

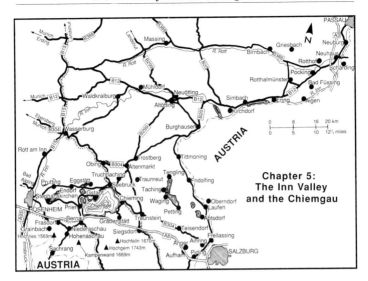

Chapter 5:
The Inn Valley
and the Chiemgau

today it is a house of the religious order of the Institute of Englischen Fräulein — an order based on the principles of the Jesuits and today devoted primarily to the education, religious instruction and upbringing of young girls. Its headquarters is in Rome and it has a membership of around 3000 sisters distributed over its several houses.

It is perhaps surprising to come across an organisation named after English girls deep in Bavaria but there is a good reason for this. In 1585 one Mary Ward was born into a Roman Catholic family near the Yorkshire city of Ripon in England. Although she is said to have been beautiful and to have had many admirers, her heart was set on a life within the Church and in 1606 she went to St Omer in France to join the community of Colletines, the severest order of St Clare. As a lay sister she was not subject to the harsh discipline she sought and she left in 1607 resolved to found a community of like-minded Englishwomen. With much opposition (to women playing a leading role in the Church) from the clergy and established orders, she had, by 1621, managed to found houses in Spitalfields, London and in Cologne and Trier. But she was not satisfied with this limited achievement and at the end of that year went to Rome to put her case to Pope Gregory XV. She was allowed to establish a house in Rome where an eye could be kept on her activities. For a time things went well but by November

1626 she had decided to return to England via Germany. In Munich, Elector Maximilian I permitted Mary and her companions to remain and even provided them with a residence and an annual allowance: he was interested in the education of girls which was one of the objects of the organisation. In 1627 the emperor of Austria invited Mary to Vienna and provided a foundation for her in that city. Opposition continued and at one stage she was arrested in Munich and imprisoned in the convent at Anger. Constant harassment undermined her health and in 1637 she returned to England where she died near York on 20 January 1645 and was buried in the churchyard at Osbaldwick where her gravestone may still be seen.

Two kilometres upstream from Neuhaus is a major technical achievement, the Schärding-Neuhaus power station with its dam which has turned the River Inn here into a 16km-long and up to 300m-wide(984ft) artificial lake. Continue to follow the Inn as it wends its picturesque way through Bavaria and reach **Bad Füssing** (population 4800), a spa with three thermal springs delivering water at 56°C (133°F), 3000 litres per minute (660 gallons)from a depth of 1000m (3280ft), the most powerful sulphur springs in Europe. These, of course, feed the spa's bathing facilities: the open-air pools have a water temperature of 36–38°C (97–100°F) and are available throughout the year but there is a thermal *Hallenbad* as well.

There are several outlying areas associated with Füssing. One is **Aigen**, close to the river, with a pilgrimage church dedicated to St Leonhard and the scene of an annual *Leonhardiritt*. It was founded in the thirteenth century to celebrate the finding of a wonder-working *Marienbild* (picture or statue of Mary) washed up from the Inn. The low saddle-tower to the south is from the first chapel built here, the Gothic west tower and the rest of the building date from about 1500.

One of the more pleasant things about Bad Füssing is the bird sanctuary on the banks of the Inn with marked nature trails. A little further upstream between Ering and Simbach, beside another Inn *Stausee* (reservoir), there is a more extensive bird protection area (*Vogelschutzgebiet*), well worth a visit.

Bad Füssing is at one corner of the so-called Rottal spa triangle, the other resorts being Birnbach and Griesbach both of which lie to the north-west. **Birnbach** — the rural spa — is 25km from Bad Füssing. Although its inhabitants number less than 1300 there is a wide range of leisure activities for every age group. The thermal springs which feed the open-air swimming pools maintain water temperatures of

PLACES OF INTEREST IN THE LOWER INN VALLEY

NEUBURG
Schloss Neuburg
Views over valley and Austria.
Fourteenth-century chapel.

NEUHAUS
(2km S). Dam for Neuhaus-
Schärding (Austria) joint hydro-
electric power station.

BAD FÜSSING
Spa with thermal springs for
year-round bathing outdoors.

Bird Sanctuary with nature
trails near river.

ROTTHALMÜNSTER (10km W of
Bad Füssing)
**Parish Church of the As-
sumption** (1472)
Outstanding altar painting.

SIMBACH
**Bird Sanctuary and Nature
Reserve**
E of town towards Ering.

BURGHAUSEN
Burg
Enormous castle complex on
terrace above old town. Interesting apartments and chapel. Part
of State Art Collection.

**Photographic Museum and
Heimatmuseum**
Within the castle complex.

**Town Hall and other
Buildings**
All with colourful façades lining
the main street.

Parish Church of St Jakob
(1360)
Later modifications. A clean,
spacious church.

Spitalkirche Heilig Geist
Fourteenth century with eighteenth-century baroque treatment.

ALTÖTTING
Gnadenkapelle
Pilgrimage church of so-called
'Black Madonna'; wall compart-
ments with hearts of kings,
queens, etc.

Near the Stiftskirche
Modern Stations of the Cross in
red marble.

NEUÖTTING
Market Area
Colourful façades and arcades.

Fine Brick Gothic Church
(started 1410)

EXCURSION FROM NEUÖTTING
MASSING (25km N.) Open-air
museum of Lower Bavarian
farmhouses, etc.

24–38°C (75–100°F). **Griesbach**, 10km east and about 20km from
Bad Füssing, was officially approved as a *Luftkurort* in 1973 and in
1977 three thermal springs producing water up to 60°C (140°F) were
tapped to supply the pools in the pleasant spa which has grown up
around the old village. The *Kur* is claimed to be specially beneficial for

sufferers of rheumatic and arthritic conditions. In addition to all the usual activities and entertainments there is an 18-hole golf course.

Some 10km west of Bad Füssing is **Rotthalmünster** whose parish church Maria Himmelfahrt was built in 1452. The mighty high altar of 1700 has an outstanding painting by Johannes Kaspar Sing. The nearby pilgrimage church, usually called the Wieskapelle, is a simple building from 1737–40 with an altar of the same period which has two good carved figures, Joachim and Anna. Another border town with a major crossing over the Inn to Austria is **Simbach** (population 5400). This pleasant country town makes an ideal base for visiting the *Vogelschutzgebiet* and for rambling in the very attractive countryside to the north between the valleys of the Rivers Inn and Rott. Fifty-three kilometres of marked *Wanderwege* are centred on Simbach and excursions into the Austrian Salzkammergut are only a matter of crossing over the river bridge. The Gothic church in **Erlach** is worth visiting and the *Heimatmuseum* has a number of items of interest. **Kirchdorf am Inn** a few kilometres up river is close to another *Stausee* which provides a natural bathing place and a broad boating lake.

Germany's great rivers are frequently dammed to provide the head of water needed for the many hydro-electric power stations. The Inn between here and Passau is a case in point but these developments have not necessarily harmed the landscape. On the contrary, the new 'lakes' provide opportunities for sailing, wind-surfing and other water activities which would hardly have been possible with a river in its natural state. At **Bergham**, 6km beyond Kirchdorf, the River Salzach takes over the frontier watch towards Salzburg and the Inn swings sharply northwards with both banks in Bavaria for a while. The B12 running west from Simbach should be followed until it crosses to the south bank of the Inn then fork left into the B20 to reach Burghausen in 10km. Although it is on the Salzach, **Burghausen** is the outstanding example of the distinctive 'Inn valley' style of architecture and a few hours should be spent here. Do not be put off by the fairly uninteresting outskirts of the modern town but seek out the *Burg* and the old town on the banks of the river. There is good parking space near the *Burg* which occupies a long, level terrace high above the town. There are fine views down to the river and the colourful houses beneath, and several paths or flights of steps lead down. Burghausen's population of 18,000 is obviously mainly accommodated in the new developments and the fortress and old town area are comparatively quiet and uncrowded.

The old town and castle, Burghausen

Much that is important -n Burghausen is at the upper level. The six sections of the ancient *Burg* extend for some 1100m along the terrace and form the largest castle complex in Germany. The present building dates from the thirteenth to fifteenth centuries and is protected on the flat north side by numerous ditches, gates and courtyards. The south buildings towering over the town include the three-storey Dürnitzstock which has a storage hall with two aisles, over which is the heated dining room, also with two aisles. The upper storey was formerly the ballroom and there is fine fifteenth-century groin vaulting in both apartments. The choir of the *Burg* chapel dedicated to St Elisabeth, was built in the Romanesque style but gave way to Gothic around 1255. The nave has net vaulting from about 1475. The Fürstenbau (Princes' Building) now houses a department of the Bavarian State Art Collection. At the entrance to the *Burg* is the municipal photographic museum and the *Heimatmuseum* is in the inner courtyard. The story is that in the Middle Ages the Lower Bavarian dukes used the *Burg* to accommodate their lawful wives while the dukes enjoyed a private life in Burg Trausnitz at Landshut without too many reflections on their matrimonial obligations.

Down in the town, the fourteenth-century *Rathaus* and the sixteenth-century Regierungsgebäude (Government Building) colourfully dominate the many fine houses which line the broad main street. This is a photographer's delight. The parish church of St Jakob (1360 with later modifications) and the Spitalkirche Heilig Geist (fourteenth century with eighteenth-century baroque) are both worth a visit. There are often concerts and exhibitions, particularly, it seems, during the spring months. The feeling of the south is very marked here in Burghausen and can be experienced to a greater or lesser degree in many other towns in this area.

Return to the Inn valley at Neuötting about 10km along a picturesque road to the north-west of Burghausen but first turn aside to see **Altötting** (population 12,000) lying a little back from the river. Pilgrims daily make their way to the Gnadenkapelle here, as they have been doing for hundreds of years. There has been a chapel here since the eighth century. The principal object of the pilgrimage is the so-called 'Black Madonna', a 64cm-high (2ft) blackened figure of Mary, probably made in Lorraine about 1300 and which was brought here in 1360. Altötting is sometimes called Herz Bayerns (Heart of Bavaria); in fact this has some validity for in wall compartments opposite the miraculous image are the hearts of six kings, two queens, two electors and Field Marshall Tilly. The continuous stream of pilgrims has resulted in a rather brash commercialism growing up around the chapel with the usual tawdry souvenirs. Those needing a little peace should seek out the modern Stations of the Cross near the Stiftskirche with its two soaring spires, an up-to-date representation in red marble of the beliefs of Christians for nearly 2000 years. The Stiftskirche St Philipp and St Jakob is worth seeing and so are the former Jesuit church of St Magdalena (sixteenth to eighteenth century) and the neo-baroque St Anna-Basilica built just before World War I. Altötting has its *Hofdult* around the end of May/beginning of June and a *Christkindlmarkt* takes place early in December when there are also concerts of Advent music.

Neuötting has none of the frantic scramble associated with its neighbour. It is a typical Inn-Salzach town and was fortunately spared by World War II so that the market area, with its colourful façades and arcades, is 'original'. It also has a distinguished church, a fine example of Upper Bavarian brick Gothic started in 1410 and not finished for some 200 years. The original plans were adhered to, however, despite the fact that tastes had changed in the meantime.

Altötting

An excursion 25km to the north from here ends at the excellent open-air museum at **Massing** in the River Rott valley. The museum is a collection of Lower Bavarian farmhouses and gives a good insight into the rural way of life in years gone by.

In contrast to Neuötting, **Mühldorf**, 12km west along the Inn, saw action at the end of the war including the blowing up of the Inn bridge. The figure of a town guard from 1659 was thrown into the river by the explosion but the fragments were recovered. The rebuilt figure now stands watch again with shield and halberd outside the Münchener Tor, one of the town's historic gateways. With around 15,000 inhabitants, Mühldorf is another typical Inn valley town with colourfully painted house fronts — some from the fifteenth and sixteenth centuries, four fountains from the seventeenth and eighteenth centuries and arcades around the long-stretched Stadtplatz or market street. The late Gothic *Rathaus* was rebuilt from three houses after a serious fire in 1640 and was complemented by the Frauenkirche in 1643.

Waldkraiburg is a larger town with the Inn snaking past it on the south side. A pleasant enough place but not one which the tourist need go out of his way to inspect. On Sundays from May to September there are concerts in the Stadtpark and there are regular concerts, drama, opera and operetta in the town theatre. Continuing upstream, **Wasserburg** (not to be confused with the Lake Constance Wasserburg) is an important centre and is the point at which the Ferienstrasse (Holiday Road) encountered briefly in Chapter 1, crosses the Inn to continue its route to the Alps. By now, the Inn has turned south to head for Austria again and a great curve of the river encircles the old town. The most striking view is obtained by entering from the south-east on the B304. The bridge over the Inn is crossed and through the Brucktor gateway is the town centre Marienplatz with the *Rathaus*, the Marienkirche and the Kernhaus with a rococo façade created by J.B. Zimmermann.

The Marienkirche is a fourteenth-century building but the baroque interior was not completed until the second half of the eighteenth century. The older furnishings include a fifteenth-century Madonna, late fifteenth-century figures of St Blasius and St Apollonaria and a font from 1520. The parish church of St Jakob has a fine baroque pulpit from 1638–9 while the *Burg* of 1531, no longer intact, has most attractive stepped gables. The *Heimatmuseum* has a fine collection of Bavarian farmhouse furniture. Civil engineers may well be interested in the Wegmachermuseum (Road-making Museum) which has some 1500 exhibits including road surfaces, bridges and every conceivable item of equipment to do with road-making, maintenance, snow-clearing and so on.

Although Wasserburg (population 13,400) may not be the place for a prolonged stay, it is certainly worth spending a night or two here in order to see the town in the evening or early morning, free from the daily throng of tourists. In February, Wasserburg is the venue of the biggest pigeon market in the world; Whitsun is the time for a big spring fair with a pleasure park; in July the wine festival includes a Venetian night when the old town is illuminated, while on the first Saturday in August there is a great flea market.

 Little **Rott am Inn**, 10km south of Wasserburg, is mainly renowned for its former Benedictine abbey church of St Marinus and Anianus. Rott was the seat of Benedictine monks from the twelfth century on. In the eighteenth century, Abbot Benedikt Lutz intended to rebuild the church using the walls of the then existing twelfth-century building but in the end commissioned J.M. Fischer to do a complete rebuild, only the old towers and some minor sections being incorporated in the new structure. The work took from 1759 until 1767,

The former
monastery church at
Fürstenfeldbruck

The monastery at
Benediktbeuern

Alpine hut above Sachrang

Steam train at Stock-Prien

Wasserburg on the River Inn

with many of the best artists of the day contributing to the decoration. The enormous fresco in the dome (M. Günther) depicts the glorification of the saints of the Benedictine order. The church, standing on the threshold of classicism, represents the mature final stages of baroque and in contrast to the plain exterior, the inside is truly magnificent. The remainder of the *Kloster* buildings fell to secularisation in 1803.

Some of the lesser-known places in the area are also rewarding. One of these is **Tuntenhausen**, 11km south-west of Rott, a village overlooked by most guide books but which has a very old (1441) pilgrimage church. The visitor should examine the interior which is lined with large pictures of numerous miracles which form a unique documentation of folklore, complemented by the many memorial tablets also inside the church. The most original picture is known as the *Tuntenhausener Tod*, a seventeenth-century painting on wood of Death with a poised arrow, illustrating the saying *'Fleuch wo du wilt, des Todes Bildt, stäts auf dich zilt'* ('Hide where you will, Death is always aiming at you.') Wherever you stand in the church the arrow seems to be aimed in your direction.

Returning to the river, enter the busy town of **Rosenheim**

PLACES OF INTEREST AS THE INN TURNS SOUTH

MÜHLDORF

Typical Inn valley town with colourful houses, historic gateways, fountains and arcades. Long market street with **Town Hall** (1640) and **Frauenkirche** (1643)

WASSERBURG

Old town in great curve of river.

Marienplatz with town hall and other fine buildings.

Marienkirche fourteenth century with eighteenth-century baroque.

Heimatmuseum
Contents include a collection of Bavarian farmhouse furniture.

Road-making Museum
Unusual exhibition of everything to do with building, maintaining, cleaning roads, etc.

ROTT AM INN
Benedictine Abbey-Church (1759–67)
Outstanding monument of the end of the baroque era. Works by famous craftsmen.

TUNTENHAUSEN (11km SW of Rott)
Pilgrimage Church (1441)
Remarkable collection of miracle pictures including famous *Tuntenhausener Tod*. Bright stucco.

ROSENHEIM
Max-Joseph-Platz
Square surrounded by fine old buildings especially No 20 and No 22, the former town hall.

Heimatmuseum
Housed in fourteenth-century town gateway.

Art Gallery
Works of local nineteenth- and twentieth-century painters.

BAD AIBLING (7km W of Rosenheim)
Heimatmuseum with studio of Wilhelm Leibl, painter.

BERBLING (3km S of Bad Aibling)
Beautiful rococo church restored in 1983. Scene of one of Leibl's most famous paintings.

(population 53,000) 27km from Wasserburg and by far the biggest town in the area. Rosenheim celebrates several festivals each year, the most important being the autumn fair during the first fortnight of September. The town stands where the old Roman road from Augsburg to Salzburg crossed the Inn and also on the old trade route from the Brenner Pass to Regensburg. Rosenheim clearly belongs to the group of Inn valley towns and the old centre around the Max-Joseph-Platz displays a similar architectural style to Wasserburg and Mühldorf, although only a few of the arcades remain following serious fires in the sixteenth and seventeenth centuries. The parish church of

St Nikolaus, Heilig-Geist-Kirche (Church of the Holy Ghost) and Heilig-Blut-Kirche all justify a visit. The *Heimatmuseum* housed in a fourteenth-century town gateway is worth a visit and the town art gallery largely features the works of nineteenth- and twentieth-century painters from Munich and the Chiemgau. Do not miss seeing the stucco and courtyard of No 20 and the former *Rathaus* (1444) at No 22 Max-Joseph-Platz.

Bad Aibling (population 12,500) just west of Rosenheim, is a pleasant spa with all the appropriate facilities. Art-lovers may be interested in the *Heimatmuseum* which includes the studio of Wilhelm Leibl (1844–1900) who lived and painted in this area for a number of years. One of his well known paintings *Drei Frauen in der Kirche* (Three Women in Church) of 1881 now hangs in the Hamburg Kunsthalle; it was painted in the church at **Berbling** just to the south and the artist is said to have spent no less than four summers working on it. The church is worth seeing anyway for it is much more than the usual village place of worship. It was restored in 1983 and shows rococo at its best; indeed, it is often called the Wieskirche of the Mangfall valley, a bit of justifiable exaggeration perhaps. During the summer, notice the flower displays on the farmhouses in this area.

East of Rosenheim, a little group of resorts south of the motorway deserve attention, for they occupy an exceptionally picturesque corner of Chiemgau. **Frasdorf** (population 1400) like many other villages, celebrates spring by erecting a maypole on 1 May. Throughout the year there are fortnightly folk-music or dance presentations but it is also an ideal centre for rambling in the Alpine foothills. The neighbouring villages of **Törwang** and **Grainbach** both have churches — originally Gothic — as their focal points. From Grainbach, the Hochriesbahn climbs to the summit of the Hochries (1570m, 5150ft). The *Bahn* is in two sections, first a chair-lift for 250m (820ft) and then a cable car for the remaining 670m (2200ft). It is cheaper to pay for both sections together and for families the *Familienkarte* offers substantial savings on a return journey. Refreshments are available at the upper station (only about half a kilometre from the Austrian border) from where there is a choice of routes to take one back to the valley on foot if desired. The summit offers marvellous views towards the Wilder Kaiser mountains in Austria to the south. Another village in this group, **Rossholzen**, is worth visiting because its church has a late Gothic winged altar and a number of naive but realistic memorial tablets portraying the one-time water traffic on the nearby Inn.

Aschau, in the valley of the little River Prien, is divided into two parts, **Niederaschau** to the north and **Hohenaschau** to the south. It is a *Luftkurort* of 4300 inhabitants and is the terminus of a branch railway from Prien on the main Munich-Salzburg line. The village is attractive with its variety of flower-bedecked houses and the twin towers of its baroque parish church. This spacious late Gothic building was given baroque treatment in 1702 and the main aisle was extended in 1752–3. However, the symbol of Aschau is not the church, pretty though it is, but the imposing castle, Burg Hohenaschau, which dominates the skyline. It is the mightiest of the many fortresses in the Chiemgau and in 1561 was converted from an uncomfortable *Burg* into a spacious Renaissance *Schloss* which was later rebuilt in the baroque style. The building is well worth a visit for its monumental 'Gallery of Ancestors' (larger-than-life stucco statues) in the state ballroom and the chapel, with works by J.B. Zimmermann and I. Günther and with an early baroque Italian high altar from Verona. Aschau has a lively programme of events from May to September for its summer visitors: in winter, attention focuses mainly on winter sports activities. In this corner of Chiemgau there are several splendid opportunities for mountain walks which, while not specially difficult, do reach fine vantage points.

From beside the main road in Hohenaschau, the *Gondelbahn* climbs up to the Kampenwand. As the car glides over the tree tops, look down into the clearings for glimpses of chamois and other wildlife. The actual summit at 1669m (5474ft) is reached along a path about 1km in a north-easterly direction from the upper station (1464m, 4800ft) (refreshments) and a little beyond that there is an *Almhütte* selling refreshments. From the Kampenwand there are wonderful views north over Bernau and the Chiemsee.Continue first north-east then north for nearly 1km. The Sulten (1473m, 4831ft) is on the left and the Gederer Wand (1399m, 4590ft) on the right. A path going sharply back to the left (west) before passing the Sulten is the shortest way back down to Hohenaschau but it is very steep. Less demanding is the path past the Sulten which gradually curves to the left (west) descending steadily and often quite steeply. After about 2.5km keep left when the path forks, continuing westwards past the Maisalm to join and follow a stream running down to the valley. The main road is reached in Niederaschau, turn left and follow it back to the starting point in Hohenaschau. Look out for posters advertising an *Almkonzert* or *Almtanz*, usually on a Sunday afternoon. There will be refresh-

H
•• ••
ΔΔΔ
7.5
or
8km

Hohenaschau castle

ments and the enjoyment of folk-music and dancing there on the mountain can make the workaday world seem very far away.

So far as Bavaria is concerned, **Sachrang** is the end of the road, which disappears into Austria just past the village. Its idyllic setting amongst the mountains close to the source of the Prien makes this a fine centre for mountain walking. Sachrang is an unsophisticated resort; the more spectacular activities are to be found down the valley in Aschau, but from 10 June the summer visitor is entertained with occasional film evenings and a fortnightly (on Fridays) *Almtanz* or *Heimatabend* (folk-evening) or guided mountain walks. The little village church was built at the end of the seventeenth century, probably a work of Lorenzo Sciasca who brought in some Italian artists to work on the stucco and paintings.

From the church (at 738m, 2420ft) walk due north up the hillside climbing steeply for nearly 2km until the path makes a T-junction with another and turn left into this. Continue climbing, now walk due west for about 1km to reach a mountain hut, the Spitzsteinhaus at 1237m (4057ft) right on the Austrian border. Refreshments should be avail-

PLACES OF INTEREST IN SOUTH-WEST CHIEMGAU

GRAINBACH
Hochries (1570m, 5150ft)
Wonderful views and mountain
walks. Chair-lift and cable car.

ROSSHOLZEN
Church with late Gothic winged
altar and memorial tablets
recalling water traffic on River Inn.

HOHENASCHAU
Castle
Former fortress now a fine
baroque palace. 'Gallery of

Ancestors' and chapel with works
by famous craftsmen.

Kampenwand (1669m, 5474ft)
Extensive views and mountain
walks. Cable railway.

SACHRANG
Village in idyllic setting close to
Austrian border. Charming little
church. Starting place for
mountain walks. Beautiful
mountain flowers.

able here. To ascend to the summit of the Spitzstein (1596m, 5235ft) go north from here on a well used steep path on the Austrian side of the border and reach the summit in about 1km. Note that this involves a climb of about 360m (1180ft) from the Spitzsteinhaus. From the summit there is a choice of return route.

1. Continue northwards along the ridge to the Brandelberg (1517m, 4976ft) and (by now back in Bavaria) on to the Feichtenalm about 2km from the summit where a path turns down to the right, east at first and then curves to the right to drop steeply down into Innerwald and Huben (refreshments) then follows the main road back into Sachrang in under 2km.

2. Return the same way to the Spitzsteinhaus, continue south on the Austrian side for 1km or so — do not take any paths going west off the ridge — and look out for signs to Café Kaiserblick. From the café there is a fine view to the Kaiser mountains and down to Sachrang below. Continue downhill, sometimes fairly steeply, on one of several obvious paths to reach the village.

Whether one chooses route 1 or 2 there is little difference in the distance covered or the time required. These are most rewarding walks and the summer visitor will be astonished at the variety and abundance of wild flowers to be found. Remember to carry your passport; the frontier guards of either country are liable to be less than delighted if you cannot identify yourself. You may not know just which country you are in, for the border is not obvious in these mountains.

From some of the heights around Frasdorf or Aschau one can look north to the 5km-long Simssee near Rosenheim, a delightful lake in pretty surroundings. The principal resort on the Simssee is **Stephanskirchen** near the south end, only 6km from Rosenheim. There are numerous bathing places including a particularly fine beach at **Krottenmühl** near the north end where there are also good eating places. **Prutting** is a village about 2.5km west of the Simssee and 2 or 3km beyond it are two more lakes, the Hofstättersee and the Rinssee, each about 1.5km long. There is a veritable network of paths and small farm roads which make for pleasant and level walking between and around the lakes. Prutting is equally well placed for access to the small lakes or to the larger Simssee, connected to the village by a direct footpath.

A little beyond the end of that lake, **Endorf** (population 5100) is principally a health resort with important mineral springs. No single large village this, but the core of a group of no less than fourteen little communities. A lively programme of entertainment is organised, especially in the summer months when *Kur* guests are joined by many holidaymakers. Concerts, theatrical productions (including a religious one June/July), film evenings and so on ensure there is always something for the visitor to look forward to. Between here and the village of Eggstätt, 6km to the east, there is another cluster of idyllic little lakes. **Eggstätt** (population 1700) is also a health resort on a modest scale. Despite the proximity of the busy Chiemsee this area is relatively unspoiled and one could spend many happy days just wandering from one little lake to another, enjoying the (protected) natural surroundings. Look out in July and August for announcements of *Almtänze* (folk dances) and *Dorffeste* (village fairs).

Now is the time to take a closer look at Bavaria's 'ocean', the Chiemsee. With an area of 80sq km, not only is it Bavaria's largest lake but it is also the largest entirely German lake. It only takes a few minutes to travel from Endorf or Eggstätt to **Prien** (population 9000) at the west end of the lake, which is not only the biggest town near the lake but is also the only one served by the main line trains. In fact, the town centre and station are 1.5km from the lake shore. A magnificent museum piece of a steam railway, the nineteenth-century Prien-Stock-Bahn connects the DB station with the pier at Stock where the lake steamers depart. The strange tramway-type locomotive is known affectionately as 'Feurige (fiery) Elias'

Prien is a *Kneippkurort* and a town worth visiting if only for the

Prien

Heimatmuseum in a house of 1681 which gives a comprehensive picture of the one-time peasant life around the Chiemsee. The parish church Maria Himmelfahrt (1735–8) is a surprisingly large building and J.B. Zimmermann was among the artists who contributed to the decoration and furnishing. There is a busy programme of events in Prien and the surrounding villages and various excursions on foot, by bicycle or by steamer are arranged from May to September. There is a bathing beach on the Chiemsee at **Stock**. Less than 3km to the south in the village of **Urschalling**, the little twelfth-century chapel is the site of remarkable Romanesque and Gothic wall paintings which were hidden for centuries under countless coats of distemper and only came to light during restoration work in 1941–2.

Travel into the mountains, to Rosenheim or even to Munich is easy from Prien but it is the steamer trips on the lake which bring many people here and in particular the opportunity to go ashore on the main islands, **Herrenchiemsee** and **Frauenchiemsee** (Herreninsel or Fraueninsel). Herrenchiemsee is the bigger of the two and most

visitors coming off the steamer hasten past the Altes Schloss towards Ludwig II's dream palace (1869–86) which, conceived during his

The interior of Herrenchiemsee palace

'French' period, is modelled on the French baroque palace of Versailles. However, the Altes Schloss (built 1700) is also of interest; it was part of the monastery which once stood here (hence the *Herren* [men or monks]in the name) and is where Ludwig stayed during his frequent visits to the island which he bought in the first place to protect it from speculators. The library hall was decorated in grandiose style by J.B. Zimmermann.

The new palace is a truly spectacular building and the great hall, the mirror gallery and the state bedroom are amongst the finest of Ludwig's creations. It is a wonderful experience to take the steamer to the island from Prien or one of the other lake resorts, enjoy a leisurely meal in the Schlosshotel and then walk through the trees to the palace for a concert of chamber music in the great hall (no seats). Then back to the mainland, if one is lucky, in the moonlight.

Frauenchiemsee is the site of a *Kloster* founded by one Irmingard in 772 for nuns of the Benedictine order. Her grave was only rediscovered in the course of excavations started in 1961. To enjoy fully the delights of this little island, it should be visited outside the peak

A quiet corner of the Chiemsee near Prien

holiday season when every calling steamer disgorges a crowd of visitors. The meringue swans are a delightful speciality of the Klostercafé where liqueurs and gorgeous marzipan are also on sale.

 Take time to walk right round the island for the wonderful views in every direction but especially southwards towards the mountains. Frauenchiemsee is a favourite haunt of artists and an exhibition of their work is held during the summer months.

PLACES OF INTEREST   AROUND THE CHIEMSEE

SIMSSEE
5km-long lake with numerous bathing places. Many other small lakes and resorts in good, level walking country.

PRIEN
Parish Church of the Assumption (1735–8)
Several famous artists involved in decoration and fittings.

Heimatmuseum
The story of peasant life around the Chiemsee.

Historic Steam Railway
Connects town and DB station with pier at Stock.

URSCHALLING (3km S of Prien)
Chapel
Romanesque and Gothic wall paintings. Twelfth century.

HERRENCHIEMSEE
Biggest island in the lake.

Schloss Herrenchiemsee
Palace of Ludwig II based on Versailles (1869–86).
Many spectacular apartments.

King Ludwig II Museum

Old Palace (built 1700)
Part of the former monastery.
Fine baroque library.

FRAUENCHIEMSEE
The island has wonderful views and is a haunt of artists.
A favourite venue for afternoon coffee and cakes.

Nunnery (founded 772)

SEEBRUCK
Heimathaus
Exhibition of Roman remains.

A circuit of the Chiemsee is a must, even if traffic is a problem at times. Going north from Prien, pass through a succession of resort villages: **Rimsting** (population 2680) is only 3km along this road and then comes **Breitbrunn** (population 1300) with its picturesque baroque church and extensive views over the lake to Frauenchiemsee and the mountains beyond. **Gstadt** is right on the shore, with steamers, boats for hire and a bathing beach. **Seebruck**, at the northernmost tip of the lake, is where the lake waters enter the River Alz on the way to the Inn. One of the lake's sailing centres, Seebruck also caters for bathing and other water activities with a large bathing beach, a *Freibad* and an enormous area for just sunning and lazing. This was once the site of the Roman settlement of Bedaium where a fortress was erected to protect the important Salzburg-Rosenheim road. Many Roman remains are exhibited in the Heimathaus.

Now, for a short while, the lakeside road becomes the Ferien-

Breitbrunn church

strasse which has come across country from Wasserburg. Pass through **Ising** which is combined with **Chieming** a few kilometres further along to make a resort with a population of 3500. Chieming marks the easternmost limit of the lake and is devoted largely to sun and water worshippers. The lake steamers call here from May to September. The Ferienstrasse now turns off east to **Traunstein** but visitors should continue south along the shore towards **Grabenstätt** (population 3100), a flower-bedecked health resort lying about 2km from the shore, because the road has to make a detour round the marshy delta of the River Tiroler Ache, a wildlife sanctuary. The nearby Tüttensee is one of Bavaria's warmest natural bathing places.

Shortly after leaving Grabenstätt join the motorway for the westward journey along the south lake shore. The next junction — **Feldwies** — gives access to a 3km-long sandy strand which is a favourite weekend goal for the *Münchners*. Before the war the Autobahn Rasthaus Chiemsee was another popular destination but it was taken over in 1945 by the Americans to use its 300-bed capacity as a 'Recreation-Center' for the forces and they are still there. At the Bernau exit from the motorway turn north to complete the circuit of the lake past Urschalling and back into Prien.

A few kilometres north of the Chiemsee on the B304, **Obing**, with its little lake and bathing beach, is worth a visit. Here in a peaceful land of little lakes, streams and woods is an environment ideal for those seeking escape from the workaday world. In the fifteenth-century parish church of St Laurentius there are three examples of the work of a notable local wood-carver, his *Mother-of-God, St Laurentius* and *St Jakobus* in the late Gothic style. Although there are works by this artist in a number of places in the Chiemgau his name is unknown and he is merely recorded in the annals as Meister von Rabenden. **Rabenden** is, in fact, the next village 5km eastwards and in the little church there, the high altar and two side-altars make an impressive unit and the principal figures, *Jakobus, Simon* and *Judas Thaddäus* are most lifelike. Even if the name of the creator is not known, art experts believe that he belonged to the top ranks of medieval wood-carvers in Upper Bavaria.

Four kilometres more, and in **Altenmarkt**, the River Traun adds its Alpine waters to the northward flowing Alz. It is a friendly little town of about 3000 inhabitants and the picturesque river with its waterfalls invites the traveller to linger. Immediately south of the town, the Klosterkirche Baumburg occupies an elevated site with good views of the countryside and can be seen for miles around with its unusual pointed domes. It is the former church of the Augustinian canons. The first building here was consecrated in 1023 and the present one was built on the Romanesque foundations in 1754–7. Externally quite plain, the church is lavishly decorated inside with rococo stucco work by the Wessobrunn school, excellent carving on the altars, pulpit and choir stalls and *Putti* (symbolic children's figures) everywhere. Concerts of sacred music are given here during the summer months.

Just north of Altenmarkt, **Trostberg** (population 6200) is known as the northern gateway to the Chiemgau. It is a pleasant town with a long history and one in which markets play an important role. In March, May, October and November there are market days on the third Saturday and Sunday in the month; from May to October there is a flea market on the first Saturday in each month. Although this romantic old town does not really make many concessions to the tourist trade, the Gothic parish church is worth seeing; the *Heimatmuseum* housed in the Heimathaus, built in 1943, is notable for its series of furnished rooms depicting the life-styles of the baroque, rococo and Biedermeier periods. Returning to Altenmarkt, follow the River Traun and the B304 southwards and arrive at

OBING, ALTENMARKT, TROSTBERG AND ALONG THE RIVER TRAUN

OBING
Church of St Laurentius
Remarkable wood-carvings by the 'Meister von Rabenden'. Fifteenth century.

RABENDEN (5km E of Obing)
Village Church
Lifelike carvings by the 'Meister von Rabenden'.

ALTENMARKT
Klosterkirche Baumburg (1754–7)
Lavish rococo stucco of the Wessobrunn school.

TROSTBERG
Heimatmuseum
Series of furnished rooms showing life-styles of baroque, rococo, etc periods.

TRAUNREUT
Huge swimming pool complex with giant chute and every amenity.

SIEGSDORF
Important all-year holiday centre. In Bergen (4km W) cable cars to Hochfelln (1670m, 5477ft) for views and mountain walks.

Traunreut (population 4500), a modern town surrounded by many villages and hamlets. Principal item of interest for the holidaymaker will probably be the extensive *Freibadzentrum*, a large complex of heated swimming pools with a jumbo-size water-chute and every amenity for a pleasant day in the water or on the extensive sunbathing area surrounding the pools.

Continuing south on the B304, bypass Traunwalchen, and in 10km reach **Traunstein** (population 17,400), the principal town in this corner of the Chiemgau, a *Luft-* and *Kneippkurort* with all the amenities. Originally settled by the Romans, Traunstein blossomed in the fourteenth century when it became a river crossing place for one of the old salt routes. There is less of a historic town centre than one would expect due to a series of disastrous fires. The second of these in 1704 even resulted in the destruction of the castle and in 1851 most of the old houses fell to another blaze. The baroque church was restored after the last fire and graces the 250m-long (820ft) and 85m-wide (280ft) Stadtplatz.

Traunstein is one of several places where the Easter Ride is still practised. Here it is known as the *Georgiritt* and the brightly decorated procession, including St George on a white horse, makes its way to the little church at nearby **Ettendorf** where the horses are blessed on behalf of all the animals on the farms, and on returning home, horses and riders are treated to a special Easter meal. In addition the town hosts a spring festival in May, a folk-festival in August and a *Christkindlmarkt* in December.

The visitor with time available should follow the Traun a further 5km south, crossing the motorway to the little town of **Siegsdorf**, focal point of a holiday region of about 7000 inhabitants. Since the region includes mountainous country reaching heights of over 1200m (3936ft) there are winter facilities with ten ski-tows. The region embraces the village of **Bergen**, 4km west of Siegsdorf, where there is a cable railway in two sections to the summit of the Hochfelln (1670m, 5477ft). Again there are group and family tickets offering substantial reductions. Siegsdorf is ideally situated for mountain walking, modest rambling round the Chiemsee or for excursions a little further afield to the Inn valley or the Berchtesgaden area for example.

From Traunstein the B304 heads directly for Salzburg and if this picturesque road is followed for about 16km, arrives at **Teisendorf**, a useful little resort with — between mid-June and end of August — folk-evenings, slide or film shows, guided rambles and mountain walks. Teisendorf is at the west point of a small diamond-shaped area known as Rupertiwinkel. The name goes back to about 700 and one Ruperti, the first bishop of Salzburg.

About 4km south of the village is Kloster Höglwörth, an ancient seat of the Order of Augustinian Canons which was refounded in 1125. After falling into disrepair it was rebuilt in the seventeenth century. The church was consecrated in 1689 and contains striking stucco work. The monastery was finally dissolved in 1817. This rural *Kloster* looks more like a fortress and there is no doubt that the monks built with an eye to their security in an isolated location.

Two kilometres below the *Kloster*, the parish church of St Peter and St Paul (1450) in **Anger** has a number of interesting sculptures from the sixteenth and seventeenth centuries. King Ludwig I was of the opinion that Anger was the most beautiful village in Bavaria and it is a very fine spot with its surrounding farmhouses, mostly from the eighteenth century, making a homely, attractive picture. Today, an important factor is the freedom of the village from traffic thanks to the proximity of the motorway. The king may have seen the place through rose coloured spectacles, of course, for this is where his beloved Lola Montez lived.

L
◆▸◆▸
▵▵
16-
18km

A pleasant walk by well defined footpaths southwards from Teisendorf brings one to the former *Kloster* and its church, then down to the little wood-fringed lake which belonged to the *Kloster*. From here the route runs south-east into Anger and then due east for about 3km to the summit of the Höglberg (827m, 2712ft). One could return by the same route or shorten the distance slightly by taking one of several paths or tracks which run more or less directly north-west back to Teisendorf.

Anger, with its close neighbour **Aufham**, south of the motorway, has a fairly ambitious programme of events from June to September. **Piding** marks the bottom point of the Rupertiwinkel area.

From here, the B20 closely follows the River Saalach (flowing north-east and marking the Austrian border) and comes to **Ainring** (population 8500) and **Freilassing** (population 13,000) on the east side of the diamond. From the visitor's point of view, Ainring is the more interesting place with an all-year programme of entertainments. For example, Mondays: candlelight evening with light music and dancing, Wednesdays and Fridays: light music and dancing, Saturdays: Bavarian evening with *Schuhplattler* (clog dancing), dancing

demonstrations and brass band. Note here the castle-like parsonage (1532) and the late Gothic church with interior baroque decoration. At Freilassing the Saalach joins the Salzach, now the frontier northwards to the junction with the Inn near Kirchdorf. The town is busy with frontier traffic and industry and the holidaymaker need not linger.

The B20 leads to Laufen at the northern tip of Rupertiwinkel but on the way a brief stop should be made in **Triebenbach** to see the remains of the Gothic *Schloss* and the Schlosskapelle Maria Schnee. **Laufen** itself (population 5000) is a town rich in tradition. It was a salt trading post in a favourable position on a bend of the Salzach. Now, with its arcades and a few lovingly restored houses, it is a charming

haven, an unexpected bonus here in the Rupertiwinkel. The parish church Maria Himmelfahrt is the oldest surviving hall church in Germany. It was built here from 1332 on the site of a Romanesque basilica, the tower of which it inherited. The painter J.M. Rottmayr, born in Laufen, was responsible for the fine painting (1690) on the south side altar. A low arcade with beautiful net vaulting and frescos

runs round part of the church and leads to the fourteenth-century Michaelskapelle which has been partly rebuilt recently.

The present *Schloss* is the result of building and rebuilding in 1424 and 1606 on the site where there has was a castle at least since 790.

PLACES OF INTEREST IN AND NEAR THE RUPERTIWINKEL

TEISENDORF
Kloster Höglwörth Church
4km S of village. Striking stucco. Seventeenth century.

ANGER
The 'most beautiful Bavarian village' of King Ludwig I.

LAUFEN
Church of the Assumption
Oldest-surviving hall church in Germany. (1332 onwards).

ABTSDORF
Village Church
Very good frescos and pictures.

Abtsdorfer See
A lovely unspoiled lake nearby.

WAGING
Seventeenth-century Church
Stucco of the Wessobrunn school.

TITTMONING
Romantic little town on River Salzach. Historic square, fountains and statues.

Town Hall (1580)
Mighty building decorated with busts of Roman emperors.

Castle
Houses museum with valuable exhibits. (Thirteenth century).

The sixteenth-century *Rathaus* received its present façade in 1865. Three towers remain from the old town walls which have otherwise disappeared. Just over the border in the Austrian village of Oberndorf that best-known of Christmas carols *Stille Nacht, Heilige Nacht* (Silent night, Holy night) was composed in 1818 by Franz Gruber in the period of peace which reigned after Napoléon had been despatched to St Helena.

There are various legends about how the song came to be written; one of them describes how, after mice had eaten through the organ pipes in St Nikolaus' church, the priest Joseph Mohr asked his friend Franz Gruber, local teacher and organist to come to his rescue and compose a tune which could be accompanied by guitar. Father Mohr wrote the words and the first performance was given on Christmas Eve. It was an immediate success and quickly spread to surrounding areas; Tirolean singers from the Zillertal sang it when on tour in New York in 1839 and thereafter it was quickly adopted all round the world.

A few kilometres south-west of Laufen, the idyllic Abtsdorfer See near the village of **Abtsdorf** is a quiet oasis among the old farms. The village church surprisingly contains a glittering world of frescos and pictures of the saints including St Urban, the patron saint of wine-growers, an indication perhaps that in some long-forgotten past there were vineyards here.

Waging, **Petting**, **Taching** and **Tengling** are the unlikely names of a group of village resorts in a miniature lake district 10–20km west of Laufen. The principal lakes are the Waginger See and the Tachinger See and the shores are liberally sprinkled with spacious camp sites. The lakes are amongst the warmest in Upper Bavaria so it is small wonder that the majority of holidaymakers here are those for whom water activities are the main attraction. Bathing, sailing, surfing and angling are the order of the day in this essentially summer holiday area. The organised entertainments too are angled towards the outdoor life, with forest and lakeside rambles, conducted cycle tours and gymnastic sessions. The lake shores are little built-up although Waging itself is a market town with well over a thousand years of history. The seventeenth-century church has stucco in the style of the Wessobrunn school.

The nearby towns of **Fridolfing** and **Tittmoning**, both on the B20, are really part of the same group. The former is a friendly rural town while Tittmoning is a romantic little place with a historic town square, fountains and statues. It is typical of the towns along this Austrian border — like Laufen it belonged to Salzburg until 1816 — and is comparatively little known so that it has many modest treasures to reveal to the visitor prepared to spend a little time here.

The mighty *Rathaus* of 1580 was renovated in 1751; the gilded busts of twelve Roman emperors over the first and second floor windows are a reminder that this too was once in Roman possession. The castle was erected in the thirteenth century as a bulwark against the Bavarians (!) whose troops besieged it and caused a lot of destruction in 1611. Today, twenty-five rooms constitute the Heimathaus, a museum with many valuable exhibits, inspection of which is limited to conducted tours during afternoons.

A glance at the map reveals that the area covered in this chapter is really but a small corner of Bavaria yet it is probably the most attractive part for those who enjoy the outdoor life. There is much of historical and cultural interest but it is not surprising that sun and water dominate the activities in an area where the climate during the summer months is usually reliably warm and dry.

6 THE EASTERN MARCHES

There is a great difference between the Chiemgau of Chapter 6 and the eastern marches of Bavaria. Much of this eastern strip is densely wooded, the Bayerischer Wald (Bavarian Forest) and the adjoining Böhmerwald (Bohemian Forest) on the Czech side of the border constituting the largest forested area in Europe. There are many communities in the forest though and it is a popular holiday area. This is a land of glorious scenery, well appointed resorts and a climate which favours summer and winter visitors alike. The northern part of the area has the Oberpfälzer Wald (Upper Palatinate Forest) and there are many smaller wooded parts in addition to the two major forests. Like a rather crooked spine, one of Bavaria's tourist roads, the Ostmarkstrasse, runs northwards from Passau and serves as a loose link between the various places to be visited.

There could hardly be a more pleasant introduction to the southern end of the Bayerischer Wald than the ramble along the well marked Ilztalwanderweg (Ilz Valley Way), a riverside nature trail of great charm. The Ilz is the smallest of the three rivers which merge at Passau to continue eastwards as the mighty Danube. The Ilz has its source near the Czech border between the Rachel and the Lusen mountains. The walk will be of particular interest to nature lovers who will find rare and often protected varieties of flora and fauna. In the river, mussels, which earlier supported a modest pearl-fishing industry, are now rare but crabs, trout and pike are amongst the commoner inhabitants. Many colourful birds flit among the branches and on the ground, lizards, including the fire-salamander, are to be found. Along the way there are information boards drawing attention to points of interest in the locality. There are plenty of seats and picnic areas, many natural bathing places and, of course, never far away, a hostelry of some sort for refreshments or an overnight stop.

The *Wanderweg* starts at Veste Oberhaus (youth hostel — see

L
↔
ΔΔ
70km
or
short
stages

also Chapter 7) high above the city of Passau on the north bank of the Danube and runs in a generally northerly direction. After a few kilometres is the first of several bridges which enable the walk to continue on either the left or right bank and, of course, to vary the route for the return. The final crossing point is at a water-mill, the Schneidermühle where there is a *Wanderparkplatz* and information board, about 35km from Passau. One can wander a little further upstream on the east bank to view the ruins of Diessenstein Castle, trespassing a little on another long-distance path, the Pandurensteig coming from the north. **Fürsteneck**, east of the river is probably the best place in this vicinity to seek refreshment or accommodation.

Tucked away in this furthest corner of Bavaria, east of Passau along the B388, the little health resort of **Wegscheid** (population 4400) offers the visitor a peaceful haven in an area which must be regarded as well off the beaten track and all the more attractive for that. The original late Gothic church of St Johannes was replaced in 1969 by a successful modern building but there are still several earlier churches of interest — St Anna Kapelle (1716) with a late baroque central part, little onion-capped towers and an octagonal cupola; the Wasserkapelle (1770) with a more than life-size Christ figure with water flowing into a granite basin from the five wounds, and on the road to Wildenranna, the eighteenth-century Johanniskapelle. The 1822 *Rathaus* incorporates some earlier parts.

Activities include roller-skating and there are many rambling opportunities; favourite excursions are to the Friedrichsberg (930m, 3050ft) about $1^3/_4$ hours' walk to the north for splendid views or to the rocky summit of the Eidenberger Luessen (733m, 2404ft) an hour to the south. At the foot of the latter mountain is a woodland nature trail, a circular walk of about 4km through the romantic Bärenlochklamm (Bear's Cave Ravine).

Hauzenberg (population 3500) is about 16km north-west of Wegscheid along a picturesque road and it too is a health resort, although at first it may seem that the principal sights in the area are the enormous quarries from which the famous blue granite is obtained. This material is in great demand all over the world and has long contributed to the Hauzenberg economy. The parish church of St Veit (1851) has a winged altar from about 1490 with the figures of Mary, Katharina and Barbara — a fine work but the creator of it is unknown. Rowing boats may be hired on the nearby idyllic Freudensee which is a favourite spot for anglers and here there are the ruins of a former

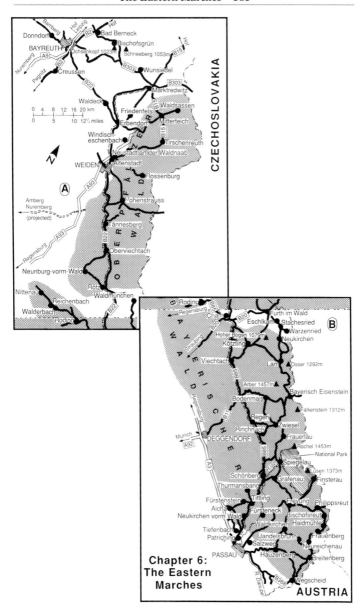

Chapter 6:
The Eastern
Marches

PLACES OF INTEREST IN AND AROUND WEGSCHEID AND HAUZENBERG

WEGSCHEID
St Anna Kapelle (1716)

Wasserkapelle (1770)
Unusual statue of Christ with water flowing from his wounds.

Johanniskapelle
On the road to Wildenranna. Eighteenth century.

Town Hall (mainly 1822)

Eidenberger Luessen
Woodland nature trail (4km) at foot of 733m (2404ft) mountain.

HAUZENBERG
Parish Church of St Veit (1851)

hunting lodge (fifteenth century) of the prince-bishops. Behind the ruin is the quarry where King Ludwig I had eighteen octagonal monoliths, each 6.70m (22ft) long, cut for his Befreiungshalle in Kelheim (see Chapter 7). They should have gone by water up the Danube but because of the weight — some 40 tons each — could not be transported to the river side and were abandoned until, in 1908, it was possible to take two of them to be incorporated in the university building in Munich's Amalienstrasse.

Rambles include the Frauenwaldberg (948m, 3110ft) the Steinberg (830m, 2722ft) and the Staffelberg (793m, 2600ft). Along this eastern fringe there are many walking possibilities and although the rambles mentioned in no way constitute mountaineering, many of them do, nevertheless, involve quite strenuous climbs.

Back near the Austrian frontier, **Breitenberg** (population 2000) is a peaceful summer resort with the opportunity of forest rambling northward to the Dreisessel (1332m, 4369ft) and to many lesser summits. Of interest here is the Webereimuseum. The growing of flax and spinning and weaving of linen are amongst the oldest occupations in this area and this little museum traces the history of the craft from the earliest times. There are demonstrations on old machines, and furniture, implements and utensils of the rural life of the past are displayed. A few kilometres north of Breitenberg is one of the many *Dreiländerecken* (literally 'three countries corners') in and around Germany; in this case all the constituents still exist and if one seeks out the location south-east of the Dreisessel one can sit in Bavaria with one leg in Czechoslovakia and the other in Austria. The frontier stone — at 1320m (4330ft) — with the inscriptions CS, Ö and B marks the point, agreed upon in 1765, by Bohemia, Austria and Bavaria.

Since it is so near, this is a good opportunity to go up through the trees to the Dreisessel for wonderful views over the forests of all three countries. The summit area is often quite busy for a motor road now terminates only a short distance below. As one climbs, the row of blue and white posts marking the border of Bavaria is seen in the trees on the right. Prominent notices in English warn American service personnel to keep well back! At the top, a narrow segment of Czechoslovakia is all that separates the track from the summit shop and *Gasthof*. One has to walk round this tip of Czechoslovakia to reach these and it is strictly forbidden to take a short cut across.

The Dreisessel, despite its prominence, is not actually the highest of the summits in the small group. Its neighbours Höchstein and Bayerischer Plöckenstein overtop it by 20m (65ft) and 50m (164ft) respectively and Böhmischer Plöckenstein over the border by 66m (216ft). Several little towns around the Dreisessel have combined to make a holiday and health resort area under the name Ferienland um den Dreisessel: **Haidmühle** (population 1000), neighbouring **Frauenberg** (population 400), a scattered place at the start of the 9km road to the summit, and **Bischofsreut** (population 900) lie at an altitude of 830–1000m (2722–3280ft). There is a good network of footpaths including a *Waldlehrpfad* (forest nature trail) and a *Trimm-pfad* (keep-fit course).

The *Hallenbad* has a sauna and a solarium and for children there are several play areas and a fairy-tale wood. Winter guests are not forgotten either and 65km of trails for cross-country skiing are serviced by several ski-lifts and the longest double ski-tow in Germany.

Neureichenau which, with its outlying villages, has a population of around 4500 is also a health resort and again caters for winter visitors as well as summer ones. Its *Hallenwellenbad* is sometimes closed to the general public during the day for use by schoolchildren. **Jandelsbrunn** (population 3200) is about 6km west of Neureichenau and is rather less developed than the other resorts in this group, relying to some extent on its neighbours to supply the various leisure needs of holidaymakers. It claims to cater especially for those who seek peace and relaxation in natural surroundings during their holidays and there is no doubt that it is well fitted for this.

The biggest town in the group is the *Luftkurort* of **Waldkirchen** with some 9000 inhabitants, a busy little centre with good shopping facilities. Waldkirchen has always been an important place, lying as it does on one of the old salt routes from Passau to Bohemia. Indeed,

PLACES OF INTEREST IN THE DREISESSEL HOLIDAY AREA

BREITENBERG
Webereimuseum
History of flax growing and linen weaving.

Three Countries Corner
8km N. Frontier stone at 1320m (4330ft) where Bavaria, Austria and Czechoslovakia meet.

Dreisessel (1332m, 4369ft)
3km NW of above. Easily accessible summit of border mountain.

FREYUNG
Wolfstein Castle (1590)

Houses art gallery for Freyung-Grafenau area.

Heimatmuseum
In the Schramlhaus (built about 1700). History of the area.

WALDKIRCHEN
Parish Church of St Peter and St Paul
Rebuilt after World War II damage. Known as the Cathedral of the Bavarian Forest. Fine organ.

---

the prosperity of the whole region was bound up for centuries with the lucrative salt trade. The town has had an unfortunate history of devastating fires so that there is little of real historic value remaining. The parish church of St Peter and St Paul built in 1861 was destroyed the following year and after being rebuilt, endured until 1945 when it fell victim to the destruction which marked the end of World War II. Once again it was rebuilt and with its impressive steeple is now a dignified church which enjoys the title 'Cathedral of the Bavarian Forest'. The fine organ is well worth hearing.

On the nearby Schulerberg (657m, 2155ft) a citizen, one Bernhard Linus, had a chapel built (1663–5) which was dedicated to his patron saint Borromäus. Rebuilt in 1756 the little church has ceiling frescos depicting the Holy Trinity, Borromäus and a view of Waldkirchen before the fire of 1782. Every Easter Sunday the men of the town are up early for the *Emmausgang* (traditional procession) and go to worship at the chapel. Later in the year the chapel is the goal of the riders taking part in the *Leonharditag* procession on 6 November. They ride three times round the chapel and the horses are then blessed by the priest. Waldkirchen's many amenities include a heated *Freibad* and a *Hallenbad* with sauna, solarium and the unique Mediterraneum — a room with Mediterranean flora and a suitably warm temperature. Waldkirchen caters for winter ramblers by keeping 25km of surrounding footpaths clear of deep snow.

These Dreisessel resorts are more or less enclosed by the B12 on its way from Passau to the Czech border near Philippsreut and thence on towards Prague. From Waldkirchen and many other resorts in the Bayerischer Wald, 2-day coach excursions are run to the Czech capital. Those intending to participate should book locally in advance and provide two passport photographs.

Ten kilometres north on the B12, **Freyung** (population 6000), a *Luftkurort*, is one of several resorts claiming to be the gateway to the Bavarian Forest National Park. It is a good centre for visiting, not only the National Park, but all the other sights in the southern part of the forest. The town takes its name (Frey=*Frei*=free) from the fact that early settlement in this corner of the prince-bishopric of Passau was encouraged by the freeing of the residents from most of the taxes and duties that would normally have been imposed upon them. The parish church Maria Himmelfahrt burned down in 1872 and was rebuilt in neo-Gothic style but it contains some treasures from the earlier build- ing. There are a few interesting houses in the town which is dominated by Schloss Wolfstein perched on a rocky eminence 37m (120ft) above the little River Saussbach. The present building dates from 1590 and today houses some government offices and the art gallery for the *Landkreis* (administrative district) of Freyung-Grafenau. Its predecessor (1199–1204) was built originally for the protection of the salt route. The *Heimatmuseum* is to be found in the Schramlhaus (about 1700) and specialises in exhibits showing the history of the area. A popular walk is through the Buchberger Leite, a rocky ravine through which the Saussbach tumbles.

The Ostmarkstrasse leaves Passau as the B85 and 10km from the city the pleasant village resort of **Tiefenbach** lies just to the west of the road. Here, as at almost every other place in this southern part of the forest, there are holiday 'packages', often with a rambling theme, which are exceptional value. Details are available from the local *Verkehrsamt* (information office). About 17km from the city, **Neu- kirchen vorm Wald** (to distinguish it from the dozens of places called Neukirchen, three in the forest), with a population of around 2000, is a peaceful resort where outdoor activities predominate; the countryside around is especially charming in spring and autumn. The Gothic parish church was given the baroque treatment in 1724 and contains some interesting relics. Half an hour's walk to the north of the village, the little baroque Kolomannkirche is also worth a visit.

Aicha (also **vorm Wald**), 7km to the west, has a parish church

PLACES OF INTEREST NORTH OF PASSAU

NEUKIRCHEN VORM WALD
(17km from Passau)
Gothic Parish Church
Baroque treatment 1724.

Kolomannkirche (Baroque)
$^1/_2$-hour walk N from village.

AICHA VORM WALD
Parish Church of St Peter and St Paul (1726–35)

Castle (built about 1600)
Courtyard with charming three-storeyed galleries.

Fürstenstein Castle
6km N. Impressive building now a boarding school.

TITTLING
Dreiburgensee

Attractive little lake for water activities.

Bavarian Forest Museum Village
On road NW to Thurmansbang. Houses of the fifteenth to nineteenth centuries.

Maria-Bründl-Kapelle (1712)
On same road. Unusual onion-domed tower over a spring.

THURMANSBANG
Parish Church of St Markus (1763)

Saldenburg Castle
4km E. Now a youth hostel.

of St Peter and St Paul (1726–35) which incorporates parts of its medieval predecessor. The *Schloss* (about 1600) is of interest for its unusual and charming three-storeyed arcades or galleries around a courtyard. It is barely 6km now to **Fürstenstein**, again a little to the west of the B85, and whose mighty *Burg* can be seen from afar on its granite ridge above the village. Rebuilt after a fire in 1860 more as a *Schloss* than a *Burg*, the impressive building now houses a boarding school of the Passau branch of the Englischen Fräulein and the interior is not normally open to the public. The nearby Englburg belongs to the same order which has a small *Pension* there. These old fortresses are two of the three castles of the so-called Dreiburgenland.

Back on the B85, the little market town of **Tittling** (population 4000) is the principal place in this Dreiburgenland and is a useful centre with a lot of activity around the little Dreiburgensee with swimming and other water pursuits. A main attraction is the Museumsdorf Bayerischer Wald, an open-air museum containing a large number of old houses, mills and other buildings representing forest life between the fifteenth and nineteenth centuries. The museum lies on the road to **Thurmansbang** (population 2000) with its baroque parish church

of St Markus (1763). Between Tittling and Thurmansbang is the little
Maria-Bründl Kapelle (1712) on the right of the road. In front of the
chapel there is an unusual little tower with onion-dome which protects
a spring. Back towards the B85 is the third of the three castles of the
Dreiburgenland, the Saldenburg, which is now a youth hostel.

The main road bypasses **Schönberg** (population 2200) so turn
off to visit this charming town with a fine market place surrounded by
houses reminiscent of the Inn valley style and a statue of St Nepomuk
dating from 1737. Schönberg enjoys a particularly mild climate and is
an ideal centre for walkers, with 200km of marked footpaths at hand,
some of which are kept clear in winter. Many of the leisure facilities are
shared with **Grafenau** (population 4000) about 6km to the east.
Grafenau was on one of the principal salt trade routes and this is
remembered each year on the first Saturday in August when the town
centre is closed to traffic for the *Salzsäumerfest*, a rural fair with demonstrations of the old crafts of spinning, pottery, woodwork, glass-
blowing, etc. Several bands provide music and there are colourful
processions, including the arrival of the salt-carriers who have wandered the salt route with their pack-horses for several days prior to the
Fest. The centre of all this activity is the spacious Marktplatz around
which the houses are again reminiscent of the Inn valley.

The fire-damaged church was rebuilt in baroque style but retains
the Gothic choir and tower of the previous building and has a number
of interesting relics. The Spitalkirche of the Holy Trinity (1759) not only
has an interesting rococo altar but also thirteen Stations of the Cross
made of sheet-zinc, colourful representations from the middle of the
eighteenth century which were only discovered in the attic of the
building in 1951. The Bauernmöbel Museum (Farmhouse Furniture-
Museum) can be found in two historic houses (eighteenth to nineteenth centuries) on the way to the *Kurpark*. A minor curiosity is the
little Snuff Museum, said to be the only one in the world, in Spitalstrasse opposite the post office. On the slopes above the park is
Grafenau's huge *Freibad* complex. A full-sized sport pool and a diving
pool are at the upper level, below is the leisure pool which caters for
paddlers and the not-so-good swimmers and at one end of this is the
Wellenbad where the wave-making apparatus operates for 10 minutes every half-hour. Toddlers have their own little paddling pool away
from the main pools which are surrounded by 25,000sq m of grass for
sunbathing. There are lockers (free) for several thousand bathers and
a restaurant, snack bar and ice-cream kiosk are at hand. Even by

Grafenau swimming pool and town

Germany's high swimming pool standards, this is an outstanding centre. Not far away is the *Sommerrodelbahn*, an exciting dry bobsleigh run, a popular venue with the youngsters and even with the not so young. The rambling possibilities here include designated walks of 11–30km which follow the old salt routes towards the eastern frontier.

The Nationalpark Bayerischer Wald is a short distance north-east of Grafenau. It was founded in 1970, is the property of the state and consists of an area of some 13,000 hectares of unspoiled forest and mountain landscape. National parks exist to protect the environment and all its living things, animal and vegetable, to inform and to educate. The first-time visitor is advised to go to the Nationalpark-Haus to learn about the area. If there are children in the party, the first priority will probably be to see the animals which are kept in large enclosures quite close to the *Haus* and parking area — brown bears, wolves, lynx, red deer, bison and many others. The park includes some 200km of *Wanderwege* and the principal routes are marked so that one may visit the areas of interest, eg forest history, geology, landscape, etc. Two prominent summits, the Lusen (1373m, 4503ft) and the Rachel (1454m, 4770ft) are good for distant views but there are many other summits in the 800–1100m (2624–3608ft) range.

The waymark *Auerhahn* (Capercailzie) leads to a rewarding walk which includes the summit of the Rachel. The starting point is the *Wanderparkplatz* called G'fäll at 950m (3116ft) reached by a good road north from **Spiegelau** in about 6km. The path goes north from the car park climbing steadily, at first through mixed woods and then through spruce. Soon after entering the spruce wood, two wayside monuments are passed; it is important to keep to the designated path and at certain seasons deviations are forbidden in order to leave the wildlife undisturbed.

H

↔

ΔΔ

9.5km

About 2km from the start is another wayside shrine and then a stiff climb for about 600m to the Waldschmidthaus, a mountain inn at (4460ft), open from May to October. Here too, is the mountain rescue centre for the Rachel. Suitably refreshed, the final climb to the summit at 1454m (4770ft) ends after 500m or so. Even if one is not breathless from the climb, the views from the top are certainly breathtaking. On a clear day, the chain of Alps far to the south can be seen, to the south-east above the lesser hills, a glimpse of the Danube between Passau and Linz. Eastwards along the frontier the Lusen and the Dreisessel are in view, and north-westwards the Grosser Falkenstein (1312m, 4300ft) and the Grosser Arber (1457m, 4780ft) can be identified. The Lusen shows up especially clearly because the whole of its summit is made up of enormous granite blocks. There are enormous boulders on the Rachel too, but in this case the vegetation reaches almost to the top and the impression is quite different. In the valleys on the west side of the frontier the cheerful red roofs of the various villages can be picked out but beyond the 'Iron Curtain' there is not a sign of habitation — nothing but the dense forest and an occasional bare strip where the invisible eastern guards keep watch.

Leaving the summit, still northwards at first, the waymark is joined for a while by the green arrowhead of the Nördlicher Hauptwander-weg, a long-distance path which links all the main summits along this border. There is a steep descent for about 1200m and a fine view at the Rachelkapelle, a tiny wooden chapel perched at the edge of a steep drop down to the little Rachelsee far below. The story goes that a rider lost in a snowstorm reached this near-precipice which was hidden from his view. His horse would not go a step further despite liberal use of spurs and whip, thus saving the life of its impatient master. In gratitude, the man had the chapel erected here and dedi-cated it, not to his horse, but to his guardian angel!

The path has now curved into a southerly direction and continues

IN AND AROUND THE BAVARIAN FOREST NATIONAL PARK

SCHÖNBERG
Market place with fine houses and Nepomuk statue (1737)

GRAFENAU
Market place with fine houses.

Parish Church
Baroque but incorporating parts of earlier Gothic building.

Church of Holy Trinity (1759)
Rococo altar and unusual Stations of the Cross.

Farmhouse Furniture Museum
Furniture etc over four centuries. Hand weaving demonstrations.

Snuff Museum
Unique history of snuff-taking.

Swimming Pool Complex
Several pools and excellent facilities. Summer bob-run nearby.

IN THE NATIONAL PARK
Information Centre
8km E of Grafenau. Essential first stop for visitors.

Animal Enclosures
0–2.5km from Information Centre. Bears, wolves, bison and many other creatures in natural surroundings.

Lusen (1373m, 4500ft)
One of the principal summits in park. Nearest car park 3km.

Rachel (1454m, 4770ft)
Another park summit, also chapel and lake. Nearest car park 3.5km.

FINSTERAU
Open-air Museum
Old farmhouses, smithy, inn.

FRAUENAU
Glass Museum
3000 years of glass technology.

Valentin Eisch Glass Factory

Church of the Assumption (1759–67)
Fine ceiling painting and rococo stucco.

to fall steeply until it passes along the east side of the Rachelsee, another essential stop to admire the view. Stand on the shore and try to spot the chapel amongst the dense trees above. Note the information board here about the Urwaldlehrpfad (Primeval Forest Nature Trail) and another a little later about the *Eiszeitlehrpfad* (Ice Age Nature Trail). The route continues to fall, less steeply now, for another 2.5km to a fork in the track near a shelter. Go right, follow the waymarks for about a kilometre then join a minor road for a few more minutes back to the starting point.

An essential piece of equipment for exploring the National Park is the 1:40,000 map *Wandern und erleben Nationalpark Bayerischer*

Wald published by Morsak Verlag, Grafenau. This map shows the degree of difficulty of the various paths; for example, the walk described above demands the stoutest footwear, preferably boots.

A little over 20km north-east of Grafenau, **Finsterau** (population 1100) is a pleasant little holiday resort on the fringe of the National Park at the foot of the Lusen. The road ends at the frontier 4km beyond the village so there is little traffic to disturb the peace. There is another rural museum here, the Freilichtmuseum Finsterau with a good range of rebuilt farmhouses, a smithy, an inn (still serving refreshments) and other items of interest. Summer visitors will come mainly to ramble in the National Park; there is a ski-school for those here in winter.

Spiegelau, already mentioned, an *Erholungsort* of 2800 inhabitants a little further west on the National Park boundary, has Erasmus Moosburger to thank for its existence, for he founded a glass factory here in 1530. The business has changed hands many times and now specialises in crystal glass, the production of which may be seen by visitors for a short time each working day. An excellent centre this with plenty for the visitor to do.

Glass-making is also an important feature in nearby **Frauenau** where the official Glasmuseum is to be found. Three thousand years of glass technology are exhibited here and there are displays of ancient and modern products. The nearby glass factory of Valentin Eisch may also be visited; it is one of only a handful of such factories left from more than sixty once working in this area. Frauenau (population 3500) is another *Erholungsort*. It was founded in 1324 by Hermann, a lay-brother from Kloster Niederalteich who sought a hermit's existence here. It became a place of pilgrimage and in 1759–67 a church was built for the pilgrims and called Zu Unserer Lieben Frauen Au from which the village derived its name, although the church is now called Maria Himmelfahrt. There is a fine ceiling painting of the Ascension by a student of the Asam school and excellent rococo stucco from 1767. A late Gothic *pietà* (1480) graces the high altar. Skiing instruction, skating and horse-sleigh rides are available in winter.

Still east of the Ostmarkstrasse **Zwiesel** (population 9300) is an important rail and road traffic centre. The railway having wended its way from Deggendorf on the Danube divides here into branches for Bodenmais, Bayerische Eisenstein and Grafenau, the latter reached through Frauenau and Spiegelau. Once again glass-making has played a significant part in the development of the town where, behind

IN AND AROUND ZWIESEL

ZWIESEL
Town Hall (1838)
Classical façade with Nepomuk statue (1767) in front.

Wald-Heimat-Glas Museum
Folk culture, everything to do with the forest and glass-making. Primeval forest diorama.

Parish Church (1891–6)
Neo-Gothic. 86m-high (282ft) steeple.

RINCHNACH
Parish Church (1729)
Called by some the most beautiful church in the Bavarian Forest.

REGEN
Town square with fine houses and attractive fountain.

Parish Church of St Michael (1655–7)
Unusual tower.

Weissenstein Castle
1 hr walk S. Mostly impressive ruin but also a small museum.

BODENMAIS
Joska Glass Factory and Exhibitions

Barbara-Stollen Silver Mine
Chair-lift to entrance. Underground tour.

Museum Bodenmais
Precious stones, minerals and fossils.

Grosser Arber (1457m, 4778ft)
6km N of village. Chair-lift.

the *Rathaus*, is the excellent museum Wald-Heimat-Glas with imaginative displays on several themes. The *Urwald* (primeval forest) diorama on the ground floor is outstanding, with models of animals and birds which have long since disappeared from the forests. The glass section includes a display of old snuff bottles while in another room there are examples of religious folk art. The three-storeyed *Rathaus* of 1838 has a classical façade and provides a backdrop for a statue of Nepomuk (1767) who is flanked by St Georg and St Florian. The neo-Gothic parish church (1891–6) has an 86m-high (282ft) steeple — unique in this area — and inside, has a more than life-size statue of the weeping Saviour. Folk music and folk singing are the subjects of competitions held in Zwiesel in late spring and September. There is always plenty going on here and winter sporting activities mean that it is always 'season' in Zwiesel. The British National Army and BAOR Nordic Ski Championships have been held here each January and February for many years. Snow then is even more certain here than in the better-known Alpine centres.

It is easy to rejoin the Ostmarkstrasse at **Rinchnach** (population

Ferry on Chiemsee

Fountain at Schloss Herrenchiemsee

Schloss Herrenchiemsee

Great Hall of Mirrors, Schloss Herrenchiemsee

3000), a peaceful summer resort. The present parish church was built on the site of, and incorporates parts of, the former Gothic *Klosterkirche*, the work being carried out in 1729 under the direction of J.M. Fischer. Lovers of baroque architecture have called this the most beautiful church in the Bavarian Forest. C.D. Asam contributed two altar pictures sometime between 1730 and 1735 and these remained comparatively unknown until they were 're-discovered' for the artist's 300th birthday celebrations in 1986.

Regen (population 11,000) is an *Erholungsort* right on the Ostmarkstrasse and it is also the *Kreisstadt* for the area, a lively and attractive town with all the facilities one would expect in a place of this size. An unusual folk festival here is the *Pichelsteinerfest* which takes place annually on 5 days around the last Saturday in July. In 1874, some youths returning from a church festival stole potatoes from the field of a man named Pichler, but when accosted by a policeman explained that they had only been collecting stones. He believed this unlikely story and the lads took their booty to the woman who was cooking up the remains from the festival and she threw the potatoes into the cauldron and concocted a nourishing stew. Making such a dish became an annual event and as more and more people came to sample it a regular folk festival gradually emerged. Today's hot-pot has a rigid recipe and must contain at least three kinds of meat — beef, veal and pork — potatoes and diced carrots all simmered slowly with parsley, onions and herbs without being stirred. The cook has a place of honour in the festival procession after which the people go to two halls to eat. Celebrations in the evenings include rides in lantern-lit 'gondolas' on the River Regen.

Extraordinarily, the village of **Bichlstein** not too far away claims to have invented the same dish in 1847 and celebrates the *Pichlsteiner Bergfest* there on the first Sunday in August to prove it!

Easter Monday is another colourful day in Regen. The event is the *Osterritt* (Easter ride) and the day starts with an open-air service. The riders assemble and process to the Wieshof and then to the town square where the gaily decorated horses are blessed. The day ends with an Easter dance in the evening. The spacious square contains a number of rather fine old houses and the attractive Marienbrunnen (fountain). The parish church of St Michael (1655–7) replaced a Romanesque-Gothic building burned down in 1648. The squat tower has an open lantern topped by the familiar onion-dome but there is also a north tower (dating from about 1270) from the earlier church.

An hour's walk south of the town, Burg Weissenstein towers over the valley, an impressive ruin. Not quite all ruin though, for the old granary now houses a small but interesting museum. This part of the castle was, from 1918 until his death in 1974, the home and workplace of the poet and writer Siegfried von Vegesack and, until 1935, of his poetess wife Clara Nordström. The ground floor has memorabilia of the couple; the first floor is mainly of geological exhibits, the second floor is given over to special exhibitions changing each year while the third floor contains literary archives with particular reference to the Bavarian and Bohemian forest areas. Finally, in the attic — Vegesack called it his paradise and used to retire there when working on a particularly demanding poem — there is a display of old equipment connected with flax growing and linen production.

Regen is a good centre for the exploration of the surrounding attractive countryside. A curiosity sometimes found in this part of Bavaria is a row of *Totenbretter*. The term cannot easily be translated into English. A *Totenbrett* is a wide board and in days gone by was used to convey the corpse to the place of burial. Unlike a coffin, the *Totenbrett* was not buried but was used as a permanent memorial to the departed. The boards were often elaborately carved or colourfully painted and often had verses or a passage relating to the life of the deceased inscribed upon them. Today the boards are no longer used for the original purpose but the old custom is not entirely abandoned and rows of *Totenbretter*, almost like an ornate fence, may be seen outside villages or around churches and chapels. Another similar practice is the production of *Votivtafeln* — memorial tablets — which take many forms and often incorporate a picture of the person being honoured or remembered. They are frequently to be found in churches and chapels which have become places of pilgrimage and a complete wall may well be covered by them.

Twelve kilometres north from Regen along a picturesque road, the *Luftkurort* of **Bodenmais** (population 3400) enjoys a favourable climate and is a recommended resort for those suffering from nervous complaints or convalescing. A map and guide to many walks stands in the Marktplatz and this is a favourite starting point for an excursion to the Grosser Arber, the summit of which (1457m, 4778ft) is 6km north of the village. Glass-making is important in Bodenmais and

visitors are welcomed at the Joska Glass Factory. There is a small charge for admission to the main factory but two exhibitions of the products — which may be purchased — are free. Bodenmais has a long history of mining silver and many other minerals. A visit to the historic silver mine of Barbara-Stollen is now possible. The parking place for the mine is at the lower station of a two-seater chair-lift and one may travel effortlessly to the mine entrance at the middle station. Alternatively walk up to the entrance along several signposted foot- paths. Museum Bodenmais in Bahnhofstrasse traces the mining history of the area and has a comprehensive display of minerals.

West of Bodenmais, back on the Ostmarkstrasse is **Viechtach**. The oldest building in the town, the Bürgerspital (1432) houses the Kristallmuseum, a remarkable collection of some 1200 varieties of crystal found naturally in the district. The rococo parish church of St Augustinus (1766) is well worth a visit for its stucco decoration by travelling craftsmen of the Wessobrunn school and fine wood-carv- ings on the choir stalls and the confessional boxes. The baroque- treated Gothic St Anna-Kapelle is close at hand as is the seventeenth- century *Rathaus*. Viechtach (population 6500) is a *Luftkurort* on the River Schwarzer Regen and has a superior camp site — Komfort- Campingplatz — with nearby *Hallenbad* and sauna and a large modern open-air leisure complex in a very attractive location.

Leaving the B85 travel north to **Kötzting** (population 6100), famous for its *Pfingstritt* or Whitsun ride, an ancient custom dating back to 1412. The actual ride takes place on Whit Monday when the residents are given a musical 'early call' at 5am. At eight o'clock hundred of horsemen assemble and ride, accompanied by solemn music, to the village of **Steinbühl** 6km away. The procession is headed by the Cross and lantern carriers, the priests and attendants are followed by the rest of the men clad in traditional costume and mounted upon splendidly groomed and decorated horses where it is greeting by fanfares and bell-ringing. The festival is officially opened the previous Saturday afternoon and on the Sunday, in addition to worship, there are various entertainments including the performance of two Whitsun plays. During the next week suitable events are arranged and the festival closes with church services the following Sunday.

Kötzting has its share of old buildings. The group in the south-west corner of the town includes the parish church (1769), the St Anna- Kapelle (seventeenth century) and the remains of the fifteenth- century *Schloss*. As a recognised *Erholungsort* with *Kneipp-Kur* facilities, this town has a good reputation for hospitality and there are a number of attractive eating places. The many well marked paths

IN AND AROUND VIECHTACH AND KÖTZTING

VIECHTACH

Crystal Museum in Bürgerspital (1432)
Huge collection of 1200 crystal forms.

Parish Church of St Augustinus (1766)
Stucco of the Wessobrunn school and fine wood-carving.

St Anna Kapelle
Gothic with later baroque treatment.

Town Hall (seventeenth century)

KÖTZTING
Attractive old buildings in SW corner of town — the **Parish Church** (1769), **St Anna-Kapelle** (seventeenth century) and the **Schloss** (fifteenth century)

Pilgrimage Church Weissenregen (built about 1758)
2.5km W, famed for its colourful 'fishermen' pulpit.

In **Lam**, 16km E of Kötzting there is a museum of minerals, fossils,

offer a choice ranging from a modest afternoon stroll to a 2-day mountain tour of 30km. Especially to be recommended is the short ramble (waymark blue fish) from the car park (also the 'bus station) near the railway to the pilgrimage church of **Weissenregen** clearly visible on its hill to the south-west. The carved *Gnadenbild* (Miraculous Image) of the fourteenth century is outshone by the remarkable pulpit known as the Fischerkanzel. This shows a boat with three apostles endeavouring to draw in the great draft of fishes which Christ has bestowed upon them. Amongst other figures portrayed on this elaborately carved, coloured and partly gilded masterpiece are Jonah and the whale. Return directly along the surfaced path to Kötzting or continue to follow the blue fish signs past the church for a longer circular walk.

Leaving Kötzting eastwards it is 16km to the resort of **Lam** (population 2500) close to the Czech border at the foot of the Osser (1292m, 4238ft) in the valley of the Weisser Regen. This is a delightful small *Luftkurort* with facilities for open-air recreation, not only in summer but in winter when many of the footpaths are kept clear for walkers and one can go ski-rambling. Guided rambles are arranged and local maps are available in the village. The summit of the Osser can be reached on foot from Lam in $2^1/_4$ hours with quite a lot of fairly steep climbing. Many *Totenbretter* are to be found in this area.

Returning again to the Ostmarkstrasse continue northwards on

PLACES OF INTEREST IN AND AROUND CHAM

Church of the Assumption
In Chammünster 2km S. From the thirteenth century on.

Parish Church of St Jakob
Gothic choir and fine rococo stucco. Fourteenth to eighteenth century.

Town Hall
Houses the *Heimatmuseum*. Fifteenth century, rebuilt 1937.

Spitalkirche (1514)
Late Gothic.

Lamberg
Near Chammünster. Red deer park.

Churpfalz-Park
8km S on B20 at Traitsching. Modern pleasure park set in lovely gardens.

---

the B85 towards Cham. In the suburb of Chammünster is the impressive church Maria Himmelfahrt with sections dating from as early as the thirteenth century and many early relics including two fonts from the Romanesque period. **Cham** (population 16,000) is a busy *Kreisstadt* with some industry but it is an old town founded in the eighth century with many reminders of the past. From the car park near the river there is a good view of an old tower topped by a stork's nest. The parish church of St Jakob has main sections dating from the fourteenth to eighteenth centuries and it was enlarged as recently as 1894. The Gothic choir and fine rococo stucco make inspection worthwhile. Nearby, the fifteenth-century *Rathaus*, rebuilt in 1937, has attractive stepped gables and houses the *Heimatmuseum*. Further along there is the late Gothic Gasthaus zur Krone, an old lodging place of the nobility.

In Schwanenstrasse the Gasthof Luckner is a reminder of a prominent son of the town, Graf (Count) Nikolaus von Luckner. Born in 1722, his title was a Danish one conferred in 1784. He later became involved in French politics and was a victim of the Revolution, dying at the guillotine in 1794. More churches: in the north-east of the town the late Gothic Spitalkirche (1514), in the north-west the neo-Gothic Protestant church and the neo-Romanesque brick-built Redemptoristen-Klosterkirche of 1908.

There is a lot to see and do around Cham. Water activities are plentiful with swimming, sailing, surfing and angling in many little lakes. On the Lamberg near Chammünster there is a red deer enclosure. South of the town on the B20 is the Churpfalz-Park at **Loifling**, a modern pleasure park with the usual attractions — Ferris wheel, old-

PLACES OF INTEREST IN THE BAVARIAN FOREST WEST OF CHAM

RODING (13km on B35)
Charming old town centre around market place.

Town Hall (1660) **and Parish Church** (1753)

WALDERBACH (24km)
Former Kloster Church and Heimatmuseum

REICHENBACH (27km)
Former Kloster Church of the

Assumption (1118–1200)
A riot of baroque colour and form (eighteenth century).

NITTENAU (34km)
Very old small town; old fortifications.

Parish Church
Gothic choir and Romanesque font.

timer train, roundabouts, boating lake and so on. What is rather unusual about this complex of 10,000sq m is that it is laid out in a garden setting with some 3km of footpaths amongst 7000 roses, herbacious borders, into baroque and 'paradise' gardens, through a dahlia display and so on. There is a good restaurant too.

Two modest festivals appear in the Cham calendar. The *Frühlingsfest* (Spring Festival) takes place from the Wednesday before Ascension Day until the Monday after. There are the usual folk activities of *Frühschoppen* (morning drinks) and clay-pigeon shooting followed by food and drink in a festival tent. The *Chamer Volksfest* lasts for 11 days starting on the Friday of the last week in July.

About 40km westwards, is the narrow neck of the forest north of Regensburg. The tourist will find much of interest in the area. **Roding** is about 13km from Cham along the B35, a very old town with many historic buildings. There are fine houses around the Marktplatz: the *Rathaus* (1660), parish church (1753) and many more. Turn off the main road shortly after Roding to **Walderbach** with its buildings around the former Augustinian and Cistercian *Kloster* or the *Heimatmuseum* for demonstrations of rural crafts; then on to **Reichenbach** for the absolute riot of glorious baroque in the former Benedictine Klosterkirche and to **Nittenau** where Napoléon made an overnight stop as he retreated westwards after his defeat before Moscow in 1812.

North-east of Cham along the B20 the road passes through the lower ground which marks the geographical division between the Bayerischer Wald and the Oberpfälzer Wald. **Furth im Wald**

Furth im Wald's famous dragon

(population 10,000) is an *Erholungsort* close to the border and the
proximity of Bohemia is reflected in the statue of St Johann Nepomuk
(1767) which stands in the town square shaded by four huge chestnut
trees around 140 years old. The old buildings include the baroque
parish church of 1727 and the eighteenth-century Leonhardikapelle,
the scene each Easter Monday of a *Leonhardiritt*. There are three
museums of interest: the Hammerschmiede Voithenberghütte
(blacksmith's workshop), the Stadtmuseum housed in the Stadtturm
(tower) of 1866 with a varied range of themes including geology,
mineralogy, botany, zoology, local history and the Furth dragon (more
about this later) and finally, the Waldmuseum covering aspects of
forest flora and fauna.

Furth has a good programme for its summer and winter visitors —
it is in a popular skiing area — and being close to a frontier crossing
point is a good starting place for coach excursions into Czechoslovakia to such places as Prague, Karlsbad and Marienbad. However,
most visitors will find plenty to do without going so far afield. Horse-
drawn coach rides — sleigh rides in winter — folk evenings, visits to
the various deer enclosures, these are the things which contribute to
a fine family holiday atmosphere far removed from the throng of

tourists found in better-known resorts.

On the second Sunday in August, the ceremony of *Drachenstich* (Spearing the Dragon) provides the theme for a colourful annual spectacle. A play tells the ancient story. It goes back to 1431 when the Imperial army was defeated at the Battle of Tans and the Bohemian hordes invaded and ravaged Bavaria. The local dragon chose this moment to emerge from the wood and the terrified inhabitants thus had a double reason to seek the safety offered to them by the noblewoman of Furth Castle. She was even prepared to sacrifice herself to the dragon to save the people but in the nick of time Sir Udo, lord of the castle, returned from the war and slew the monster. This is the climax of the play and a wedding follows to celebrate the heroic deed.

From 1912 until 1939 a redundant dragon from the Munich theatre, previously used in Wagner's *Siegfried* , represented the historic beast. After World War II a new dragon was built, 18m (59ft) long, 3m (10ft) high and weighing over a ton. It is a fearsome blood and fire spewing creature propelled by an internal combustion engine but it is nevertheless finally killed by the modern Sir Udo to the accompaniment of church bells, trumpets and applause. The grand procession which follows has about 1100 participants in costume and about 200 horses. The present version of the play was written by the Bavarian author Martin Bauer in 1952.

Furth is the biggest of a cluster of resorts in the *Feriengebiet* (holiday area) called Hohen-Bogen-Winkel, to the north of the Schwarzriegel or Hoher Bogen (1079m, 3540ft). **Neukirchen bei Heilig Blut** (population 3450) was, until the sixteenth century, called Neukirchen vor dem Böhmerwald and it is said that around 1450 a zealous follower of John Huss, the Bohemian religious reformer, split open the head of a wooden figure of Mary with his sabre and blood flowed from the 'wound'. The inevitable pilgrimages to the miraculous place started in 1452 and later the name was changed to include the Holy Blood reference. The pilgrimage and parish church Maria Geburt has a lantern tower with onion-dome from the fifteenth century and achieved its present form by 1720. In 1660 the Franciscan *Klosterkirche* was built on to the west end and the churches share the same space divided only by a double-sided altar which contains a carved wooden image of Mary and child and a sabre-swinging Hussite.

The other resorts of this group are **Eschklam**, **Warzenried** and **Stachesried** and all share the various facilities of the area including the Hoher Bogen leisure centre with activities the year round. A two-

```
         PLACES  OF  INTEREST  IN  THE
         HOHEN-BOGEN  HOLIDAY  AREA
```

FURTH IM WALD
Charming town square.

Parish Church (1727)
Excellent baroque.

Blacksmith's Workshop Museum

Town Museum
Housed in Town Tower of 1866.

Forest Museum
Aspects of flora and fauna.

NEUKIRCHEN BEI HEILIG BLUT
Pilgrimage and Parish Church of Maria Geburt
(Fifteenth century)
Home of the Miraculous Image.

Franciscan Klosterkirche
(1660)
Adjoining the above.

Hoher Bogen Leisure Centre
Summer and winter bob-runs.
Chair-lift. Restaurant.

stage chair-lift (total length 1358m) takes the hard work out of the ascent and one alights at the middle station for the exciting run downhill by the *Sommerrodelbahn* (dry bob- run, at 750m), the longest dry run in the Bayerischer Wald) or in winter for the conventional bob-sleigh run on snow. Skiers can also alight at the middle station or can go right to the top where the Berghaus provides refreshments. The chair-lift is supplemented by two ski-tows.

Waldmünchen, 12km north-west of Furth, is a *Luftkurort* of 6000 inhabitants in the Oberpfalz (Upper Palatinate). Here again there is a statue of Nepomuk (1769) in the Marktplatz together with fountains from 1776 and 1790. The parish church of St Stephan (1553) has been rebuilt many times and has little of the original about it. On the parish office (former Gasthaus Alte Post) there is a memorial tablet to the French writer and politician Châteaubriand who had an enforced stay here on his way to Prague in 1833 having mislaid his passport. He was, however, suitably impressed by the town's hospitality.

In 1742 during the war of Austrian succession, Bavaria was invaded in the name of Empress Maria Theresa by the Baron of Trenck with an army raised at his own expense. These violent soldiers were called Pandours — a word implying brutality — and they played havoc in the nearby town of Cham but it appears that Waldmünchen bought itself comparative peace by paying Trenck 'fifty gold coins'. Needless to say, this historic event is celebrated in the twentieth century by a pageant, *Trenck der Pandour vor Waldmünchen*, which is staged at 8.15pm usually on Saturdays during July and August. There are spectacular wild riding scenes and an accompanying colourful folk-festival.

The same event provides the theme for a long-distance walk *ohne Gepäck* called 'Der Pandurensteig' which runs from Waldmünchen to Passau, the last section joining with the Ilztalwanderweg mentioned earlier. The route touches many of the places of interest already mentioned. More details in 'Further Information'.

After Cham, the B22 becomes the Ostmarkstrasse and at Rötz a short deviation 4km west provides an opportunity to visit the Oberpfälzer Handwerksmuseum where there is a collection of tools and machinery from as far back as the fifteenth century with enormous circular saws, grinding stones, mechanical hammers and so on, as well as many smaller items. Well worth a little time and the modest admission charge.

Eighteen kilometres further along the B22, the skyline above the town of **Oberviechtach** is dominated by the grey profile of Burg Murach which even the Hussites were unable to overthrow. It is a pleasant little place, although a history of fires means that there are fewer medieval buildings remaining than might be expected. After one such fire, the Catholic parish church of John the Baptist was rebuilt using the choir and tower of the previous Gothic building. It contains excellent rococo decoration from 1775–6 and the choir-stalls should be specially noted. The parish church of St Andreas was also rebuilt (1826) after a fire and has two rococo altars from 1750 which were a gift from the church of St Martin in Amberg. The pilgrimage church of St Johann and Nepomuk on the nearby Johannisberg has some noteworthy carving.

Honoured by the town is the Catholic priest Maximilian von Müller who, in 1705, organised the resistance of the Oberpfälzer farmers against the Austrian occupation. He succeeded in freeing Cham but was thrown into prison in Straubing and died there in 1706. A better-known son of the town is the remarkable Dr Johann Andreas Eisenbarth, a physician and surgeon who appears to have been well ahead of his time. His methods were sometimes ridiculed — as in a popular student song from 1803— but he nevertheless achieved considerable fame and served the British royal house as well as the Prussian one as adviser and court oculist. A memorial fountain is dedicated to him and the *Heimatmuseum* is largely given over to a permanent exhibition 'Dr Eisenbarth and his Time' where some of his bizarre surgical instruments — for example, a brace and bit — are displayed.

PLACES OF INTEREST IN AND EXCURSIONS FROM OBERVIECHTACH

Parish Church of John the Baptist
Rebuilt from the original Gothic. Excellent rococo decoration (1775–6) and choir stalls.

Parish Church of St Andreas (1826)
Rococo altars (1750).

Pilgrimage Church of St Johann and Nepomuk
On the Johannisberg. Noteworthy carving.

Heimatmuseum
Includes exhibition about famous physician and surgeon Dr Eisenbarth.

Upper Palatinate Open-air Museum
In Nabburg 18km W. Houses and buildings including former twelfth-century parsonage.

Museum of Early Industrial Machinery, Hand Tools, etc.
In Rötz-Hillstett 15km S.

Tännesberg lies just to the east of the Ostmarkstrasse after about 12km and here in the idyllic Pfreimdtal there is a hut belonging to the Oberpfälzer Waldverein (Forest Association) for the use of youth and family rambling groups. The accommodation is provided on a self-catering basis and there is a river bathing place nearby, also a camp site. See 'Further Information'. A turning to the east leads into a pretty road to **Vohenstrauss** (20km north of Oberviechtach), a resort of nearly 7000 inhabitants and a place for a peaceful, relaxing holiday. The emblem of this little town is the unusual Renaissance Schloss Friedrichsburg (1586–93), its symmetrical layout having six round towers, one at each corner and one in the centre of each of the longer sides. The pretty Marktplatz with its shady trees invites the visitor to rest awhile. The interesting little *Heimatmuseum* (admission free) is to be found on the third floor of the *Rathaus* and there is a glass factory which may be visited.

About 16km north-west of Vohenstrauss, **Weiden**, on the Ostmarkstrasse, is the biggest town in the area with 42,300 inhabitants. It lies in the valley of the River Waldnaab and is one of the principal cultural venues of eastern Bavaria. It has been an important centre of communications since early times for the trade routes between Nuremberg and Prague and between Regensburg and Leipzig crossed here. The organist and composer Max Reger (1873–1916) came here as a one-year-old and received his musical education from

The town square, Vohenstrauss

Church at Moosbach near Vohenstrauss

PLACES OF INTEREST IN WEIDEN

Culture Centre
Houses the town museum and Max-Reger Collection.

Michaelskirche
(Fifteenth century).
Rococo pews.

Railway Museum
Run by the Model Railway Club.

Town Hall (1539–45) with Modern *Glockenspiel* (chimes)

Max-Reger-Haus
Home of the composer.

---

the organist Adalbert Lindner. In the Kulturzentrum is the Stadtmuseum and the Max Reger-Sammlung (Max Reger Collection) and the composer is also remembered through the Weiden *Musiktage* (music festival) which takes place in spring every fourth year — 1988, 1992, etc.

Other regular festivals here are *Frühlingsfest* around May Day, *Bürgerfest* (Citizens' Festival) the last Sunday in June, Children's Festival the last Sunday in July, *Volks- und Schutzenfest* (Folk and Shooting Festival) around mid-August and *Christkindlmarkt* about 3 weeks up to 23 December. There are regular market days on Wednesdays and Saturdays and occasional Sunday fairs in the old town pedestrian zone. There is a programme of concerts of all types of music, also exhibitions and art shows in several galleries. The Eisenbahn museum of the Model Railway Club should not be missed by those interested in the subject.

The buildings and monuments of earlier centuries are lovingly cared for here and there are many which the visitor will find worth seeing. Amongst them the *Rathaus* (1539–45) with its modern *Glockenspiel* (chimes), the Altes Schulhaus (1529) now the culture centre, the fifteenth-century Michaelskirche and, of course, the Max-Reger-Haus. Many well marked footpaths and cycling routes lead to other places of interest in the vicinity. The town is remarkably well endowed with restaurants, cafés, bars and discos and free car parking is available in the town centre.

Only a few kilometres separate Weiden from its northern neighbours **Altenstadt** (population 4100) and **Neustadt** (population 5300), both '**an der Waldnaab**', attractive little towns in a sparsely populated area of considerable charm sandwiched between two *Naturparke*. Altenstadt is near the Süssenloher Weiher (lake), good for bathing and sailing. Neustadt is known for its lead-crystal industry and visits may be made to some of the factories. There are a number

Historic watermill near Georgenberg, east of Weiden, close to the Czech border

of well preserved old buildings; in the town centre are both the Altes Schloss (about 1558) with its external staircase, arcades, balconies and high, pointed gable and the Neues Schloss (1698–1720) in Italian baroque at the east end of the Marktplatz. Some rooms on the third floor have stucco and ceiling paintings from 1710–20. On a little hill outside the town is the rather unusual pilgrimage church of St Felix originally built in 1735 but enlarged 1763–5 and at the same time fully renovated. There is a rectangular church with rounded corners for the laity while the monks have a clover leaf-shaped choir. The ceiling is painted with numerous scenes from the life of St Felix. Another pilgrimage church, St Quirin (1680) could be the goal of a modest

> ## PLACES OF INTEREST IN AND AROUND ALTENSTADT, NEUSTADT AND WINDISCHESCHENBACH
>
> ALTENSTADT
> **Süssenloher Weiher**
> 1.5km from centre. Lake for bathing and sailing.
>
> NEUSTADT
> **Lead Crystal Factory** (visits)
>
> **Altes Schloss** (built about1558) Palace with external staircase, arcades, balconies, etc.
>
> **Neues Schloss** (1698-1720) Italian baroque. Many fine houses between the palaces.
>
> **Pilgrimage Church of St Felix** (1735) Unusual layout; ceiling paintings.
>
> **Pilgrimage Church of St Quirin** (1680) 2km NE. Good viewpoint.
>
> **Flossenburg and Gaisweiher** 15km E. Very ruined castle and lake for bathing and sailing.
>
> WINDISCHESCHENBACH
> **Lead Crystal Factory**
> Visits. Good value factory shop.
>
> **Lead Crystal Museum**
>
> **Burg Neuhaus**
> Unusual tower. Houses the Waldnaabmuseum.

ramble from the town. Go north-east past Rastenhof to the Botzerberg where the church commands a good view. The route needs no detailed description but if in doubt inquire at the information office.

L

↔

Δ
5km

There is a very fine camp site — claimed to be one of the best in Europe — on the little Gaisweiher (lake) at the foot of the Flossenburg, a castle ruin 15km east of Neustadt. A little aside from the Ostmarkstrasse **Windischeschenbach** (population 5900) some 8km north of Neustadt, is another place famed for its lead-crystal industry. Factory visits are possible and there is a sales point where crystal, porcelain, ceramics and pewter may be purchased at favourable prices. There is also a lead-crystal museum. A speciality of the town is *Zoiglbier*, a traditional brew rich in hops and free from carbonic acid which is best sampled in a *Zoiglbier-Stub'n* (bar) with a tasty home-made snack. Windischeschenbach is the gateway to the nature preservation area of Waldnaabtal. At nearby Burg Neuhaus is the Waldnaabmuseum and the 'Butter-tub' tower, so-called because of its unusual form.

The B22 continues to *Erholungsort* **Erbendorf** at the south end of the Steinwald *Naturpark* which has at its centre the 946m-high (3100ft) Platte. From about 1200, Erbendorf was a significant mining centre, silver, lead, copper, zinc and coal having emerged from the

The Hackelstein rock in the Steinwald near Friedenfels

same workings. Production fell off after 1400 and many miners supplemented their wages by panning for gold in nearby streams. The mines gradually fell into disuse, various attempts to revive them over the centuries were only partially successful and they were finally abandoned in the 1930s. Friedrich Schiller's maternal ancestors came from Erbendorf and Max Reger stayed here with his uncle, head teacher of the Catholic school, and wrote his choral fantasy *Ein' feste Burg* which was to bring him acclaim as a composer of organ music. The melody was set to words by Martin Luther and became the familiar hymn 'A safe stronghold our God is still'.

The Ostmarkstrasse now leaves the B22 to head for Marktredwitz which lies due north. The route now is through the Steinwald *Naturpark* to the *Erholungsort* of **Friedenfels**. The landscape is charming and there are many well marked paths. These can be followed without difficulty to the ruins of Burg Weissenstein at 63m (2830ft) between the Platte and the Plössberg (820m, 2690ft) north of the village. The watch-tower can be climbed for an even better view. This walk is suggested as a limbering-up exercise for those arriving in Friedenfels for a 7-day, 140km *Wanderung ohne Gepäck* called Burgenweg which, as its name implies, covers many of the old castles in the area.

L
••
ΔΔ
8km

PLACES OF INTEREST IN THE NORTH END OF THE OBERPFÄLZERWALD

TIRSCHENREUTH
Renaissance Town Hall
(1582–3)

Parish Church of the Assumption (rebuilt 1669)
Rare late Gothic carving.

MITTERTEICH
Town Hall

Church Square
Tower and columns featuring Mary and Nepomuk.

WALDSASSEN
Stiftland Museum
Minerology, geology, sacred art, etc.

Baroque Basilica of the Cistercian Order (1681–1704)

Library in the Cistercian Abbey (1724–5)
Outstanding carvings.

Church of the Trinity, Kappel
(Seventeenth century.) 4km NW. Church of very unusual design.

The countryside between Friedenfels and Tirschenreuth (population 9500) 18km to the east is speckled with thousands of little lakes — some hardly more than fish ponds — in what is known as the *Teichpfanne* (Pond Pan), a quite amazing landscape where holidays are geared towards water-orientated activities. Angling and sailing are popular and there are many other facilities. **Tirschenreuth** has much to offer the gastronome and it is not surprising to find that fish, especially carp, features prominently on the menus here. Buildings of interest include the *Rathaus*, a Renaissance building of 1582–3 and the parish church Maria Himmelfahrt dating from the end of the thirteenth century but completely renewed in 1669. There is a wooden relief *Heimsuchung Mariens* from the early sixteenth century which is much valued because examples of local late Gothic carving are rare in the Oberpfalz.

Ten kilometres north of Tirschenreuth, **Mitterteich** is another resort of similar size and characteristics except that the landscape is rather less influenced by water. Once again, fire has robbed the town of most of its old buildings so that there is little apart from the *Rathaus* and a church tower. **Waldsassen** on the other hand, only 8km away and again of similar size, has much for the visitor to admire. Not least the baroque basilica built 1681–1704 following the return of the Cistercian monks from Fürstenfeld. Their previous stay here lasted from 1133 until about 1560 when they were banished as a result of the Reformation. The principal architect of the basilica was Abraham

The Teichpfanne near Tirschenreuth

Leuthner from Prague whose assistant Georg Dientzenhofer became more important as the work progressed. No doubt the Jesuit church in Prague was what Leuthner originally had in mind for his pattern but Dietzenhofer's ideas, probably influenced by Fürstenfeld, are evident in the later stages. The interior decoration is striking with rich stucco work by G.B. Carlone who produced 200 angels and angels' heads and many other masterworks to complement the frescos. In the adjoining *Kloster* the splendid library, built at about the same time, lost most of its valuable store of books during secularisation in 1803. Now the shelves are well filled again thanks in part to purchase and in part to the 'loan' of some of the stolen books from the state archives.

Apart from the principal resorts above, there are many more equally attractive smaller places in the area. Four kilometres north-west of Waldsassen is the unusual pilgrimage church of the Heilige Dreifaltigkeit (Holy Trinity) built in the seventeenth century on the site of earlier chapels. The design was by Dientzenhofer and consists of three semi-circular niches with half-domes or conches in the angles of the basic trefoil, above each of which is a round tower capped with an elongated onion-dome. The church, atop the bare Glasberg (628m, 2060ft), appears to be more often known as the Kappel than by its formal name. The first chapel dated from the twelfth century; it

Holy Trinity Church, north-west of Waldsassen

was burned down during the Hussite wars and its successor fell victim to the Landshut war of succession in 1504. The third chapel, shown in a picture on the high altar, was only built in 1645.

In 1683 the war with the Turks resulted in more pilgrims coming here and the Cistercians in Waldsassen wanted a large 'chapel' which Dientzenhofer began in 1685. Later the three external half-circles were roofed over and protection provided for the many memorial tablets. The interior is richly endowed with sacred treasures and the work of many artists of the period including G.B. Carlone. The valuable organ has been beautifully restored but since the church now sees more tourists than pilgrims, Mass is only celebrated once a month and on the Sunday after the Feast of the Holy Trinity (3 June).

The route now leaves the Oberpfalz in a westerly direction and enters Oberfranken (Upper Franconia). **Marktredwitz**, the final place on the Ostmarkstrasse (population 20,000) is essentially an industrial town but has several sights of interest. The Protestant parish church of St Bartholomäus has a Renaissance pulpit with inlaid work from 1613 and a late Gothic tabernacle from around 1490. The old *Rathaus* (fourteenth century) is enhanced by a pretty balcony while the new *Rathaus* is a late eighteenth-century building in the classical style.

PLACES OF INTEREST IN THE FICHTELGEBIRGE

MARKTREDWITZ
**Parish Church of
St Bartholomäus**
Fine Renaissance pulpit and late Gothic tabernacle.

Old Town Hall
(Fourteenth century).

New Town Hall
(Late eighteenth century).

WUNSIEDEL
Fine market place and many fountains.

Fichtelgebirgsmuseum
Memorabilia of Jean Paul and Max Reger.

BISCHOFSGRÜN
Ochsenkopf (1023m, 2256ft)
Chair-lift, viewing tower, café.

The B303 west to Bad Berneck is the Fichtelgebirgsstrasse and passes through the attractive scenery of the Fichtelgebirge Nature Park. **Wunsiedel** (population 10,000), a little to the north of the road, is the regional capital and economic centre of its area and although it is quite industrialised has some attractions for visitors. Some 100,000 people come each year to see the festival play which has been performed since 1890 in the rocky labyrinths of the Luisenberg on the north slopes of the Kösseine (939m, 3080ft), a unique natural stage encircled by the forest.

On the Saturday before Johannistag (24 June) there is the *Brunnenfest*. The twenty or so fountains in the town are decorated with garlands, and ornaments. In the evening people gather in the Marktplatz and the fountains are illuminated with lanterns and candles. The crowd moves from fountain to fountain and at each there is music and folk singing. The festival goes back to the ancient ceremony of *Brunnenputzen*, the essential annual cleaning in days when the fountains were the source of the town's water supply. The ceremony can be likened to that of 'Dressing the Wells' in parts of England. Wunsiedel was the birthplace of the poet Jean Paul (1763–1825) and he is remembered, along with Max Reger in the Fichtelgebirgsmuseum.

Continuing on the B303, the summit of the Schneeberg (1053m, 3454ft) can be seen on the right. If time permits, the 20-minute ascent of nearby Ochsenkopf by chair-lift is a rewarding excursion. At the top there is a café and a stone tower with extensive views over the countryside. The Fichtelgebirge is an area rich in semi-precious stones and one could quite easily form a small private mineral collection here. Nearby **Bischofsgrün** (population 2500), a *Luft-*

kurort and winter sports centre, is a good base for a relaxed and peaceful interlude. The modern hotel Berghof has a pleasant restaurant.

The long journey from Passau ends at **Bad Berneck**, 41km from Marktredwitz. This is an attractive little spa with around 4500 inhabitants and it is encircled by seven hills. The town is a *Kneippheilbad* and *Luftkurort* and its praises have been sung by many famous people including Jean Paul the poet and the composer Carl Maria von Weber, who concluded that the place was 'just made for artists'. The town's rise to fame is actually fairly recent. From 1857 a health establishment offered a cure based on skimmed goat's milk and vegetable juices, a recipe that seems to have been very successful. The benefits of the climate were becoming apparent and in about 1900 a factory owner from Waldsassen fell in love with the place and gave the whole of his fortune to the town for its development. A *Kurhaus*, chapel and the *Kneipp* centre were built and a town garden was laid out. In 1950 the town was rewarded with the prefix *Bad* to its name. Nowadays there are many facilities from minigolf to a modern *Hallenbad* in the sports centre near the River Main.

The B2 leaves Bad Berneck in a southerly direction and enters the Richard Wagner festival town of **Bayreuth.**

In 1848 Wagner started to think about a setting for his projected music drama (he preferred the term to opera) *Siegfried* and made a plea for quality, if necessary at the expense of number of performances. His efforts to persuade existing managements to reform were fairly unsuccessful so he decided he needed a completely new setting for his work. Wagner first thought of Zurich and then started to consider some of the smaller German cities, especially Weimar. How then, did he finally settle on Bayreuth? The answer can be found in a letter he wrote to Friedrich Feustel, in 1870: 'The place must not be a large city with a permanent theatre, nor one of the larger summer resorts where during the season an absolutely undesirable public would offer itself; it must be centrally located in Germany and moreover be a Bavarian city, as I intend to take up my permanent residence in the place and consider that I could do this only in Bavaria, if I hope to enjoy the continued patronage of the King . . . this pleasant old city with its surroundings made an indelible impression on me years ago and the fact that I am an utter stranger to the citizens of Bayreuth gives me no cause for alarm.'

Wagner confirmed this impression during a visit in spring 1871.

The Margrave's Opera House, Bayreuth

When he fell ill he was treated by Dr Carl Landgraf with whom he struck up a firm friendship. Writing to Landgraf in May of that year '. . . it is now decided that my great Stage Festival Play shall take place in the summer of 1873 in Bayreuth, at which time I also intend to take up my permanent residence in your city . . . His Majesty the King of Bavaria has granted his permission . . . and will give considerable financial support . . . .'

The next few years were dogged by financial and other problems but on 22 May 1872 Wagner laid the foundation stone of his Festival Theatre on his 59th birthday. Building was finished in 1875 and the first festival was planned for the following year but even this was in doubt because of the difficulty in obtaining the quality for which Wagner was striving. However, all was ready in time and the opening celebrations included the complete 'Ring' cycle. Famous visitors to Bayreuth for the occasion included Kaiser Wilhelm I and King Ludwig II. Many musicians also came to pay honour including Bruckner, Grieg and Tschaikovsky. A full house at every performance was still insufficient to generate enough income to cover the costs and even the costumes had to be sold afterwards to help the funds. It all looked like a gigantic flop but Wagner, although disheartened, did not give up and in 1882 the festival resumed with a performance of *Parsifal*. Richard Wagner died in Venice on 13 February 1883. His wife Cosima — daughter of Franz Liszt — carried on the work and the survival of the festival owes much to her. Later his son Siegfried took over the reigns of management from 1906 until 1930 and was in his turn succeeded by his English wife Winifred whom he had married in 1915. She kept the festivals going in splendid style but was discredited by her friendship with Hitler — a great admirer of Wagner's works — and her public career ended at the close of World War II. She lived on until 1980 and did a lot of work behind the scenes.

Those wishing to attend performances of Wagner's works in the Festival Theatre must be prepared to book a very long time in advance.

This town of 70,000 inhabitants is good for a visit at any time; there is always plenty to see and do. The Festival Theatre can be visited as can the Margrave's baroque opera house (1745–8), a little gem of a theatre. It was built at the suggestion of the Margravine Wilhelmina (1709–58) who was no mean musician herself and did much to foster the cultural life of the town.

Wagner was not the only famous resident. Johann Paul Friedrich Richter (1763–1825), known as Jean Paul, spent much of his life here and with Franz Liszt (1811–66) is buried in the town cemetery. The Wagners' graves are behind his house Villa Wahnfried in the Hofgar- ten. A little outside the town is the Eremitage with its spectacular fountains, cascades and extensive park. It was created between 1715 and 1750 to enable court society to spend time pretending to be

The sun temple at the Eremitage, Bayreuth

hermits or shepherds, an eighteenth-century social game.

The Eremitage has its own Altes Schloss and Neues Schloss and the sun temple, a magnificent example of late rococo work with its fine rotunda surmounted by a gilded chariot drawn by four horses. Back in the town, the Altes Schloss has an octagonal tower (1565–6) with a spiral ramp for horses; the three wings are from the seventeenth century. The Schlosskirche was added in 1753–6 with rococo stucco and contains the graves of the Margravine Wilhelmina and her husband Friedrich. The Neues Schloss (1753–4) has room decorations which reveal Wilhelmina's inclination towards natural motifs, trees, birds, insects and dragons! — things Chinese were in vogue at the time. The building now houses the Stadtmuseum and a branch of the Bavarian State Collection of paintings of the sixteenth to eighteenth centuries. The Schreibmaschinen-museum (typewriter museum) and the Freimaurer Museum, a library and exhibition on the history of freemasonry in Germany are also worth seeing.

Six kilometres west of Bayreuth in the village of **Donndorf** on the B22 is the Schloss Fantaisie with a fine park. Fourteen kilometres to the south on the B2, **Creussen** is the home of the Krügemuseum, a historical display of Creussen stoneware in colourful array.

7 THE DANUBE AND THE GERMAN HOLIDAY ROAD

This chapter explores the long corridor lying right across the centre of Bavaria. The 1785km-long Holiday Road (Deutsche Ferienstrasse Alpen-Ostsee) is the longest of Germany's named roads; its northern terminal is at Puttgarden on the Baltic coast and its southern at Berchtesgaden near the Austrian border. One of the routes outlined in this chapter embraces part of the Holiday Road which is joined at Dinkelsbühl. About 70km south of Dinkelsbühl in the west of Bavaria, the River Danube, which has its source in the Black Forest, enters Bavaria and the course of this river is traced eastwards into Austria.

From their respective starting points on the western border of Bavaria the Holiday Road and River Danube draw steadily closer until they finally meet and cross at Kelheim, west of Regensburg, after which the Holiday Road leaves the river to go south to Landshut.

Dinkelsbühl to Kelheim

The first route begins by leaving **Dinkelsbühl** and heading eastwards along the Ferienstrasse; this is a route to be enjoyed in a leisurely fashion. The small towns follow closely upon each other and most are worth a brief sightseeing stop.

The hill named Hesselberg (689m, 2260ft) is soon seen on the left, a site of significant historical discoveries including the remains of a bronze casting workplace dating from about 1800BC. The main access road to the Hesselberg starts in the village of **Gerolfingen** about 14km from Dinkelsbühl and climbs steadily to the parking area near the summit. Walkers can start from the preceding village of **Wittelshofen** and follow the geological trail to the summit, 5–6km. Near the car park there is an information centre with detailed drawings and descriptions (only in German) of the many features of interest.

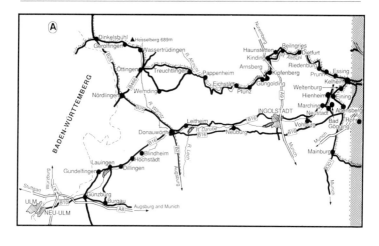

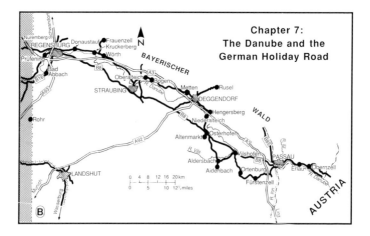

As one explores the area it is obvious why this has been a fortified place since the earliest times for the steep slopes alone would have been sufficient to deter all but the most determined attacker. Even today the hill is not without strategic importance for the American army has occupied and fenced off an area at the top which includes the old

Gasthof. Even if one is not interested in the historical aspect, the detour to the Hesselberg is worthwhile just to reach a pleasant picnic spot with spectacular views all round.

About 20km from Dinkelsbühl is the former Margrave's town of **Wassertrüdingen** (population 6000) lying between quiet forests and soft hills. A short pause here to visit the moated castle and the town church is worthwhile. The little River Wörnitz is good for fishing. A folk festival takes place in the 8 days following Whitsun. This is a good walking area and there are conducted rambles, often with a geological theme. Information is available from the *Rathaus*. The Holiday Road follows the Wörnitz a mere 10km to **Öttingen**, a small Swabian health resort with a good range of facilities for young and old and well preserved timbered and baroque houses. In July there is a water festival on the Wörnitz.

Ten kilomentres or so in a south-easterly direction is the resort of **Wemding** (population 5200), reached after passing the pilgrimage church Maria Brünnlein built in 1748–52, one of the most beautiful rococo churches in Bavaria. Every town and village seems to have its annual festival and here in Wemding this starts on the Wednesday before Ascension Day and lasts for 5 days.

Fifteen kilometres north-east of Wemding, like nearly every other town in this area, **Treuchtlingen** (population 12,000) is a health resort; there is a thermal open-air pool, a *Hallenwellenbad*, a leisure centre, a highly acclaimed central play area for children, nature trails, keep-fit paths, a museum, churches and a deer park. The town's folk festival is during the week from the second to third Sundays in July. The information office in the *Rathaus* can provide itineraries for rambles in the vicinity. Some of these are conducted and have a theme.

The River Altmühl here is one of Bavaria's lesser known but nevertheless very beautiful waterways and it is followed through its finest scenery until it joins the Danube at Kelheim. River, road and railway keep close company through the first 20km or so of the Altmühltal. The river has carved a broad cleft deep into the Franconian Jura; on the fringes are rocky cliffs and the river winds through meadows, fields, woods and colourful settlements.

Pappenheim, but a stone's throw from Treuchtlingen, is a small resort (population 2400) where numerous hostelries offer specialities of the region for travellers following the Holiday Road. The ninth-century church of St Gallus is worth a visit as is the fourteenth-century

PLACES OF INTEREST ON THE HOLIDAY ROAD BETWEEN DINKELSBÜHL AND EICHSTÄTT

GEROLFINGEN (14km E of Dinkelsbühl)
Hesselberg (689m, 2260ft)
Former fortified hill with historical and geological significance. Geological trail from nearby Wittelshofen.

WEMDING
Pilgrimage Church Maria Brünnlein (1748–52)
Beautiful rococo.

EXCURSION FROM TREUCHT-LINGEN

Monheim (16km S)
Historic steam railway to Fünfstetten.

PAPPENHEIM
Church of St Gallus
(Ninth century.)

Kloster Church
(Fourteenth century.)

EICHSTÄTT
Baroque town centre with **Cathedral**, **Residenz** and **Parish Church**.

Kloster church. There are also many leisure facilities. From May to October there are various conducted rambles. The annual folk festival is during the third week in July.

Since Wemding, the route has forged through the Naturpark Altmühltal, with 290,800 hectares one of the biggest nature reserves in West Germany; the route stays in the *Naturpark* until Kelheim on the Danube. The autumn colours in the Altmühltal are very spectacular and the natural attractions and the cultural and historical sights are pressed closely upon one another with a richness seldom found elsewhere.

Nowhere is this more true than in **Eichstätt** some 25km along the twisty valley road from Pappenheim. Eichstätt, the last town on this part of the route directly accessible by train, is a place of some 13,000 inhabitants, a former bishop's seat and the home of numerous ecclesiastical and government institutions. There is a church high school and several *Klöster*. The baroque town centre, the cathedral, the Residenz, the parish church and numerous other buildings make an attractive picture with the imposing castle Willibaldsburg dominating the skyline. There are conducted rambles and thematic excursions in the vicinity as well as a number of recommended cycle tours using some of the 140km of designated cycling paths.

The 'Twelve Apostles' in the Altmühl valley below Solnhofen

Pfünz with its ancient castle is only 5km away. Before Arnsberg with its prominent castle on a rocky outcrop is the Gungolding landscape preservation area with its juniper bush-clad slopes. At Arnsberg catch a glimpse of the lovely Schambachtal to the south and before the health resort of **Kipfenberg** cross the remains of the Limes, a Roman fortification built during the first and second centuries. Kipfenberg has a romantic castle perched on steep rocky slopes. The medieval and earlier fortifications including the Limes provide the theme for a festival in August. Although it has little more than 4000 inhabitants, this attractive resort caters well for visitors.

Turn north for a few kilometres, pass beneath the Nuremberg–Ingolstadt motorway near the Altmühltal junction and almost immediately reach the picturesque village of **Kinding** (population 2000). Although not an officially designated health resort it offers a considerable range of facilities. The Erholungszentrum Kratzmühle is a kind of health centre with a lake for bathing and all appropriate facilities for the ailing guest. Kinding is a good centre for excursions — two side valleys feed into the Altmühltal here — and amongst other sights the fourteenth-century Kirchenburg Castle and the haunted ruin Rumburg may be visited.

From Kinding there are two possible routes to Beilngries, 5 or 6km

PLACES OF INTEREST ON THE HOLIDAY ROAD BETWEEN EICHSTÄTT AND KELHEIM

GUNGOLDING
Landscape preservation area with juniper bushes.

KIPFENBERG
Medieval and other fortifications including the Roman Limes.

KINDING
Recreation Centre Kratzmühle
Health facilities and bathing lake.

Kirchenburg Castle
(Fourteenth century.)

Rumburg
'Haunted' ruined castle

HAUNSTETTEN
Hirschberg
Stately baroque palace.

BEILNGRIES
Attractive medieval centre and town wall.

DIETFURT
Five Gothic Town Towers

Parish Church of St Ägidius

Market Place with Chinese Fountain

RIEDENBURG
Rosenburg (1112)
Fine castle/museum and home of hunting falcon organisation. Birds of prey fly daily.

PRUNN
Schloss Prunn
Castle on steep cliffs above River Altmühl. Furniture, paintings and tapestries. The place where the Lay of the Nibelungs was discovered in 1575.

MARKT ESSING
Unspoiled old village with ancient wooden bridge. Centre for exploration of many caves in the vicinity including the Schulerloch with rare rock drawings.

KELHEIM
Parish Church of the Assumption
Late Gothic Madonna over south portal.

Liberation Hall
Monument to the ideal of German unity and in memory of wars of liberation, especially against Napoléon. Magnificent views of Danube and Altmühl valleys.

to the north-west. The Holiday Road closely follows the river but the scenic road via Haunstetten goes past the stately baroque palace of Hirschberg which may be visited although the opening hours are somewhat restricted due to use of the building as offices for the Diocese of Eichstätt. **Beilngries** is a health resort of 3500 inhabitants; the medieval centre is very attractive and there is a well preserved town wall. There is a wide range of facilities for the holiday-

The market place and town hall, Markt Essing

maker with many marked paths for walkers and routes for cyclists.

The Ferienstrasse now enters the lower Altmühltal. There are usually many anglers along the river bank for this is a fine fishing river. Pike, carp, tench barbel and other fish may be caught here.

The road now crosses the southern tip of the Oberpfalz and, still following the River Altmühl, **Dietfurt** is reached in about 10km. This town of seven valleys is another little health resort, a meeting place of roads and rivers and the place where the original canal of King Ludwig I joined the Altmühl. It is a place which will become of increasing interest with the development of international traffic on the waterway. Five of the original six Gothic town towers still exist, overshadowed by the 65m-high (213ft) spire of the parish church of St Ägidius (Giles) the interior of which is decorated in the baroque style. There are relics from the fifteenth and sixteenth centuries. Do not miss the famous Chinese fountain in the Marktplatz. In the Franciscan *Kloster* church on Thursday afternoons during Lent there is a dramatic and musical performance recalling the happenings on the Mount of Olives. Dietfurt is an excellent centre for walking — routes from the information office — and the rivers are a paradise for anglers.

Continuing downstream pass through or stop in several pleasant little villages and arrive, in about 14km, at **Riedenburg**, known either as 'the pearl of the valley' or the 'town of three castles'. Either way, the

Rosenburg (built 1112) is the jewel in the crown of this delightful town which is noted for its scenic beauty and its hospitality. The Falconry Museum in the Rosenburg is unique in Bavaria. Daily flying displays by eagles, vultures and falcons are a spectacular sight. In another 3km, Schloss Prunn towers above the valley; this is where the *Nibelungenlied* (Lay of the Nibelungs) was discovered in 1575. In the next 4km to **Markt Essing** (population 1100) pass a series of natural monuments, rocks and caverns. Essing itself huddles beneath towering cliffs and is a useful centre for exploring the various caves in the vicinity including the Schulerloch with its rare rock drawings. The old village centre is bypassed but one can park and walk into the market place over an ancient wooden bridge for a worthwhile visit.

A few minutes later reach **Kelheim**, the end of this first stage of the journey along the Holiday Road and the end, too, of the Altmühl which now loses its identity as it merges with the Danube. Kelheim (population 15,000) is on the site of an early Stone Age settlement.

Otto I, first duke of the Wittelsbach dynasty was born here and the old town is typical of the Wittelsbach era with the remains of fortifications, town gates and decorative house fronts on the main streets. Worthy of note is a late Gothic Madonna over the south side portal of the parish church Maria Himmelfahrt. In and around Kelheim, the Befreiungshalle (Liberation Hall) comes repeatedly into view, which is, of course, exactly what the founder of this monument intended. The 45m-high (147ft) building tops the Michelsberg, which itself rises 100m (328ft) above the town.

King Ludwig I was a great believer in things German and in German unity; he wanted to erect a monument in memory of the *Befreiungskriege* (Wars of Liberation). He was travelling in Greece in 1836 (which had, in 1821–30, freed itself of Turkish rule and had adopted his son Otto as its king), and decided on the construction of a 'Byzantine' hall in this commanding position at the confluence of Altmühl and Danube. Work progressed slowly and in 1847, Leo von Klenze (builder of the Glyptothek and Pinakothek in Munich) took command and changed the style to that of Roman antiquity. Work was completed in 1863, just in time for the 50th anniversary of the Battle of Leipzig (16–18 October 1813). The colossal round temple includes memorials to the victories and victors of the wars against Napoléon (1813–15). The climb up to the Befreiungshalle is well worthwhile just for the splendid view in all directions even if one is not particularly interested in the historical symbolism of the monument.

Bavarian band at Grafenau

The sun temple at Eremitage, Bayreuth

Interior of the Benedictine monastery church in Reichenbach

The old town hall at Bamberg

*The Liberation Hall,
Kelheim*

The remarkable caverns in the Altmühltal are best visited on foot then one can move easily from one to another. Start from the car park beside the Danube quays in Kelheim. Enter the town through the medieval Donautor (Danube Gate). Go left via the Altmühltor and over the river bridge through Riedenburger Strasse and Brandner Steig. The footpath proper starts after passing the last houses and climbs up to the Maria-Fels, a rocky viewpoint. The path is then followed until it drops down into the Heidental. Take the path (waymark red N) which leads directly into the wood until the main Schulerloch is reached 5km from Kelheim. 40,000 years ago this giant stalactite cave was used as a dwelling place and it was inhabited again in the Bronze Age. From Easter until 1 November there are guided tours into the cave. In the nearby small Schulerloch the only Ice Age drawings in Central Europe are scratched on the walls.

Continue up the valley to **Essing** (8km from Kelheim); the ruined castle Randeck nearby has a fine view over the valley and far beyond, even to the Alps in clear weather. Return from here by the same route or by going down to pick up the track (waymark red bar) along the river. However, the path continues forward to Felsenhäusl hut and from there, bears right and upward to the Höhenweg (Hill Way) marked by a blue dot. Turn left and follow it to Schloss Prunn (12km from Kelheim) where there is a welcome terrace café. Down then to **Einthal** and over a pretty bridge to the Klammhöhle (more caves)

M

ΔΔΔ
16
or
25km

and a prehistoric earthwork. The way back is along the river (red bar) which forms part of the great international waterway. It is possible to return to Kelheim by 'bus from Einthal but the walker can visit two more caves on the way, the Kastlhängehöhle and the Klausenhöhle.

Neu-Ulm to Kelheim

A hundred kilometres westwards at **Neu-Ulm** the Danube is joined, soon after its entry into Bavaria. This is Swabia and there is a noticeable difference in architectural style compared with Franconian Dinkelsbühl 70km to the north.

Since 1971, Ulm in Baden-Württemberg and Neu-Ulm in Bavaria have been one administrative unit and are regarded as a 'double town' like several others in Germany. The Danube is the dividing line. Train travellers will probably have arrived at the *Hauptbahnhof* in Ulm, the converging point of no less than ten passenger routes with a total of some 270 trains per day.

Neu-Ulm, as its name implies, is a comparatively new town. In 1815 its population was no more than 260; by the time of the merger it was able to add its 48,000 to the 99,000 of Ulm across the river. Needless to say, there is much friendly rivalry between the two parts and the respective merits of Württemberg and Bavarian beer or the Catholic white sausage and the Lutheran red are always good topics for discussion. The holidaymaker need not linger long although the Catholic parish church of St John the Baptist, rebuilt between 1922 and 1926, is worth a visit. The musem in the Edwin-Scharff cultural centre is noted for its display of locks and fastenings.

Take the B10 eastwards to **Günzburg** (population 19,000) where the Hotel Lamm in Hofgasse has a selection of specialities which have earned it a Michelin star. In the old upper town there is a pleasant historic atmosphere with buildings from the Middle Ages surrounding a fine market place. The palace of an Austrian margrave with its court church of 1579 and a rococo chapel justify a visit and the Liebfrauen-kirche, built between 1735 and 1741 to the designs of Dominikus Zimmermann, is one of the most impressive rococo churches in Swabia. In the *Heimatmuseum* there is a large collection of archaeological finds. This is a popular cycling and rambling area and there is angling in the Danube for carp, tench, pike and trout. Fishing permits are available from Josef Sixti, Schlachthausstrasse 60.

Burgau

It would be a pity to stay too close to the Danube and miss a pleasant place like **Burgau** (population 7900) just 11km further along the B10. The town church (1791) shows the transition from rococo to classical style and has a fine ceiling painting (1829). The *Heimatmuseum* is located in yet another Margrave's palace (1787) and there is a fine fountain, the Marienbrunnen (1728). The Auto-Motorrad-Museum has a collection of over seventy vintage cars and motorcycles including such classics as the 1902 Peugeot and the Mercedes 'Stuttgart' of 1928. From November until March an ice rink provides ice hockey, skating and curling. A good network of well kept and well marked footpaths provides pleasant rambles in the neighbourhood.

An agreeable 16km drive brings one back to the Danube which is crossed to reach medieval **Lauingen** (population 10,000), a former duke's seat with picturesque corners and some impressive sights. The late Gothic minster, with its princes' burial vault and cloister paintings, should be visited and the classical *Rathaus* (1782–91), facing what is said to be the finest market place in Swabia, should not be overlooked, except that is, by climbing the Schimmelturm, a 55m-high (180ft) tower giving a splendid bird's eye view of the town. The concerts which take place in the great hall of the *Rathaus* have a good reputation and there are various other entertainments in this lively little town. There is a *Heimatmuseum* and a notable exhibition of

PLACES OF INTEREST ALONG THE DANUBE BETWEEN NEU-ULM AND DONAUWÖRTH

NEU-ULM
Edwin-Scharff-Museum
In the cultural centre. Unusual display of locks and fastenings.

GÜNZBURG
Fine market place with historic buildings around.

Margrave's Palace and Court Church (1579) **with Rococo Chapel**

Liebfrauenkirche (1735–41)
Impressive rococo.

Heimatmuseum
Archaeological collection.

BURGAU
Town Church (1791)
Transition from rococo to classical style.

Auto-Motorrad-Museum
Over seventy vintage cars and motor-cycles.

GUNDELFINGEN
Motor Museum
Vintage cars and motor-cycles.

LAUINGEN
Town Hall (1782–91)
Faces the 'finest market place in Swabia'.

Minster
Late Gothic with princes' burial vault and cloister paintings.

Heimatmuseum
Exhibition of minerals.

DILLINGEN
'Golden' Hall of Former University

Former Jesuit Church (1610–17)

Franciscan Church (1736–8)
Rococo.

HÖCHSTÄDT
Market Place surrounded by fine patrician houses.

Renaissance Palace housing branch of **Bavarian National Museum.**
Sculpture, textiles, furnishings, etc.

minerals. There is an annual *Faschings* procession and a summer folk festival. Sports enthusiasts have tennis, riding, sailing, a bowling alley and swimming and there is fishing in the Danube and in several small lakes — Leo Mack, Donaustrasse 14 will provide permits. At **Gundelfingen**, a few kilometres to the west, there is another motor museum with a collection of vintage vehicles.

Only 5km eastwards along the B16 is another town with very similar characteristics and equally well endowed with interesting sights. This is **Dillingen** (population 12,000), formerly the residence of the prince-bishops of Augsburg and from 1549 until 1804, a university town, a fact which had considerable influence on the

Former Jesuit church at Dillingen on the Danube

buildings. More than a short stop is required to see and appreciate the *Schloss*, the Studienkirche (former Jesuit church) (1610–17), the rococo Franciscan church (1736–8) and the golden hall of the former university, to name just a few of the architectural treasures. The town's many attractions include concerts and theatre and again there is fishing in the Danube — permits from Gästehaus Noll, Georg-Schmid-Ring 47 close by the camp site at No 45.

Six kilometres more and **Höchstädt**, at first glance rather less attractive than the two previous stops, is nevertheless, well worth closer inspection. Of particular interest to English visitors is the memorial to the fallen of the great battle of the Spanish Succession on 13 August 1704 when the 'allied' forces of Austria and Holland, with the English under the duke of Marlborough, defeated the combined armies of Bavaria and France here and at nearby **Blindheim** which — as Blenheim — became the name of the well known family seat of the dukes of Marlborough in England. The Gothic parish church has a baroque high altar and a richly decorated pulpit and once again the Marktplatz, surrounded by old patrician houses, makes a fine centre. The Renaissance palace is being converted to become an external branch of the Bavarian National Museum where the exhibits will

PLACES OF INTEREST ALONG THE DANUBE BETWEEN DONAUWÖRTH AND INGOLSTADT

LEITHEIM
Seventeenth-century Palace
Lovely rococo banqueting hall. Church (1696) with rich stucco and museum with eighteenth-century works of art.

NEUBURG
Renaissance Palace
(1530–45)
Chapel with frescos from 1543.

Court Church (1607)

St Peter's Church (1641-6)

Church of the Holy Ghost (1723–6)

Town Hall and Mint

Provinzialbibliothek
Library with fittings from former Kloster Kaisheim.

include a collection of Swabian sculpture, textiles and rooms furnished in the style of the eighteenth century.

Donauwörth was visited in Chapter 1 so there is no need to linger. Towns, rather than scenery, have provided the theme since leaving Neu-Ulm but from Donauwörth, the motorist has to choose between the fairly fast B16 south of, but not near, the river and the quieter road on the north side running in part along the fringe of the Altmühltal *Naturpark*. The latter is really more pleasant and allows a stop to visit the fine seventeenth-century *Schloss* at **Leitheim**.

 From 1680 to 1803 this was the summer seat of the abbots of Kaisheim and its rococo banqueting hall has fine ceiling and wall paintings executed from 1751. The *Schlosskirche* has rich stucco from 1696 while the *Schlossmuseum* exhibits important works of art from the eighteenth century. Concerts are given in the *Schloss* every Saturday from May to October at 8pm, usually chamber music or solo artists. Advance booking is essential.

Both roads converge on the Danube at **Neuburg** in Upper Bavaria (population 20,000) a rather pleasant town with the usual range of leisure activities. The *Neuburger Barockkonzerte* organised by the local Mozart club each September are well thought of. The Renaissance *Schloss* was built between 1530 and 1545; in the *Schlosskapelle* are frescos from 1543. Neuburg has many places of worship and the Hofkirche (1607), St Peter (1641–6), Church of the Holy Ghost (1723–6) and the Studienkirche (1700–1) are all worth seeing if time permits. Secular buildings of note include the *Rathaus*, the Münz (mint) and above all the Provinzialbibliothek (library) which

PLACES OF INTEREST IN INGOLSTADT

Palace   (1418–1500)
Home of the Bavarian Army Museum. 16,000 'tin' soldiers in world's largest diorama.

Minster (started 1425)
Fine late Gothic church.

Former Oratory Maria de Victoria (1732–5)
Fine work by C.D. Asam and J.M. Fischer.

Moritzkirche   (fourteenth century), **Franciscan Church** (begun 1275) and **Spitalkirche** (begun fourteenth century).

German Medical History Museum

Kreuztor   (1385)
Part of the remaining fourteenth-century fortifications.

Town Theatre (1966)
Example of modern theatre architecture.

has the fittings of the former Kaisheim abbey library.

The remaining 21km leads to **Ingolstadt**, a city of 100,000 inhabitants. Pipelines, refineries and power stations are likely to be the visitor's first welcome here, but there is much to see and do. Like most other German cities, Ingolstadt has a rich and varied cultural life to which the autumn concerts (*Musik-Herbst*) make an important contribution. It was the first university town in Bavaria and although the university ceased to function as such in 1800 there are still a number of educational establishments. The devastating bombing of the town on 9 April 1945 at the end of World War II inflicted heavy damage on many fine buildings. The most important have since been painstakingly restored and today's visitor will find many historic structures again in their pre-war glory. Indeed, the *Schloss* (1418–1500) is even better than it was, for in the course of restoration, the towers have been built to the height originally planned. The *Schloss* today houses the Bavarian Army Museum. The minster (begun in 1425) is amongst the finest examples of late Gothic church architecture in Bavaria. The former oratory Maria de Victoria (1732–5) is another building involving C.D. Asam and J.M. Fischer and the fourteenth-century Moritzkirche, the Franciscan church (begun 1275) and the Spitalkirche (begun in the fourteenth century) are worthy of inspection.

Die Anatomie (1723–36) is the home of the German medical history museum but is of general interest. The Kreuztor (1385) and other parts of the fourteenth-century fortifications still exist. Coming up to date, the Stadttheater of 1966 is a good example of modern

Fifteenth-century palace in Ingolstadt, home of the Bavarian Army Museum

theatre architecture.

The rail traveller must now follow a more southerly route to Kelheim, perhaps interrupting the journey in **Neustadt an der Donau** (population 6500) which has a fifteenth-century church. The next station is at **Abensberg**, a little town of about the same size which could make a pleasant stop for a night with a visit to the little Aventinusmuseum housed in the former Carmelite *Kloster* where relics of the historian Johannes Thurmair, known as Aventinus, are on display. Nearby is the Lower Bavarian Bird Park.

The motorist should leave Ingolstadt along the road called Schlosslände on the north bank of the Danube and follow signs for Regensburg, shortly joining the B16a and continue along this for about 10km to turn left into **Vohburg** just before the road crosses the river. The route continues through **Pförring**, **Marching** (for a short excursion to the church in Neustadt south of the river) and **Irnsing** to **Hienheim**.

8.5km

There is an opportunity here for two short rambles. Leaving the village in an easterly direction, follow the small road towards Essing for about 2km to Hadriansäule, a monument in memory of the Roman emperor Hadrian who was responsible for building the Limes, the fortified wall marking the one-time boundary of the Roman Empire.

PLACES OF INTEREST ALONG THE DANUBE BETWEEN INGOLSTADT AND KELHEIM

ABENSBERG

Aventinusmuseum
In the former Carmelite *Kloster.*
Memorabilia of historian Johannes
Thurmair known as Aventinus.

Lower Bavarian Bird Park
Extensive collection of birds including fifty different birds of prey.

BAD GÖGGING

Church of St Andreas
Built on foundations of former
Roman bath.

EINING

Abusina Roman Fort
On road to Bad Gögging.

HIENHEIM

**Monument in memory of
Roman Emperor Hadrian**
2km NE. Remains of Roman wall.

WELTENBURG

**Benedictine Abbey and
Church** (1716–18)
Outstanding work by Asam brothers. High altar of St George and
dragon. Restaurant. Beer garden.

Danube Gorge
Remarkable natural spectacle.
Best seen by boat from Wel-
tenburg or Kelheim.

During the years 117–138, Hadrian and his successors built this
166km-long buttress, the remains of which are still to be seen in a
number of places. To the locals the Limes was known as Teufels-
mauer (Devil's Wall). Hadrian is probably better known for the great
wall he constructed across Britain in 122–127. Turn left at the monument into a field track and follow the visible remains of the wall for a
further 2km before turning left into a track out of the wood and into the
village of **Weiler Ried** in about 1.5km. Visit the baroque chapel
before returning to Hienheim along a minor road in about 3km.

The other ramble includes a ferry crossing of the Danube. It is only
a short walk from the village to the landing stage from where a small
boat plies across to the village of **Eining**. Now the route goes south-
west along a minor road in the direction of Bad Gögging and very soon
the remains of a Roman fort called Abusina are reached. It is about
2.5km to **Bad Gögging** where the Norman-style church of St Andreas, with its richly decorated portal, is built on the foundations of a
former Roman bath. Although it is thus one of the oldest German
spas, it is only since 1976 that new 650m-deep (2132ft) borings have
tapped important reserves of therapeutic mineral waters which have
resulted in the development of the town as a modern health resort.

Return to Hienheim by the same route or, on the south side of the

L
↔
Δ
8km

river, use the alternative field paths.

Leave Hienheim by the Essing road and follow signs to reach **Kelheim** in about 16km. The map shows that the Danube gorge, where the river cuts through a spur of the Franconian Jura, has been bypassed. However, during the main holiday season, passenger boats leave Kelheim every half-hour for an excursion as far as Kloster

Weltenburg through an outstanding example of European scenery. Each year on the first Saturday of July, the spectacle called *Flammende Donau* takes place and the gorge is illuminated by thousands of Bengal lights. Early reservation of a place on the cruise boats is essential.

M
↔
△△△△
10km

To fully appreciate this delightful area, one should also explore it on foot. Begin beside the Danube in Kelheim. Walk a little way west and leave the river bank near the end of the old Ludwigskanal to join a path up through the parkland of the Michelsberg and past the Befreiungshalle. The way ahead is clearly marked. On the west side of the Michelsberg there are remains of the Keltenwall, another ancient fortification and shortly after this the path divides. The right fork (waymark 6) goes ahead through the wood on a pleasant little road and is slightly shorter than the left fork (7) which goes closer to

the gorge with several fine view points. The hostelry 'Klösterle' provides for a rest and refreshment on the way. Just after passing another portion of the Keltenwall, both routes meet at a road. Join this and turn left down to **Stausacker** on the river bank where — from April to October — a boat goes across to **Weltenburg**.

The *Kloster* here was the first in Bavaria and is considered to be where the Christianisation of the country began. In the seventh century, monks founded a mission station on the tip of the tongue formed by a huge curve in the river and in the year 760, this became a Benedictine abbey. The present *Klosterkirche* was built by the Asam brothers (begun 1716). It is a masterpiece of their work and the visitor should not fail to see it. Refreshments are available here; the *Kloster* has it own brewery and a glass of its *Weltenburger Klosterbier* is very welcome under the trees on a warm summer day.

Return to Kelheim by the same route — with the choice of paths 6 and 7 — or along the hill path (9) on the south side of the river. Or from April to October, save about 4km walking distance by travelling at least one way between Kelheim and Weltenburg by boat.

Kelheim to Landshut

The interrupted journey along the Holiday Road can now be resumed. From Kelheim, the first 10km or so lead back, parallel with the river, to Weltenburg and Eining but then the road turns south out of the Altmühltal *Naturpark* to reach **Abensberg**. From here join the B301 and pass through extensive fields of hops, for this is the Hallertau or Holledau, the largest hop-growing area in Europe. There are other crops and the general impression is of prosperous agricultural land interspersed with dark woodlands. This area is rich in art and cultural monuments — brick churches with onion-domed towers, well preserved *Klöster* and *Schlösser* and solid houses in the towns.

Another outstanding example of church architecture is to be found in **Rohr** some 11km south-east of Abensberg. A house of the Augustinian canons was founded here in 1133. Little remains now of the Romanesque building and in 1717 the site was more or less cleared to allow E.Q. Asam free rein in the construction of a new church which was consecrated in 1722. There is some painting by brother Cosmas Damian but otherwise practically every detail of the church Maria Himmelfahrt was planned by Egid Quirin and executed in his workshops. The quite fantastic high altar depicts the Assumption of the Virgin, borne up by angels towards an opening where the choir of angels and the figures of the Trinity await her. The apostles are gathered below in amazement and awe around the empty marble sarcophagus. During a service or organ recital, the atmosphere is tremendous and the whole creation is seen as Asam conceived it. The 1803 secularisation brought the usual problems but mercifully the church survived. In 1945 the former buildings were taken over as a Benedictine abbey and the monks are now responsible for the care of this lovely building.

Some 20km from Abensberg, the Ferienstrasse reaches the centre of the hop industry, **Mainburg** (population 11,000). The folk museum is of interest as is the largest hop preparation plant in Europe. After Mainburg the road leaves the B301 to turn east for the final 40km to Landshut. **Landshut** is the perfect picture of a medieval old Bavarian town. The colourful façades of the buildings face each other across the broad Altstadt and the skyline is dominated by the 130m-high (426ft) tower of St Martin's Minster. Through the simple entrance beneath the tower is the brick-built three-naved church, 92m (302ft) long and about 29m (95ft) wide and high, begun in the fifteenth

PLACES OF INTEREST ALONG THE HOLIDAY ROAD TO LANDSHUT

ROHR (11km SE of Abensberg)
Benedictine Abbey Church of the Assumption (1717)
Outstanding baroque church mainly by E.Q. Asam.

MAINBURG
Centre of the hop industry with interesting folk museum.

LANDSHUT
Colourful houses along the Altstadt, centre of the old town.

Town Residenz
First Italian Renaissance palace north of Alps. Art gallery, especially works of sixteenth to eighteenth centuries.

St Martin's Minster
(Begun fifteenth century.)
130m-high (426ft) tower. Fine Gothic brickwork.

Trausnitz Castle
(Earliest parts thirteenth century.)
Many fine apartments. Gothic chapel.

century. The pulpit and high altar are original and are examples of the best of Gothic stonemasonry.

From the earliest days, Landshut, now with a population of 58,000, has been a place of royal residence and Burg Trausnitz provided the necessary accommodation. That it also served as a fortress is shown by the drawbridge. Parts of the complex date from the thirteenth century but many of the royal occupants introduced their own ideas of decoration and furnishing. From 1868 onwards, King Ludwig II had rooms on the second floor magnificently fitted out for his own use but these were destroyed in a serious fire which engulfed a large part of the building in 1961. Much has been restored and Trausnitz today houses part of the state archives.

The university, transferred to Landshut from Ingolstadt in 1800, only had a short life for, in the years 1826–7, it was moved again and was absorbed into the Munich university. A surgical school and a religious establishment for teacher training remained however.

Historical too is the famous pageant, the *Fürstenhochzeit* (Prince's Wedding) which takes place every 4 years in June (1989, 1993, etc). This is probably the greatest folk festival in all Europe and is in memory of Ludwig, Duke of Bavaria (1450–79) who successfully claimed the hand of Hedwig, the 17-year old daughter of Kasimir IV, King of Poland, for his son Georg. Hedwig came to Landshut in the autumn of 1475 with her parents and a 'court' of no less than 642 persons. The wedding celebrations included church-going, jousting and feasting and all this is recalled today when the wedding 'guests' in authentic costume walk from the new to the old town to the sounds of music and bell-ringing with 'Ludwig' in a sedan chair and 'Hedwig' in the golden bridal coach drawn by eight white horses with knights, jesters and gypsies all joining the merry throng.

Because there is so much to see and do in Landshut it is a very good base for the holidaymaker. There are many places of interest within easy touring distance and as the junction of several railway lines, it is equally good for those without their own transport. By train, Munich can be reached in less than an hour, Regensburg in $^3/_4$ hour and Passau in about an hour and twenty minutes.

From Landshut, the Ferienstrasse continues southwards into territory already explored so return to Kelheim to resume the journey down the Danube.

Kelheim to Passau

For the 20km or so to Regensburg the motorist must choose between the pretty rural road on the north bank or the B16 on the south side direct into the heart of the city. The former is more pleasant but the latter provides the opportunity to visit the attractive spa of **Bad Abbach** which lies in between. The usual health resort facilities are available and since 1949, the Bavarian Red Cross has established a Rheumatism Centre here which has won international acclaim as a model clinic. This is no recently developed spa, for as long ago as the sixteenth century the Emperor Karl V came here for the *Kur*. A stop should be made in **Prüfening** on the western outskirts of Regensburg to visit the Benedictine abbey of the same name founded in 1109. In 1114 the bishop introduced monks from the *Kloster* at Hirsau in the Black Forest together with Abbot Erminold from the same place, a supposedly moderate man of God whose discipline was so hard however, that in 1121 he was slain by an enraged monk. The former *Klosterkirche* is now the parish church of St Georg, famed for its ceiling and wall paintings (1130–60) discovered in 1897.

Regensburg is the biggest centre of population in this chapter. With some 135,000 inhabitants it is a busy city and a lively one. It is a bishop's seat and the seat of the government of the Oberpfalz. For a large part of its history it has been a place of royal residence and a centre of trade. The building of the huge cathedral was begun in the

The Prinzess-Conditorei in Regensburg

middle of the thirteenth century but the main work was not finished until 1525. In fact, development, re-development, restoration and improvement have continued right until the present day. It is a curious fact that at the time of its building, the cathedral would have accommodated every citizen of Regensburg three times over.

The former Benedictine *Kloster* of St Emmeram was one of the spiritual centres of Regensburg from the eighth century and was equipped and decorated by the Asam brothers between 1731 and

1733. This is sufficient guarantee of a stimulating visit. The so-called Schottenkirche (Scottish Church) of St Jakob (1160–80) is the best-preserved Romanesque church in Regensburg. In fact, the Benedictine *Kloster* of St Jakob goes back to the wandering Irish monks of the eleventh century who settled here and were followed by countrymen who were wrongly called Scottish. However, at the beginning of the sixteenth century, Scottish Benedictine monks did arrive and they occupied the *Kloster* until 1862. The church now serves as a seminary for the priesthood and is well worth inspection.

The Stadtmuseum has been housed since 1931 in the former Minoritenkirche (1250–70). It must be counted amongst the most comprehensive 'local' museums in Europe with more than 100 rooms of exhibits on three floors of the old church and in two modern

PLACES OF INTEREST IN AND AROUND REGENSBURG

Cathedral
(Thirteenth–sixteenth centuries.)
One of the finest large churches in Bavaria.

Church of St Emmeram
(Eleventh–eighteenth centuries.)
Works by the Asam brothers 1731–3.

'Scottish' Church of St Jakob
(1160–80)
Best-preserved Romanesque church in Regensburg.

Town Museum
Housed in former Minoritenkirche (1250–70). A varied art and culture collection in more than 100 rooms.

Diocesan Museum
Religious art, etc.

Domschatz Museum
Enter through cathedral. Cathedral treasures and religious art.

Town Gallery
Paintings, sculpture, etc. Changing exhibition of modern art.

Palace of the Princes of Thurn and Taxis

Museum showing history of the famous postal service.
Also carriages and stables.

Town Hall
Concerts given in the splendid *Reichssaal*.

Stone Bridge over the Danube (1135–46)

Historic Sausage Kitchen
Close to the stone bridge. Sausage specialities of the region.

Danube Shopping Centre
Near Nibelung bridge. Extensive under-cover complex with shops, banks, bars and restaurants.

Danube Waterfront
Floating museum of river transport in historic paddle-wheel tug. Steamer excursions.

Parish Church of St Georg
In Prüfening 3km W of centre. Former *Klosterkirche*. Ceiling and wall paintings from 1130–60.

Walhalla
In Donaustauf 8km E of centre. Remarkable memorial to national heroes. Copy of the Parthenon.

annexes. The Stadtmuseum is, however, only one of half a dozen museums to be found in the city. Philatelists may learn something of the famous Thurn and Taxis postal service by visiting the museum in the *Schloss*.

Under Franz von Taxis (died 1517), a postal service between west and middle European states had been organised with Brussels–Vienna as its main artery. In 1695 the princely rank was bestowed upon the heads of the family. The headquarters of the postal service had been in Brussels but in 1731 it was moved to Frankfurt to be more central and finally, in 1748, to Regensburg. The various states gradually took over the postal functions for themselves, Bavaria in 1812, Württemberg in 1851 and Prussia finally bought out the rest of the family holdings in 1867 which is the last year the now rare Thurn and Taxis stamps appeared. The full story of this early example of international private enterprise is told in the museum.

Music plays an important role in the life of the city. The famous boys' choir, the Domspatzen (Cathedral Sparrows) sings regularly; in June there are serenade concerts in the cloisters of the museum; June to August is the time for organ recitals in the *Dom* following the April to June concerts in the splendid *Reichssaal* of the town hall.

There is a wide range of eating places in Regensberg and visitors should not fail to sample the delights of a speciality fish inn on the riverside and the Historische Wurstküche (Sausage Kitchen) near the 310m-long (1016ft) Steinerne Brücke, the old stone bridge built in 1135–46. Legend has it that the sausage kitchen was first built to provide meals for workmen building the bridge and the nearby cathedral. On the subject of sausages, a Regensburg speciality is *Schweinebratwürste über Buchenholzkohle gebraten,* little pork sausages grilled over a beechwood charcoal fire. On a quite different level, a call at the Prinzess-Conditorei-Café — said to be the oldest confectioners' shop in Germany — for coffee and cakes is most pleasant. Some of this shop's famous hand-made chocolates such as *Regensbürgerinnen* (Ladies of Regensburg), *Donaumuscheln* (Danube Shell Fish) or *Barbaraküsse* (Barbara's Kisses) make a lovely gift. The excellent shopping facilities in the old town are supplemented by the Donaueinkaufszentrum, an enormous indoor shopping complex north of the river near the Nibelungenbrücke. The *Fremdenverkehrsverein* publishes a useful and inexpensive booklet of suggested outings and rambles.

The turbulence of the Danube water around the piers of the stone bridge is known as the 'Regensburger Strudel' (commemorated in a well known student song) and it follows that the river steamer trip called '*Strudelrundfahrt*' (round trip) has nothing to do with the well known apple pie! There are many river excursions from here, even a voyage as far as Weltenburg beyond Kelheim is possible.

On his way to Italy in 1786 Goethe wrote in his journal, 'Regensburg's situation is enchanting.' Four years later, Mozart was also favourably impressed, recording that he '. . . had a delicious lunch and drank an excellent wine to the accompaniment of divine music.'

A few kilometres downstream from Regensburg at **Donaustauf**

Walhalla

is the gigantic national monument Walhalla. From Easter until the end of October it can be reached from Regensburg by steamer — 358 marble steps to climb from the pier! Walhalla, on a small hill called Breuberg, is a copy of the Parthenon in Athens. Fifty-two columns 9m high (30ft) and 1.7m (5ft) wide at the base and the temple walls are also of marble. The building is 20m (66ft) high and covers an area of 2100sq m. Double doors 6.7m (22ft) high close the entrance, each leaf weighing 2.1 tons.

Why is a Greek temple on the banks of the Danube called Walhalla, the name of the place where according to Norse legend, Odin received the fallen heroes? Inevitably it was another brainchild of Ludwig I who wanted to create a shrine where German 'heroes' could be honoured for all time. Busts of the famous were installed and by the time of the opening in 1842 no less than 162 suitable persons had already been identified. The 'German' qualification is interpreted freely and the busts include those of Dutch, Swiss and other national notables. The king laid an obligation upon his successors to continually review the ranks of the famous and since 1945 the Bavarian government has added nine more marble busts. This impressive monument occupies a very fine vantage point above the river. A car park near the top saves the motorist the steep climb.

It is possible to make the rest of the journey to Passau by steamer but most holidaymakers would find this too time-consuming. The motorist has the advantage of flexibility over this section but the train traveller can still reach many worthwhile places. After leaving Walhalla the motorist should continue eastwards and after passing the vineyard village of Kruckenberg in about 8km, turn left to arrive after about another 6km at the Benedictine Kloster Frauenzell. Of the fourteenth-century church only a tower remains. The rest was pulled down in 1747 to make way for a new church to be built by 'the most famous and excellent artists' of the day. The abbot had the Asam brothers in mind but they were occupied with the Ursulinen church in Straubing and a somewhat motley collection of artists — although all of good repute — was assembled instead. It is well worth making the short detour away from the Danube to see this fine church.

Back on the main road, arrive at the little town of **Wörth** (population 2000); its *Schloss* was originally built in the twelfth century but most of the present building is from the sixteenth and seventeenth centuries. Since 1812 it has been owned by the princes of Thurn and Taxis. The artist Albrecht Altdorfer painted the Danube landscape with Schloss Wörth in 1520 and his painting (now in the Munich Alte Pinakothek) is regarded as the earliest landscape of the European school. Wörth is a pleasant place for a peaceful holiday and well sited for excursions into the Bavarian Forest.

Leaving Wörth, pass under the motorway (A3) to reach **Straubing** (population 45,000) in about 20km. Perhaps the biggest surprise is that Straubing is the home of an ancient festival which, in scale, comes a close second to the famous Munich *Oktoberfest* and yet is virtually unheard of outside Germany. The *Gäubodenvolksfest* takes place every year for 2 weeks in mid-August. In 1812 the king directed that there should be a regular agricultural show to display the achievements of the fertile area known as Gäuboden; the agricultural aspect is still of prime importance with some 400 exhibitors showing their wares and there are numerous specialist exhibits and displays. Over the years, the show has gradually come to be supported by a folk festival featuring an enormous fairground with a Ferris wheel, roundabouts, dodgems etc. Seven beer halls cater for nearly a million visitors to the show each year. Then every 4 years (1988, 1992 etc) there is a production of the Straubing folk play *Agnes Bernauer* which tells of the tragic death in 1435 of a beautiful girl of humble parentage who had fallen in love with Duke Albrecht III — and he with her — but for whom there was no happy ending due to family objections.

The former monastery church at Frauenzell

Straubing was once the Roman fort Sorviodurum, where a detachment of the Third Italian Legion from Regensburg was stationed. The Romans fled before Alemannic invaders in 233 but before doing so somebody buried a valuable hoard of beaten gold masks, leg protectors, etc, no doubt with the idea of retrieving the booty later. He did not do so and it was only in 1950 that the valuable relics were unearthed and they are now in the Gäuboden Museum.

The oldest church in Straubing is St Peter's, originally founded in 1029 and rebuilt in the late twelfth century as a three-naved Romanesque basilica. The cemetery of St Peter is worth inspection; there are three chapels there and the Agnes Bernauer chapel is of special interest for its memorial to that unhappy girl. Several other churches, including St Jakob and a Carmelite church are well worth seeing but the visitor should at least visit the Klosterkirche St Ursula, a remarkable work by the Asam brothers. The jubilation of the colours, frescos and altars has been compared with the 'Hallelujah Chorus' from Handel's *Messiah* which received its first performance in 1742, the year in which this beautiful church was consecrated.

From September to May there are regular performances in the town theatre and from time to time chamber music and other concerts are given in the historic town hall. There is also the near-unique spectacle of trotting races which take place regularly and, once a week, by floodlight. Straubing is a stopping place for the passenger ships between Regensburg and Passau but the river is mainly busy with commercial traffic. The town has the only zoo in east Bavaria.

Continuing downstream leave the town over the Danube bridge and follow signs for Bogen until, in about 8km, **Oberalteich** is reached. Here, the former Benedictine abbey (731) is the site of the present *Klosterkirche* of St Peter (1622–9) with rich baroque and rococo decoration including two altar paintings by C.D. Asam. This imposing double-towered church is one of the notable memorials to Bavarian baroque. **Bogen** is a town of 7000 inhabitants on the edge of the Bayerischer Wald overlooked by the Bogenberg (432m, 1417ft) with splendid views all round. The Bogenberg has prehistoric ramparts and unusual plants are to be found here but most visitors make the climb to visit the late Gothic pilgrimage church of 1463.

True to a vow made in 1492, a special 2-day pilgrimage takes place each Whitsun. On the Saturday, farmers from Holzkirchen 60km away, set off early in the morning, two of them carrying the 13m-high (43ft) Whitsun candle — a tree trunk coated in wax and weighing 60kg. They take a midday break at the monastery brewery in Niederalteich and then continue to Deggendorf for an overnight stop, leaving the candle in the Church of the Holy Sepulchre. On arriving at the Bogenberg on Whit Sunday, the candle is then carried upright by one man for the last stage of the journey. Several picturesque roads go from Bogen into the heart of the forest but those without transport will find ample scope for walking on well marked paths within 10 or 15km.

The route continues in a general south-easterly direction (signs 'Deggendorf') and in about 20km, before entering the town, reaches the Benedictine *Kloster* of **Metten**. The *Kloster* church is yet another example of Bavarian baroque at its best. Once again the artistic achievements of C.D. Asam are in evidence. In the east wing of the *Kloster* buildings is the library, a little jewel of baroque ornamentation, which should not be missed. There are numerous other richly decorated apartments and the visitor will be rewarded for a little time spent here.

Deggendorf (population 22,500) is one of several towns claiming the title 'Gateway to the Bavarian Forest' and in this case with very good reason. It is a busy market town and shopping centre, the market place — Luitpoldplatz — being dominated by the free-standing late Gothic *Rathaus* with its distinctive stepped gable. The building dates from 1535 and embraces the town tower, begun in the fourteenth

PLACES OF INTEREST ALONG THE DANUBE EAST OF REGENSBURG — 1

FRAUENZELL (7km N of Wörth *Autobahn* exit.)
Benedictine Kloster Church
(1747)
Beautiful baroque in a rural situation.

WÖRTH
Palace
(Mainly sixteenth–seventeenth centuries.) Owned by princes of Thurn and Taxis. Subject of famous painting by Altdorfer.

STRAUBING
Market Place, Town Hall

Gäuboden Mueum
Exhibits include valuable Roman relics.

St Peter's Church
(Twelfth century.) Cemetery with Agnes Bernauer Chapel.

Kloster Church of St Ursula
(1742)
Joyful baroque by Asam brothers.

Zoo
1km W of town centre. Wide variety of animals. Tropical bird house.

OBERALTEICH
Kloster Church of St Peter
(1622–9)
Rich baroque and rococo.

METTEN
Kloster Church
Baroque at its best. Beautiful library.

DEGGENDORF
Market Place with distinctive late **Gothic Town Hall**

Heimatmuseum
Rural implements and folklore.

Church of the Holy Sepulchre (1337–60)
Beautiful baroque bell tower (1727).

Parish Church of the Assumption
Near the Danube bridge. Canopied high altar (1749).

Pilgrimage Church of Maria Schmerzen (1486–7)
On the Geiersberg (379m, 4874ft). Memorial tablets, wonderful view.

NIEDERALTEICH
Benedictine Abbey Church of St Mauritius
Charming baroque with interesting frescos. Buildings house educational establishments.

OSTERHOFEN/ALTENMARKT
Damenstiftskirche (1138)
Later works by the Asam brothers including some of C.D's finest painting.

century and reaching its present form in 1790. Opposite is the *Heimatmuseum* with a comprehensive display of rural implements and folklore. The Church of the Holy Sepulchre is a Gothic basilica

PLACES OF INTEREST ALONG THE DANUBE EAST OF REGENSBURG — 2

ALDERSBACH
Cistercian Abbey Church
Rebuilt about 1720 with baroque ornamentation by Asam brothers.

AIDENBACH
Worth a visit for its attractive market place.

VILSHOFEN
Renaissance Tower (1747)
A prominent feature of the interesting old town centre.

ORTENBURG
Renaissance Palace and Museum
Fine wooden ceilings (seventeenth century) and wall paintings. Deer park. Inn nearby.

FÜRSTENZELL
Cistercian Kloster Church (started 1739) **and buildings** (1687)
Beautiful library.

built between 1337 and 1360. The slender bell-tower was added in 1727, one of the most beautiful baroque towers in Bavaria. The parish church Maria Himmelfahrt in the lower town near the 416m-long (1364ft) Danube bridge has a canopied high altar (1749) originally intended for the cathedral in Eichstätt. The late Gothic pilgrimage church of Maria Schmerzen (1486–7) in the nature reserve on the Geiersberg (379m, 1243ft) has a collection of votive tablets and a wonderful view as well.

Leisure activities are well provided for and there are 70km of *Langlauf* (cross-country) skiing trails. In **Rusel**, 10km north-east of the town, there is a *Langlauf* centre — details from the *Verkehrsamt* in Deggendorf. This is outstanding rambling or cycling country and there is ample rural farmhouse accommodation. Tour suggestions from the *Verkehrsamt*. The annual folk festival takes place at the end July/beginning of August, events — including horse racing — taking place over about 10 days. For those wishing to spend a holiday in a place with a good range of facilities and interests yet not in one of the larger cities, it would be hard to better Deggendorf.

About 8km beyond Deggendorf is the *Erholungsort* **Hengersberg** (population 5500) with modern facilities and looked down upon by two hill-top churches, Michaelskirche on the Rohrberg and Maria Himmelfahrt on the Frauenberg. Both of are of interest.

Nearby is the Benedictine abbey Niederalteich whose continuous and rich history came to an end with secularisation in 1803 when many of the interior appointments were stolen and the buildings partially destroyed. Only in 1918 was it possible for the abbey to be re-occupied and today it is a centre for education and the furthering of Christian unity. New buildings erected in 1965 house an ecumenical institute, a boarding grammar school and an educational centre for the dioceses of Regensburg and Passau. The church, dedicated to St Mauritius, is a charming baroque building with frescos honouring all those who previously led the order here, amongst them St Gotthard, abbot and later bishop of Hildesheim. The famous St Gotthard Pass and tunnel in Switzerland is named after this first Bavarian-born saint.

The motorist could now join the *Autobahn* to reach the city of Passau in about half an hour but there are several more places of interest on the south side of the Danube. In fine weather there is a ferry near Niederalteich or the next bridge is a few kilometres downstream. A route taking in some of the following is recommended: **Oster-hofen/Altenmarkt** (Damenstiftskirche — works by the Asam brothers), **Aldersbach** (another fine 'Asam' church), **Aidenbach** (attractive *Marktplatz*), **Vilshofen** (old town centre and churches), **Ortenburg** (*Schloss* and deer park), **Fürstenzell** (Cistercian *Kloster* church and buildings).

And so to **Passau**. It is difficult to know what to say first about this delightful city. Passau has more than 52,000 inhabitants and is the most easterly Bavarian city. It stands at the confluence of the Danube, Inn and Ilz rivers and there has been a settlement here from the earliest times; the Romans, with an eye for strategic locations, built a fort here in AD 80. Today, this lively city stands with one foot in Austria, for that part known as the Innstadt is the only part of Germany south of the rivers, the Austrian border having been obligingly bent inland to accommodate it. Upstream, the Inn itself forms the border and downstream, the Danube does so. It is hardly surprising that the rivers have played an important role in the history of the place and that today they continue to have considerable influence on its life and culture.

A cruise to the Orient can begin here, for from the middle of March until the middle of October there are sailings to places as far distant as Yalta on the Black Sea and Istanbul. The longest of these cruises takes 3 weeks, possibly on a Russian ship; in some cases the return journey can be made by air. Thus does Passau claim the title 'Gateway to the Balkans'; it could equally be the Gateway to the Bavarian Forest or to the upper Danube, of course.

Few European cities can boast a finer situation and not only the river and hill scenery around but the architectural treasures of the city itself are a constant delight to the eye. As one might suspect, there is something not quite 'Bavarian' about it. The Inn has brought a taste of the building styles of its valley downstream but, at the same time, some of the streetscapes are reminiscent of towns south of the Alps or perhaps Passau has been influenced by the mysterious east.

Passau is sufficiently small and compact to be explored on foot — indeed, this is the only way and there is no better place to start than at the *Dom* of St Stephan. There is a convenient multi-storey car park just north of the cathedral. There was a church on this site at the beginning of the sixth century and already in the middle of the eighth a church was built which carried the name of St Stephan; of the late Gothic building (1407–1530) parts of the choir and transept, later overlaid with baroque decoration, were incorporated in the later cathedral. A serious fire in 1662 almost totally destroyed the main aisle; financial considerations did not allow construction of a completely new building so parts of the old were used. The 'join' is undetectable and in the course of 20 years' work, the biggest high baroque church in Bavaria with a length of 101m (330ft), width 33m (108ft), dome 69m (226ft) high and two west towers 68m (223ft) high was created. G.B. Carlone was entrusted with the stucco work with his partner Paul d'Aglio and sixteen workers and this took 8 years to complete. The frescos were painted at the same time.

The exterior of the cathedral has been 'improved' on several occasions over the years and the west towers were only given their present domes (based on Salzburg Cathedral) in 1897. A thorough renovation of the building was completed in 1980 and during the work the opportunity was taken to catalogue the thousand or so figures which Carlone had created. Sheer size apart, this church may not have as much impact on the visitor as do some of the smaller, more intimate and more colourful baroque churches of Bavaria but it does have one outstanding asset. It is the home of the biggest church organ in the world, a modern instrument built 1978–81 by Ludwig and Wolfgang Eisenbarth as a development of the Steinmeyer organ of 1928. In fact it consists of no less than five independent organs, all of which can be played from the main five-manual keyboard. To the left of the main altar area is the choir organ, invisible above the main aisle the 'echo' organ, in the gallery at the west end there is the main organ and keyboard in the centre, in the north side nave the so-called 'gospel' organ and in the south side the 'epistle' organ. The potential of this vast instrument with its 17,388 pipes and 231 registers is

Passau   Cathedral

demonstrated each weekday from the beginning of May until the end of October between 12 noon and 12.30pm with a longer concert on Thursdays from 7.30pm. There is a modest admission charge at these times and to be sure of obtaining entry it is advisable to be there about half an hour before the recital is to start.

From the cathedral west doors face the rectangular Domplatz, originally intended to provide a clear view of the imposing façade but now often full of parked cars. The finest baroque façade of the sur- rounding buildings belongs to the Palais Lamberg (1724) which today houses the Diocesan Museum. Round the south side of the *Dom* (Zengergasse) are historic buildings with ecclesiastical origins. Enter the Residenzplatz which takes its name from the 'new' bishops' Residenz of the seventeenth century. Leaving behind the Wittelsbach fountain turn eastward into the Grosse Messergasse from which several narrow alleys lead steeply down to the Danube and to the *Rathaus* facing the river and steamer quays across its courtyard.

Some small but excellent restaurants are to be be found in the alleys and the town hall has its own fine restaurant, the Ratskeller. As in many other towns which were the seats of bishops or prince-bishops, the citizens had difficulty in obtaining land for their own town hall and it was not until 1393–1405 that they were able to construct a purpose-built *Rathaus*. That building had to be demolished in 1811

PLACES OF INTEREST IN PASSAU

Cathedral of St Stephan
(Earliest parts 1407.)
Later baroque treatment. World's biggest church organ.

Palais Lamberg (1724)
Now the Diocesan Museum. Stands with other baroque buildings round the cathedral square.

Town Hall (1890)
Superior restaurant, the Ratskeller.

Former Jesuit Church of St Michael
Ornate interior decor (seventeenth century).

State Library in former St Michael buildings
Italian stucco.

Church of the Holy Cross
(Thirteenth century.)
Various architectural styles.

Inn Promenade and Schaiblingsturm
Favoured spot for artists.

Veste Oberhaus
Former fortress on N bank of Danube, now the city museum and art gallery.

and the present town hall with its mighty tower was only built in 1890.

With the Danube behind, a few minutes walk through the Milchgasse leads to the former Jesuit church of St Michael with ornate interior decoration of the seventeenth century, in part, at least, by associates of Carlone. The associated buildings now house the Leopoldinum grammar school and the state library. The old library with stucco decoration in the Italian style is worth seeing. Nearby Kloster Niedernburg dates from the eighth century. Its buildings now provide homes for two girls' schools under the auspices of the Englischen Fräulein and only the Church of the Holy Cross is normally open to the public. It was mainly built in the thirteenth century but has been much altered at different times and thus exhibits architecture from many different periods.

From here it is a pleasant short walk right out to the tip of the tongue of land between the two big rivers. A walk back beside the Inn leads to the picturesque Schaiblingsturm, a relic of old fortifications and a favourite subject for artists. Returning to the Danube quay opposite the *Rathaus* boats leave for the Three Rivers Excursion — Danube, Ilz and Inn. The trip takes about 45 minutes and boats leave every 30 minutes during the high season. High above the Danube on the north bank is the fortress Veste Oberhaus which today contains the town museum and art gallery. Here, with magnificent views, is a 200-bed youth hostel. The art gallery and museum are well worth a visit and from May to October there is a regular bus service (No 9) from the town centre, avoiding the stiff climb. Incidentally, to avoid the hassle of town centre parking, the motorist could leave his vehicle up here at Oberhaus and use the bus service to reach the town.

Music plays an important part in the rich cultural life of Passau. In addition to a major international festival from mid-June until the beginning of August there are concerts, operas, operettas, etc throughout the year. There is a consumers' fair in April and the *Maidult* at the beginning of May. On the first Sunday of the *Dult* there is a procession with about 4000 participants in costume and some twenty bands from different parts of Bavaria and Austria. About the second week in September is the *Herbstdult* (Autumn Fair) while December sees the great Christmas fair, the *Christkindlmarkt*.

The traveller determined to follow the Danube out of Bavaria can travel the remaining 20km along the quite pretty north bank to the Austrian border. Of interest on the way is **Obernzell** (population 3600) where the fifteenth-century recently restored *Schloss* is now a museum of ceramics. The Marktkirche is a baroque building from 1745 and has a carved wooden pulpit, while the fifteenth-century late Gothic parish church above the village has a pulpit of granite, a material obtained in the nearby hills. Many fairly easy walks can be started here including one into the Erlautal where there is a *Wald-lehrpfad*. Boat hire, water-skiing and angling are amongst the Danube-based activities here. Around 370km in river distance from its entry into Bavaria at Neu-Ulm the Danube disappears now into Austria to flow eastwards for another 2200km to its mouth in the Black Sea.

8 FRANCONIAN SELECTION

In previous chapters, the fringes of Franconia (Franken) have been briefly touched upon but the central part of this largest constituent of Bavaria remains to be discovered.

Between Bayreuth and Bavaria's northern boundary lies the Frankenwald (Franconian Forest), an area of peace and beauty. Less than 20km north of Bayreuth and reached quickly on the A9 to the Bad Berneck exit, then the B303, is the outstanding Deutsches Dampf- lokomotiv Museum (Steam Locomotive Museum) at **Neuenmarkt** with dozens of engines from all over Germany, a must for every railway enthusiast. A little to the west, the Plassenburg in **Kulmbach** houses the Deutsches Zinnfiguren Museum, a collection of over 300,000 'tin' soldiers and other figures.

The B85 is a picturesque road to **Kronach** (population 12,000). Seek out the upper town, the old part, with its 800-year- old castle, the birthplace of the famous painter Lukas Cranach and many other historic sights. From Kronach, road and railway disappear together into the forest, dense between the small towns and villages. The B85 now leads right up to the barbed wire of the 'Iron Curtain'. From **Pressig** an alternative westerly route closely follows the frontier through splendid scenery. Around **Ludwigsstadt** the forest retreats a little, making way in summer for a colourful array of tents in this favourite camping and bathing area. Just a kilometre or so before the Federal Road is snuffed out by the arbitrary frontier, the village of **Lauenstein** lies at the foot of the hill topped by the Mantelburg, an attractive castle taken over by the state and restored at considerable cost for the pleasure of today's sightseers. In the Burghotel, a year-round 7-day package holiday enables guests to live for a little while in a genuine medieval atmosphere, surrounded by hunting trophies, ancient weapons, antique furniture and four-poster beds. As a concession to the twentieth century, central heating has been installed

PLACES OF INTEREST NORTH OF BAYREUTH

NEUENMARKT
German Steam Locomotive Museum

KULMBACH
German Museum of 'Tin' Soldiers etc.
In the Plassenburg. More than 300,000 figures in 220 dioramas.

KRONACH
Historic upper town with ancient castle. Birthplace of painter Lukas Cranach.

MARKTRODACH
Logging Museum
History of timber rafts etc in Frankenwald. Working models.

LAUENSTEIN
Mantelburg Castle
Now a comfortable hotel.

and the picturesque tiled stoves put into retirement. Lauenstein, with its Mantelburg landmark, is known as the 'Pearl of the Frankenwald'. The southern part of the Frankenwald is drained by the Weisser (white) Main and Roter (red) Main rivers, soon to merge and become the Main proper for the westward journey to the Rhine.

The River Main forms the south border of an area to the west with the city of **Coburg** (population 50,000) at its centre. It lies beneath its immense fortress, Veste Coburg, one of the biggest castles ever built. The fortress was a bulwark against the incursions of the Slavs: today it is a bulwark of German culture and art, for the enormous building is a museum of massive proportions with collections of treasures of all kinds and works of the great masters of the past. The Coburgers are proud of their connection with the British royal family for Albert of Coburg was the consort of Queen Victoria. Her statue now stands in the town which also boasts the 'Edinburgh Palace' and the 'Windsor Castle' façade of the royal riding school. Even earlier is the 'English' Gothic of Schloss Ehrenburg, the imposing seat of the dukes of Coburg, with interior decoration from the seventeenth to nineteenth centuries. From the Schlossplatz in front of Ehrenburg, enter the highly esteemed *Hofgarten* for a pleasant walk up to the fortress above — a little over 1km. The town centre contains many buildings of interest in a compact area but with a maze of one-way streets the motorist would be wise to leave his vehicle on the outskirts and walk the remaining short distance.

An excursion to **Neustadt bei Coburg**, 12km north-east, is recommended for a visit to the Trachtenpuppenmuseum with over 1000 dolls dressed in national costumes from all over the world.

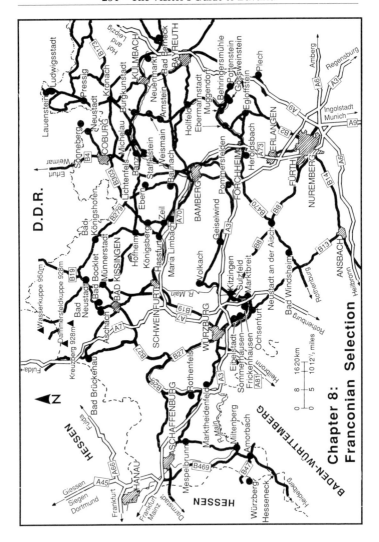

Neustadt, known as the 'doll town', is barely 5km from the old south Thuringian world toy centre of Sonneberg in East Germany.

Many of the places along the Main valley are worth visiting: **Burgkunstadt** is a little town of old timbered houses, **Michelau**, the

*The fortress
Veste Coburg*

'basket town' with the world's only basket museum, **Lichtenfels**
(population 14,000), another basket town with remains of fortifications from the fourteenth century and a pretty baroque *Rathaus* from
1743 (Heinrich Dientzenhofer). The big attraction here is the pilgrimage church Vierzehnheiligen overlooking the valley from the south
slope. Its history goes back to a shepherd who, in 1445–6, had visions
of the Christ Child and the fourteen auxiliary saints or helpers to whom
the faithful prayed for their earthly needs. Pilgrims soon started to visit
the holy place where first a cross was erected, later a chapel and then

---

PLACES OF INTEREST IN AND NEAR COBURG

Veste Coburg
Enormous castle, now a magnificent museum and art gallery.

Ehrenburg Palace
'English' Gothic. Interior decoration of seventeenth to nineteenth
centuries.

Court Garden
Fine gardens leading up to the
fortress.

Statue of Queen Victoria

**Royal Riding School with
'Windsor Castle' façade**

**Museum of Dolls in National
Costumes**
In Neustadt 12km NE. More than
1000 dolls from all over the world.

The pilgrimage church of Vierzehnheiligen

a church. For the 300th anniversary of the vision it was decided to build a new church and Balthasar Neumann created here his most beautiful church in Franconia with the aid of such famous craftsmen as the Feuchtmayr brothers and J.G. Üblherr. The ceiling frescos are considered to be amongst the finest achievements of the period.

Facing Vierzehnheiligen from the north bank of the Main is the former Benedictine abbey of **Banz**. A church was consecrated here in 1114 but it was destroyed in the Thirty Years' War. J. Dientzenhofer was responsible for the present building (1710-19) while his brother J.L. was in charge of the rebuilding of the *Kloster* complex. The gatehouse wing in the main courtyard (1752) was to plans by Balthasar Neumann. The rich architectural style of the church is late baroque with the interior decoration in early rococo. Approaching the façade, note the dramatic expressions of the saints in the various niches. Inside, the ceiling frescos are most striking and there are outstanding choir stalls, high altar, choir altar and pulpit. Banz is best approached from **Staffelstein** (population 6000) by a road to the

Detail on a building in Sulzfeld

The pilgrimage church of Maria Limbach

Hotel Riesen,
Miltenberg

Berg Rothenfels

SOME PLACES OF INTEREST IN THE MAIN VALLEY

MICHELAU
Basket Museum
Unique history of basket-making
through the ages.

LICHTENFELS
Town Hall (1743)
Pretty baroque.

**Pilgrimage Church
Vierzehnheiligen** (1745)

Beautiful baroque by Balthasar
Neumann.

STAFFELSTEIN
Town Hall
(Seventeenth century.)
Picturesque timbered building.

**Former Benedictine Abbey
of Banz** (1710–19)
Impressive late baroque and early
rococo.

right of the picturesque seventeenth-century timbered *Rathaus*.

South of the River Main, the so-called Fränkische Schweiz (Franconian Switzerland) runs for some 60km south towards Nürnberg (Nuremberg). South of Burgkunstadt (see above), a route through the rocky, romantic Kleinziegenfelder Tal enables the traveller to stop briefly in **Weismain** with its beautiful Renaissance *Rathaus,* or in **Arnstein** with the Catholic parish church of St Nikolaus (1732–4) by Balthasar Neumann. The charms of the countryside have attracted many artists and people of leisure with a taste for good living. Fürst Pückler, creator of famous gardens and gourmet of repute, found 'trout, cherries and crayfish nowhere better than in **Muggendorf**', a delightful little town and health resort which can still provide a memorable meal. The charming valley of the River Wiesent with derelict water mills, narrow gorges, rocky cliffs topped by grim castles, caverns, towns and villages and fine old *Gasthöfe* is an experience in itself. The pilgrimage church of **Gössweinstein** was created by Neumann around 1730. Apart from the religious significance, the delightful stucco — now in new delicate colours — and the early rococo sculptures attract art lovers from all over the world. The nearby palace-like 'parsonage' was erected as the summer residence of a later prince-bishop.

The crenellated Burg Gössweinstein nearby is thought by some to have been the inspiration for the Gralsburg in Wagner's *Parsifal*. This may be unlikely although the great composer did have a summer retreat in Muggendorf where a popular viewpoint is called Wagnershöhe. The castle is occupied, but from time to time, the Rittersaal (Knights' Hall) is thrown open for musical entertainment.

PLACES OF INTEREST IN FRANCONIAN SWITZERLAND

WEISMAIN
Town Hall
Beautiful Renaissance building.

ARNSTEIN
Parish Church of
St Nikolaus (1732–4)
By Balthasar Neumann.

RIVER WIESENT VALLEY
Delightful route of gorges, cliffs,
castles and caverns.

GÖSSWEINSTEIN
Pilgrimage Church (about
1730)
Another creation of Neumann.
Very fine early rococo sculptures.

Pretty Hill-top Castle

POTTENSTEIN
Charming town under steep cliffs.

Devil's Caverns
Splendid caves with stalactites
and stalagmites.

BEHRINGERSMÜHLE
Lovely little health resort. Terminus of steam railway to Ebermannstadt.

NEAR EGLOFFSTEIN
Wildgehege Hundshaupten
Zoo with many varieties of deer
and birds, also bison and other
animals in natural surroundings.
Trout and carp ponds.

PLECH
Franconian Wonderland
Leisure park with fairy -tale
themes, miniature railway, *Rodel-*
bahn, etc.

Pottenstein (population 3000 is another charming little town
nestling under steep cliffs. An annual spectacle takes place on the
festival of the Three Kings, 6 January, when there is a torchlight
procession and the hills and cliffs all round are ablaze with bonfires
and there is a sea of flickering light from thousands of torches. Close
to Gössweinstein, the *Luftkurort* of **Behringersmühle** on the River
Wiesent is beautifully situated amongst hills and woods at the conver-
gence of four valleys.

An interesting ramble from here also takes in Gössweinstein and
Pottenstein. From the Hotel Stern, walk along the Promenadenweg
above the Wiesent (waymark red X) to the Gasthof Stempfermühle.
In front of the Gasthof a well kept path with serpentine curves (waymark blue dot) goes off to the left and leads through woods with rocky
outcrops to the car park at Gössweinstein. Two hundred metres along
the main street is the great basilica. The Pottenstein road is then followed down to the end of the village to a filling station where the
Wanderweg (vertical blue stripe) goes off to the left. After passing a
Waldcafé continue through the hamlet of **Bösenbirkig** at the south

L-M
••••
△△△
15km

end of which the path goes sharp left to quickly reach tiny **Hühnerloh**. Continue to follow the waymark, cross a road and enter the wood again. About 100m later, watch for the waymark where the path goes left into a small forest track and follow it until it crosses a little road. The path goes through fields for about 200m and then along the edge of a wood. A gentle climb leads to the hill, the Kreuzberg, with its Kreuzigungskapelle above Pottenstein. There is a wonderful view here into the Püttlachtal and down on to Pottenstein .

Walk down to Pottenstein.This is a much-visited town with fine old timbered houses. Behind the Catholic church there is a steep path (350 steps) up to the Teufelshöhle, splendid caves with stalactites and stalagmites, the biggest in the Fränkische Schweiz and well worth a visit. From Pottenstein leave the town on the Behringers-mühle road (B470) and in about 250m turn left onto a beautiful path (red X), passing the Bärenschlucht (ravine) with its camping place and in about 4km reach **Tüchersfeld**, sometimes called the 'Rock Village of the Fränkische Schweiz' with its impressive cliffs reminis-cent of the Dolomites and houses perched in apparently precarious situations. Below the mill, cross the B470 and in about 150m bear right into the continuation of the *Wanderweg* following the red X back into Behringersmühle. The map for this area is the Fritsch edition, 1:50,000 *Innere Fränkische Schweiz*. Between Behringersmühle and **Ebermannstadt** to the west, 16km of former Federal line has been taken over by a railway preservation society, making it possible once more to travel by train through part of the delightful Wiesenttal.

A large variety of animals and birds in natural surroundings can be found in the Hundshaupten *Wildgehege* 10km south of the B470 and midway between the A73 and A9 motorways. Close to the **Plech** exit on the A9 is the Fränkisches Wunderland, a leisure park with many different amusements for the family — fairy-tale themes, a miniature railway, Wild West scenes, a *Rodelbahn* and so on. Another similar place is the Familien-Freizeitpark Schloss Thurn at **Heroldsbach** near Forchheim westwards along the B470.

Near the south end of the Fränkische Schweiz is **Nuremberg**, the Franconian metropolis, with well over half a million inhabitants and the second city in Bavaria. The visitor would find no difficulty in spending many days sightseeing here, visiting the numerous muse-ums, enjoying the gastronomic specialities of the area or just wander-ing through the old streets, now beautifully restored from the destruc-tion of World War II. Nuremberg is famous for many things and only a small selection are mentioned here but more details of museums etc

The Nuremberg Christmas market by night

can be found in 'Further Information'.

The well known *Nürnberger Lebkuchen*, spicy little cakes or biscuits, come in many guises and are exported the world over but are sold here in all sorts of attractive containers. The city has long been known as a toy-making centre and there is an annual fair. The Spielzeugmuseum (Toy Museum) is a wonderful experience but those with a special interest in railways or philately should visit the Verkehrsmuseum (Transport Museum), Germany's foremost exhibition of transport — especially railway — and postal history. The first railway in this country, between Nuremberg and Fürth nearby, was opened on 7 December 1835 and the locomotive *Adler*, built by George Stephenson in Newcastle-upon-Tyne in England, supplied the motive power. The original engine no longer exists but the museum has an excellent replica. That railway may be travelled upon in miniature from Easter until October in Nuremberg's excellent zoo.

Art lovers may wish to visit the Albrecht Dürer House built in 1450–60 in the Gothic style where the artist lived from 1509–28. The National Museum exhibits German art and cultural history from prehistoric times to the present. Significant churches in Nuremberg include St Sebaldus (Protestant) (1230–40) based on Bamberg Cathedral with many works of art. St Lorenz, Protestant and begun in the

Nuremberg old town with St Sebaldus' church and the castle

late thirteenth century, looks very similar . The Catholic Frauenkirche was built on the site of an old synagogue which had been destroyed along with the Jewish quarter in the fourteenth century. Kaiser Karl V made the present building his court church in 1355. The only baroque building in Gothic Nuremberg is the church of St Egidien (1696).

The *Christkindlmarkt* in Nuremberg is usually reckoned to be Germany's oldest Christmas market. It started in 1639 and begins each year on the Friday nearest to St Barbara's Day (4 December) and remains open until Christmas Eve. It is held in the square by the Schöner Brunnen (fountain). Every 2 years a local 'Christ Child' is chosen to open the market by reciting a prologue from the outside gallery of the Frauenkirche to an accompaniment of festive music and church bells. Be warned that on the opening day at least, Nuremberg is a very crowded city indeed.

North from Nuremberg, the A73 provides a speedy means of reaching **Bamberg** 63km away. Bamberg (population 80,000) escaped relatively unscathed from World War II and now has probably the finest concentration of historic buildings in original condition in Bavaria. One can wander happily through the streets and alleys but it is a pity to visit Bamberg without spending some time enjoying the various works of art and architecture. As in other towns, it is best on foot and a suitable circuit can be started at the Löwenbrücke (Lion

PLACES OF INTEREST IN NUREMBERG

German National Museum
Art and culture, sculpture, paintings, toys, etc.

Toy Museum
Comprehensive display of toys through the ages. Large model railway.

Transport Museum
Strong in railway and postal history.

Zoo
One of the best in Europe. Children's zoo. Miniature railway operates Easter–October.

Albrecht Dürer House
(1450–60)
Home of the artist 1509–28.

St Sebaldus Church
(1230–40)
Based on Bamberg Cathedral. Many art works.

St Lorenz Church
(Thirteenth century.)
Many art works.

Frauenkirche
Court church of the Emperor from 1355.

Church of St Egidien (1696)
The only baroque building in Nuremberg.

Schöner Brunnen
Beautiful fountain in square near the Frauenkirche.

Bridge) over the right arm of the River Regnitz. The motorist can park in the nearby Weidendamm *Parkplatz*: the rail traveller should walk west from the station to reach the bridge. From here Markusstrasse runs directly to the Markusbrücke over the left Regnitz arm in about 400m. From the bridge, to the left, is so-called Klein Venedig (Little Venice) with the colourful backs of old fishermen's houses on the water's edge, a favourite photographer's scene. At night, a coin in a slot machine will switch on the flood-lighting!

Over the bridge turn left into Sandstrasse and into the first alley on the right (Schrottenberggasse). In Ottoplatz, turn right again and keep bearing right up to the Michaelsberg. Continue forward along the left side of the church for a fine view over the Bamberg basin and turn back to leave the Michaelsberg via the Storchsgasse and then left to go down the Jacobsberg when this is reached. Go through an arch and to the right in front of the archbishop's palace to explore a quiet medieval area of ivy-clad and timbered buildings, the canons' houses where time seems to have stood still. A gateway leads to the inner courtyard of the Alten Hofhaltung (Residenz) and out into a wide square with architecture hardly equalled in Europe. Here is the great cathedral of Emperor Heinrich II and opposite, the new Residenz.

PLACES OF INTEREST IN BAMBERG

Little Venice
Colourful old fishermen's houses on River Regnitz.

Cathedral (1215–37)
Romanesque three-aisled basilica. Noted portals and sculptures and famous 'Bamberg Horseman'.

St Michael's Church (1121)
Famous 'botanical garden' ceiling.

Upper Parish Church (1338)
Famous 'marriage' doorway.

Diocesan Museum
Cathedral treasures, etc.

Karl-May-Museum
Memorabilia of the author.

Old Residenz
Renaissance building now housing the history museum.

New Residenz (1697–1703)
Early palace in baroque style. Now houses part of Bavarian State Art Collection.

Town Hall
Striking building on an island in river.

Continue through the Judenstrasse at the end of which, on the right, is the charming patrician Böttingerhaus. The Palais Concordia (also probably built for the Böttinger family) is to the right in its town park laid out in the so-called 'English' style. Go left down to the river at the Nonnenbrücke but turn left along the bank of the old King Ludwig I canal back towards the town centre. The Regnitz water still foams around the bottoms of old mills and, turning right to cross the river, see what must surely be one of the most photographed buildings in the north of Bavaria, the old town hall perched on a tiny island in the river, joined to the banks either side by bridges with the road passing through the middle of the building. The citizens wanted some land for their town hall and the prince-bishops reluctantly agreed to make a plot available, only for the townsfolk to find that the plot was in the middle of the river! To the left, 'Little Venice' can be seen from the opposite direction. Walk through Grüner Markt past the Maxplatz to the end of Kleberstrasse. Opposite is the *Verkehrsamt*, the town information office. The Weidendamm *Parkplatz* is reached in a few minutes by turning left through Kleberstrasse. Needless to say, the $1\frac{1}{2}$ hours or so needed for this walk do not allow time for visiting the cathedral or any of the notable churches and buildings.

The thirteenth-century *Dom* owes its fame largely to its series of sculptures and its portals. It is a three-aisled basilica with four towers, a typical Romanesque building with choirs in the east and west. The most famous sculpture is the *Bamberger Reiter* (Bamberg Horse-

The old town hall, Bamberg

man). In front of the east choir the double sarcophagus of Emperor Heinrich and Empress Kunigunde (1499–1513) is by Tilman Riemenschneider in late Gothic style. The Bamberg altar (1520–5) in natural wood is by Veit Stoss. The church of St Michael on the Michaelsberg was built in 1121 to replace an earlier building destroyed by earthquake in 1117. The present west façade was erected in 1696 in front of the towers and in 1723 the wide steps and balustraded terrace were added. The vaulted ceiling is painted with the 'botanical garden', pictures of over 600 native and foreign plants, and is the outstanding feature of the church. The Obere Pfarrkirche, basically from 1338, is a fine building; entry from the north side is through the so-called marriage doorway, a portal with the 'wise and foolish virgins' and the Assumption and Coronation of Our Lady (from about 1330).

The Diocesan Museum at Domplatz 5 contains the many treasures of the cathedral and other relics of early Christianity. The collection of medieval textiles is of particular significance. The Karl-May Museum has a room representing the famous author's study which forms the basis of the little museum. In the Alte Hofhaltung at Dom-

PLACES OF INTEREST BETWEEN NUREMBERG AND BAMBERG

HEROLDSBACH (6km W of Forchheim (B470))
Leisure Park Schloss Thurn
Fairy-tale land, Wild West town, steam railway, boats, etc.

POMMERSFELDEN (19km S of Bamberg. 'Bamberg' exit on A3.)

Weissenstein Palace (1711–18)
Magnificent building housing college of music but open to public.

platz 7, the impressive rooms of the Renaissance building are the home of the Historisches Museum which exhibits the history of Bamberg and its surroundings from the Stone Age to this century.

The Neue Residenz (1697–1703) was largely built by J.L. Dientzenhofer and was one of the first such palaces built in Germany in the baroque style. In addition to having richly furnished rooms with valuable furniture it houses part of the Bavarian State Art Collection.

Bamberg, like that other Franconian city Rothenburg, is an essential element of the Bavarian experience and the first time visitor should plan his itinerary to include at least one of these places.

At **Pommersfelden**, 19km south of Bamberg, at the foot of the slopes of the Steigerwald stands the enormous palace known as Schloss Weissenstein. Seen from afar across the green fields, the sparkling white building — a sort of Franconian Versailles — makes the origin of its name obvious. There is an interesting story about Weissenstein; it appears that Prince-Bishop Lothar Franz von Schönborn himself designed the spectacular entrance hall and staircase with its fine balustrades, lanterns supported by exquisite cherubs and so on. He then demanded that the architect — J. Dientzenhofer — compose the rest of the palace around his masterpiece. Dientzenhofer was assisted by the Austrian Lukas von Hildebrant who had made his name with the Belvedere in Vienna and Schloss Mirabell in Salzburg. However, it is with music that Weissenstein has come to be mainly associated. Dr Karl Graf Schönborn founded his 'Bach weeks' here (later transferred to Ansbach) and the establishment of the Collegium Musicum Schloss Pommersfelden ensured international recognition. Much of the *Schloss* is open to visitors. At the close of the academic year the splendid marble hall becomes the venue for public concerts when the students display their talents.

A motorway service area may seem an unlikely place to start a ramble to Schloss Weissenstein but this is where the next ramble

L
••
ΔΔ
15km

begins. Rasthaus Steigerwald is on the A3 some 60km east of Würzburg and 40km north-west of Nuremberg. Head north-east from the service area and in about 500m the roofs of **Weingratsgreuth** village come into view. By the first houses follow the *Wanderweg* to the right (SE) towards the *Autobahn* but before reaching it turn sharp left onto a footpath northwards through a wood to **Horbach.** From here a minor road leads to nearby **Simmersdorf**; do not go through this village but turn right into a footpath to reach another minor road for the kilometre or so to **Mühlhausen**. The little River Reiche Ebrach is seen from time to time on the left. Go into the centre of Mühlhausen, crossing over the river, and turn right to leave it again (take care not to follow the road which crosses the railway) and after passing the last house, turn left into a footpath over meadows to Lempenmühle — a water mill. Here, the Reiche Ebrach is crossed again and the route continues east towards Schloss Weissenstein, soon seen in the distance and reached in about 7km from the start.

After visiting the *Schloss* continue by turning left along a footpath which more or less follows the park wall and then joins a minor road into **Limbach** in a very few minutes. Follow the road and leave the village mostly to the left; the road swings gently left when about level with the last houses but leave the road and follow a footpath straight ahead (S-SE) towards a wood. The wood goes right up to the *Autobahn* but the path curves to the right to take a westerly direction towards **Schirnsdorf**. About 500m after this village leave the road and go left into a footpath through woods and meadows back to Weingratsgreuth and to the starting point.

Bamberg lies at one point of the rough triangle which encloses the Hassberge to the north-west, a small area of soft, peaceful hills. The other corners lie at Schweinfurt and Bad Königshofen. There is a whole string of little towns with unspoiled images of old Franconian timbered houses. The motorist could see some of the most attractive by making a tour from **Hassfurt** on the Main, north to **Königsberg**, **Hofheim** and **Bad Königshofen**, returning via **Ebern**, **Baunach** and **Zeil am Main**. Königsberg is particularly fine; Bad Königshofen is another new spa. In Hassfurt the principal, although not the only sight, is the late Gothic Catholic Ritterkapelle (Knights' Chapel) of St Maria built for the Franconian nobility at about the same time as the nearby parish church of St Kilian. The choir has a three-tiered frieze of 248 coats of arms of the knightly noblemen. The many fine works of art in St Kilian include a wooden figure of John the Baptist by

PLACES OF INTEREST IN THE HASSBERGE

HASSFURT
Knights' Chapel of St Maria
Late Gothic. Frieze of knights'
coats of arms.

Parish Church of St Kilian
John the Baptist carving by
Riemenschneider.

KÖNIGSBERG
Beautiful unspoiled old centre with
timbered houses.

BAD KÖNIGSHOFEN
**Fairy-tale and Leisure Park,
Sambachshof**

Western city, old-time railway,
boating, pony-rides, etc.

ZEIL AM MAIN
Town Hall
Sixteenth century and many fine
houses

LIMBACH (6km SE of Zeil)
**Pilgrimage Church Maria
Limbach** (1751–5)
One of Neumann's latest and finest
works.

Riemenschneider. Zeil am Main has many proud timbered houses and the commanding sixteenth-century *Rathaus,* while nearby on the south side of the river, is the outstanding pilgrimage church Maria Limbach (1751–5) one of the last works of the famous Balthasar Neumann and well worth making a slight detour to see.

The Hassberge is, above all, an ideal rambling area with a remarkable network of paths, many of which are designed to lead the walker to the dozen or so historic ruined castles or the thirty-five *Schlösser.* The open-air enthusiast will be happy near the Ellertshäuser See, a little lake with provision for bathing, sailing, angling and other water activities. Not yet a victim of mass tourism, the Hassberge can be recommended as a district for those seeking a peaceful holiday location. As in the Fränkische Schweiz, the altitude in the Hassberge rarely exceeds 500m (1640ft) but the last corner to be mentioned, in the north of Franconia, is the Bayerische Rhön whose more significant summits include the Dammersfeldkuppe and the Kreuzberg, both 928m (3044ft). This could be described as Franconia's health centre, resorts in the area including the spas of Bad Kissingen, Bad Bocklet, Bad Neustadt and Bad Brückenau.

The healing properties of the **Bad Kissingen** waters have been known at least since the ninth century but it was not until the sixteenth that it developed as a resort. The distinguished buildings of the *Kur* quarter were begun in 1834 and gradually extended along the River Saale, the final elements not being added until 1913. The Catholic

PLACES OF INTEREST IN THE BAVARIAN RHÖN

BAD KISSINGEN
Classic spa with distinguished buildings along River Saale.

**Old Town Hall
(Sixteenth century.)**

New Town Hall (1709)

Parish Church of St Jakobus
(Fourteenth and eighteenth centuries.)

MÜNNERSTADT
Unspoiled medieval town with walls and towers.

Late Gothic Town Hall
In market place surrounded by timbered houses.

Parish Church of St Mary

Magdalena
Riemenschneider altar (1492)

Former Kloster Church of Augustinian Hermits (1752–4)
Rococo with many treasures.

BAD NEUSTADT
Former Carmelite Kloster Church St Petrus and Paulus
(Fourteenth century.)
Good interior fitments.

ASCHACH (5km W of Bad Bocklet)
Aschach Palace
Good collection of furniture, glass, paintings, etc. Café.
In this area fine examples of wayside 'shrines'.

parish church of St Jakobus (fourteenth and eighteenth centuries) and the Catholic cemetery church of St Burkard are worth seeing.

The Altes Rathaus of the end of the sixteenth century and the Neues Rathaus (1709) by J. Dientzenhofer are of interest. Prince Bismarck, the famous statesman, had problems with his weight and came here to take the *Kur* and lose 45 of his 245 pounds! Today's overweight visitor can stay — at a price — at the Hotel Fürst Bismarck. Kissingen (population 25,000) is a classic spa and has a casino, a theatre for opera or drama and many other entertainments. The visitor can take an excursion by genuine old post coach to Schloss Aschach. It is not difficult to find the starting place for this historic ride with the colourful postilion on the coach box prominent over the heads of the spectators and photographers. Passengers experience the unusual motion of this ancient vehicle and the accompanying sounds of hoofbeats and the rattle of harness as they roll along the avenues towards **Bad Bocklet** (population 2500) where the healing waters are said to have been revealed by a deer bathing a wound in them — a similar legend to that at Wildbad in the Black Forest.

Münnerstadt

In **Aschach** there are some *Bildstöcke* (poles surmounted by a portrayal of the Virgin or a saint) said to be amongst the finest examples of this custom in all Franconia. The arrival of the post coach at the *Schloss* is quite spectacular as it draws up before the external staircase of the castle to the sound of the post-horn. The *Schloss* contains a rich art collection — furniture, glass, paintings, carpets, ceramics and so on. A visit is recommended.

North-east of Bad Kissingen on the B19 is **Münnerstadt** with its well preserved medieval townscape, defensive walls and fine entrance towers from the mid-thirteenth century. Old timbered houses with pointed gables surround the Marktplatz with its late Gothic *Rathaus*. The little town has some significant historical gems, like the Catholic parish church of St Mary Magdalena which has Riemenschneider's great Magdalenenaltar of 1492, coloured by Veit Stoss in 1503, and excellent glass in the choir windows (about 1420–50). The rococo church (1752–4) of the former *Kloster* of the Augustinian hermits also has its treasures, in particular the altar and pulpit.

Nearby **Bad Neustadt** (population 13,500), a popular resort with a combination of spa and industry, has become an important north

Franconian centre. Remains of the town's defensive walls can be seen and the former Carmelite *Klosterkirche*, St Petrus and Paulus (fourteenth century) near the *Rathaus* is worth seeing for its good interior fitments, especially the rococo pulpit from around 1750.

Bad Neustadt is on the eastern fringe of the Rhön and 35km west is **Bad Brückenau** (population 7000) just beyond the A7. It too has a long history as a spa and its waters are noted for the broad spectrum of complaints they benefit. A disastrous fire in 1876 almost completely destroyed the town which is thus poor in historic architecture. This is compensated for by the modern *Kur* developments started after 1900 and the resort today can offer its guests every comfort and convenience and a varied programme of leisure activities.

The principal resorts have been mentioned but for the foreign tourist the many smaller towns and villages have a lot to offer. In the Rhön, as indeed in all Franconia, there are many walking possibilities and almost every place has its suggested excursions; details can be obtained from the local tourist information offices. In many cases, guided rambles are arranged. A comprehensive booklet *Wandern in Franken* is available from the main tourist office in Nuremberg. There is a corresponding publication for cyclists, *Radeln in Franken.*

Close to the A8, midway between Erlangen and Würzburg, is the pleasure park Freizeit-Land Geiselwind, reached by the *Autobahn* exit **Geiselwind**. There are exotic birds, highland cattle, prehistoric monsters, a model exhibition, a model railway and a 'Wild West' train for children, to mention just a few of the dozens of attractions here.

The Franconian vineyards are mostly to be found along the valley of the Main, and **Volkach**, some 20km east of Würzburg, is in the heart of them. The village (population 6000) is Bavaria's biggest wine community and holds its annual festival, the principal wine festival in the state, in mid-August. This is when the Bavarian wine-queen for a year is chosen and crowned. Franconian wine is usually sold in the dumpy bottles called *Bocksbeutel*; from this comes the name of a course, run in Volkach for those wishing to better their knowledge of the wines of the area. The Bocksbeutel-Akademie claims to raise participants to a high level of proficiency by the end of its 5 days of tuition.

On the outskirts of the village, the little pilgrimage church of Maria im Weingarten rises from the vineyards, reached by a track marked by the Stations of the Cross. One of the treasures of this church is a famous limewood Madonna by Tilman Riemenschneider. This was taken hostage some years ago and only retrieved from the robbers by

Rose-wreath Madonna by Riemenschneider in the church of St Mary in the Vineyards, Volkach

payment of a ransom of 100,000 Marks. Twenty kilometres down the Main, **Kitzingen**, with more than 18,000 inhabitants, is another place connected with the wine trade. Its landmark is the Falterturm, a tower with a crooked cupola; legend has it that the mortar was mixed with wine! It now stands over a museum dedicated to the carnival tradition, only open at the weekend however. Kitzingen straddles the Main but the old town is on the west bank.

The fifteenth-century Catholic parish church of St Johannes is a three-aisled hall church; the figure-decorated tabernacle, the beautiful choir-stalls and the late Gothic frescos are notable. The baroque seventeenth-century Protestant parish church should also be seen with, east of the river, the Kapelle Heiligkreuz (1741–5). A pleasant stroll is along the flower-bedecked promenade on the river bank.

Sulzfeld, about 5km from Kitzingen, on what for the moment is the west bank, is an unspoiled wine village where it seems as if almost every house is adorned with figures from the Bible. The church of St Sebastian is worth the short climb and outside is a large representation of the scene on the Mount of Olives, a theme quite common in Franconia. The wine festival here takes place the first weekend in

PLACES OF INTEREST IN THE VINEYARD COUNTRY ALONG THE RIVER MAIN

GEISELWIND (Near A3 40km E of Würzburg)

Leisure Land Pleasure Park
A mixture of reality and fantasy. Highland cattle, exotic birds, Wild West town, model railway, etc.

VOLKACH (20km E of Würzburg)
Large vineyard village.

Pilgrimage Church Maria im Weingarten
Famous Riemenschneider Madonna.

KITZINGEN (20km SE of Würzburg)
Falterturm
Tower with crooked cupola. Houses the carnival museum.

Church of St Johannes
(Fifteenth century.)
Very fine interior.

Protestant Parish Church
Seventeenth-century baroque.

Holy Cross Chapel (1741–5)
E of river. A pleasant church by Neumann.

SULZFELD (5km from Kitzingen)
Unspoiled vineyard village. Many houses adorned with Biblical characters.

Church of St Sebastian
Mount of Olives scene outside.

MARKTBREIT
Romantic old town, fine buildings.

Town Hall (1579) flanked by attractive houses

Lion Hotel (1450)
Timbered façade; second oldest inn in Bavaria.

Old Harbour with Historic Treadmill Crane (1773)

OCHSENFURT
Historic town with walls and towers.

St Andreas Church (1288)
Fine interior with St Nikolaus carving by Riemenschneider.

Town Hall (1488–99)
Imposing building with external staircase and unusual clock tower.

FRICKENHAUSEN (3km E of Ochsenfurt)
Delightful vineyard village with walls and towers.

Town Hall
Late Gothic with external staircase.

St Gallus Parish Church
Well appointed interior on twelfth-century foundations.

SOMMERHAUSEN
Picturesque vineyard village. Fifteenth-century palace and two fine fountains in main street.

EIBELSTADT
Charming town centre with late baroque town hall (1706).

Parish Church of St Nikolaus
Parts from thirteenth century. Fine font and Riemenschneider crucifixion scene.

The Falterturm, Kitzingen, home of the carnival museum

August. The Main flowing southwards makes a huge arc in order to turn towards Würzburg.

Downstream again, in a few kilometres is **Marktbreit** (population 3500) on the other bank, one of the best examples of a romantic German town. In the Middle Ages there was a busy inland harbour and later it was an important European trading centre for coffee. The remains of the old commercial harbour, the warehouse and the tread-wheel crane of 1773 are to be seen beside the river. The *Rathaus* dates from 1579 and is complemented by two fine patrician houses. The Hotel-Löwen (Lion) has a splendid timbered façade and claims to be the second oldest *Gasthaus* in Bavaria. It was built in 1450 as a hostelry for the gentlemen of the von Schwarzenberg family. After-noon coffee and cake in the Löwen can be highly recommended.

On the same bank, the lovely town of **Ochsenfurt**, with a popu-lation of around 13,000, has much for the visitor to see. Some of the narrow streets do not favour the motorist but there is ample free parking space a few minutes away beside the river. The general view of the town with its old walls, towers and timbered houses makes a lasting impression. One of the towers, the Klingenturm is now a youth hostel. The Catholic church of St Andreas was built over a period from 1288 until the late fifteenth century. There is an extremely high nave and lavish tracery is a dominant feature of the interior. Riemenschneider contributed the excellent wooden figure of St Nikolaus.

The late Gothic *Rathaus* (1488–99) is one of the finest in Franconia. The clock tower with its comical figures has a mechanism dating from 1560 and has become the unofficial emblem of the town. Ochsenfurt celebrates a number of local festivals including, from Easter Sunday until the following one, the *Frühlingsfest* (Spring Festival) on the Festplatz near the old Main bridge with fairground and firework displays and at Whitsun, the Sausage Festival — *Bratwurstfest* — when traditional Franconian costumes can be seen. On Whit Sunday every odd year there is *St Wolfgangs-Ritt* with a traditional procession of horses to St Wolfgangs-Kapelle. Usually on a mid-July weekend there is the street wine festival which is held mainly on the bank of the Main. During the first weekend in September, the town centre is closed to traffic for the roasting of an ox — it features on the town's coat of arms — and the *Altstadtfest* (Old Town Festival). The last September weekend sees a 3-day autumn fair with a big programme of entertainments and the year ends with the Christmas celebrations when the old town is decorated and illuminated.

Across the river and a little way upstream is the exceedingly picturesque wine village of **Frickenhausen** with its encircling walls and four entrance towers. The late Gothic *Rathaus* has an original external staircase and there is a memorial to St Kilian nearby. The three-aisled St Gallus parish church is on twelfth- century foundations and is well appointed inside. The wine festival takes place the second weekend in August.

Downstream the river now heads north, but before reaching Würzburg, there are several more vineyard village resorts. **Sommerhausen** has its wine festival during the first week of June and a church festival with costume procession at the beginning of August. The village is sometimes compared with Rothenburg and with some justification. The fifteenth-century *Schloss* and two fountains known as 'Katharina' and 'Hansjörg' embellish the main street. **Eibelstadt** has similar festivals, wine mid-June and church the second weekend in August. The late baroque *Rathaus* (1706) presides over a town centre of great charm. The oldest parts of the parish church of St Nikolaus are from the thirteenth century and there is a richly ornamented font and a crucifixion scene by Riemenschneider.

A little time should be spent in the broad neck west of Würzburg. The area is called Spessart and the visitor might well visit one or two

Rothenfels with its castle overlooking the River Main

places of interest here. The River Main still has a great influence on the landscape and a short distance upstream from **Marktheiden-feld** is **Rothenfels**, a small town with a long history. It was already documented in 1050 and by 1148 a castle had been built on the *roten Felsen* (red cliffs) above and still dominates the skyline today when it serves as one of the biggest youth hostels in Germany. Despite the traffic passing through, the town has retained its medieval character, with wrought-iron inn signs, narrow alleys and religious figures on some house fronts. The motorist may park his car near the castle to take a pleasant walk. Walk in a westerly direction up through open country (waymark blue circle) to the Hainmarter, a modest ridge at 275m (900ft) where there is a wayside shrine and fine views up and down the River Main. The path curves to the right to run roughly north-west for nearly 2km through pretty woods.

M
↔
ΔΔΔ
12.5km

Descend into the Hafenlohrtal and on reaching the meadow ground in the valley, turn left to cross the little River Hafenlohr and the main road and immediately turn right to resume the north-west direction up through the woods. Gradually the path curves left and by the time Jagdschlösschen (Little Hunting Lodge) Karlshöhe is reached in about 2.5km from the river and road, the route is going due south. The lodge is in a woodland clearing and the forester's house here con-

The fifteenth-century moated castle at Mespelbrunn

ceals a neat little *Gaststätte*. From here, walk south-east in a dead straight line for a good 3km until the marked path branches off to the left for the very steep descent back into the Hafenlohrtal.

On the main road in the valley is the Hotel Sankt Hubertus, the famous 'Wirtshaus im Spessart' known through the story of that name by Wilhelm Hauff, the film of the same name and another film *Das Spukschloss* (Haunted Castle) im Spessart. This hostelry is highly recommended for a break as the walk nears its end; it is almost a little museum with historical objects the landlord has gathered together. The wayside shrine of St Hubertus outside the door is more than 300 years old and the doorway itself deserves special note. The objects of interest are listed on the menu which becomes a sort of visitor's guide to the Wirtshaus. From the hotel the ramble continues half-left over the river again and steeply up through the woods north-easterly to regain the open ground and so directly back to Rothenfels.

The B8 westwards from Marktheidenfeld is a picturesque road and the parallel A8 has some striking views. About 60km from Würzburg (Weibersbrunn exit on the A3) is the much-visited Wasserschloss **Mespelbrunn**, originally erected in the fifteenth century. In

PLACES OF INTEREST IN THE SPESSART

ROTHENFELS (28km W of
Würzburg)
Small medieval town on west bank
of River Main.

Castle
On imposing cliff W of town. Now
a large youth hostel.

Hotel Sankt Hubertus
In Hafenlohr valley W of town.
Famous as the 'Haunted Castle in
Spessart'.

MESPELBRUNN (60km W of
Würzburg)
Castle (Fifteenth century)
Outstandingly attractive moated
little palace with interesting apart-
ments and furnishings.

MILTENBERG
Extremely fine timbered buildings.
Superb market place.

The Riesen Hotel
Possibly oldest inn in Germany.

its pretty wooded surroundings it is just made for the photographer.
The Rittersaal (Knights' Hall) reached from the small courtyard is the
principal room on the ground floor. Above, the Gobelinensaal contains a famous Gobelin tapestry from 1564. The Chinese salon and
other rooms with interesting furnishings are open to view.

Almost due south on another great bend in the Main, the little town
of **Miltenberg** (population 10,000) is one of the gems of Bavaria and
another 'must' for the visitor. The fact that it is claimed to be one of the
most photographed towns in Germany speaks for itself. The superb
Marktplatz is often thronged with sightseers but there are many other
less busy attractive corners. One could go a long way to find finer
timbered buildings, which include the famous Gasthaus zum Riesen
(The Giant) claiming to be one of the oldest hostelries in Germany. It
was another lodging place of the nobility and is known to have been
in use as early as 1504. From the Riesen through the long main street
to the Marktplatz is a pedestrian zone. Car parking is available along
the Main river front which is a hive of activity with steamers and small
pleasure craft. St Johann Nepomuk stands watch in a shady corner
at the south end of the Main bridge. Finds from the Bronze Age reveal
that this area has been settled from very early times and later Miltenberg was a key location on the north-eastern edge of the Roman
Empire.

Ten kilometres south on the B469, **Amorbach** is an essentially
baroque town (population 5000), the outstanding sight in which is the
former Benedictine abbey church of St Maria, founded by Abbot St
Amor in 734. There was rebuilding in the ninth century and the west

The main street and Hotel Riesen, Miltenberg

towers were added in the twelfth. In 1742 the basilica was demolished except for the towers, and baroque rebuilding was completed in 1747. Secularisation in 1803 took it out of the hands of the Roman Catholic church and it is now the Protestant parish church. Rococo decorations on walls and ceiling are by the Wessobrunn artists J.G. Üblherr and J.M. Feuchtmayer. Of particular note are the wrought-iron railings between the nave and the transept and the organ built in 1774–82. The Catholic parish church of St Gangolf (1752–4) is also very fine and it too has a lovely organ on which recitals are given from time to time. Amorbach also has connections with British royalty. After the death of her husband Ernich, Prince of Leiningen, in 1814, Marie Louise Victoria (daughter of Francis, Duke of Saxe-Coburg-Saalfeld) travelled to England in 1817 to marry Edward, Duke of Kent and thus became Duchess of Kent. Their daughter was also given the name Victoria and it was she who became Queen of England in 1837 and reigned until her death in 1901.

A short excursion could be made westwards from Amorbach to the village of **Würzberg** (not to be confused with Würzburg) in the Odenwald, right on the Bavarian border and on the line of the Roman

PLACES OF INTEREST IN AND NEAR AMORBACH

Former Benedictine Abbey Church of St Maria (1747)
Now the Protestant parish church. Baroque with fine rococo decoration.

Catholic Parish Church of St Gangolf (1752–4)
Beautiful interior and fine organ.

WÜRZBERG (10km W)
Bavarian border village on line of Roman wall, the Limes.

THROUGH FOREST SOUTH FROM WÜRZBERG TO HESSENECK (10km)
Restored Roman Bath and other remains

Wild Boar Park

Three Countries Corner
A stone marks the spot where Bavaria, Baden and Hessen met.

defensive wall, the Limes, mentioned earlier.

The Gasthaus zum Adler (*Ruhetag* Tuesday) can be recommended for a meal and from here, a short way into the forest, are the restored remains of a Roman bath and other relics of the period. The forest road leads on through a wild boar park until, near the village of **Hesseneck**, an insignificant monument amongst the trees marks another 'three countries corner' where the former independent Kingdom of Bavaria and the Grand Duchies of Baden and Hessen came together.

From Miltenberg, the Main turns northwards towards **Aschaffenburg** (population 60,000) where the red sandstone façade of the Johannisburg (1605–14) dominates the scene. It can be reached along the tree-lined path of the broad old fortification wall. The view reveals the industrial area of the city but the yacht harbour below adds a touch of gaiety to the scene.

Three times a day the carillon from the castle tower sends a joyful baroque sound over the town. The *Schloss* houses a fine collection of works of art including the town collection of paintings. Just beyond, the yellow profile of the Pompejanum enhances the skyline. The Pompejanum was, in fact, another romantic idea of King Ludwig I who had it erected in 1840 as a copy of the villa of Castor and Pollux excavated in Pompeii. The building is decorated with friezes of classical symmetry and is surrounded by Mediterranean-style gardens; ivy-clad conifers, fountains and statues in rose beds ornament the vineyard sloping sharply down to the river.

The new *Rathaus*, a cubic stone and glass representative of

PLACES OF INTEREST IN ASCHAFFENBURG

Johannisburg(1605–14)
Red sandstone castle above River Main. Now houses works of art and city art gallery.

Pompejanum (1840)
King Ludwig I's copy of villa of Castor and Pollux in Pompeii.

Church of St Peter and Alexander (Started 950.)

Famous painting by Matthias Grünewald.

Hotel Post
Earlier post station of the Thurn and Taxis postal service.

Schönbusch
3km from centre over river. Classical landscaped gardens, palace,

modern architecture, stands in strange contrast to a few veteran timbered buildings. Here in the heart of the town is the 1000-year-old Stiftskirche St Peter and Alexander with Norman cloisters. Inside there is a famous and startling painting by Matthias Grünewald, *Beweinung Christi*. It is not far to Park Schöntal and 3km away across the river is Schönbusch with classically landscaped gardens, a *Schloss*, temples and lakes. The Hotel Post was a royal Bavarian 'Post Station' used by the princes of Thurn and Taxis for their postal service mentioned earlier. The Post has earned a Michelin star for its specialities which include one named after the princes.

Aschaffenburg is the terminal for river cruises sailing between here and Nuremberg and occasionally to Mainz. They are usually of 9–11 days duration and some are purely pleasure cruises while others are study tours with a theme such as 'Franconia's Hidden Treasures' or 'On the Trail of Tilman Riemenschneider'. The cruise prices are fully inclusive of travel, overnight accommodation in good hotels, meals and excursions. Those who have enjoyed the better-known Rhine cruises would almost certainly enjoy these on the Main equally well, with the beautiful scenery and visits to historic towns. This indeed opens up another possibility for an 'Introduction to Bavaria' for the first time visitor.

FURTHER INFORMATION

Note: The postcode for German addresses appears immediately before the place name, eg 8400 Regensburg. To telephone the Federal Republic from the UK, dial 010-49- then omit the first '0' of the telephone code.

Accommodation

Accommodation is available throughout Bavaria in hotels, inns, *pensions,* private houses, farmhouses, holiday flats or houses, youth hostels and camp sites. Accommodation lists for the principal resorts are obtainable from German National Tourist Offices (GNTO) overseas but often exclude private houses, farms, holiday flats and camp sites. More detailed lists which include these may be requested from the local tourist information office (*Verkehrsamt*).

Once there, accommodation in private houses is often indicated by a sign *Zimmer frei* (rooms available). A holiday flat to let can be recognised by a notice *Ferienwohnung zu vermieten.* Inns and *pensions* may display a sign *Fremdenzimmer* to show that they have rooms for casual guests. A comprehensive book *Urlaub auf dem Bauernhof* (Holidays on the Farm) should be available from GNTOs or in case of difficulty write to local offices. Some of the 'farms' are really riding schools and others

cater for unaccompanied children, usually from 10 years upwards.

The Germans were pioneers of self-catering and such accommodation is very widely available in Bavaria, both in farmhouses and elswhere. There are numerous camping and caravan sites. Advance booking is advisable in the summer months and this also applies to the many youth hostels. Here is a list of useful terms.

Aufenthaltsraum — lounge; sitting-room
Bad — bath
Bauernhof — farm
Doppelzimmer (Dz) — double room
Dusche — shower
Einzelhof — isolated farm, ie not in a village
Einzelzimmer (Ez) — single room
Endreinigung — cleaning after departure of visitor from self-catering accommodation
Feriendorf — holiday village, usually with specially built bungalows
Ferienhaus/Ferienwohnung (Fewo) — holiday house or flat
Fernseher — television
Frühstück — breakfast
Gasthaus — restaurant, inn, tavern
Gasthof — hotel or inn
Halbpension (HP) — half-board
Hotel-garni — hotel which does not serve meals (except breakfast)
Kinderermässigung — reductions for children
Mehrbettzimmer (Mz) — family room

Nebenkosten — extras
Pension — boarding house; board and lodging
Ruhige Lage — peaceful situation
Strom — electricity
Übernachtung mit Frühstück (ÜmF) — bed and breakfast
Vollpension (VP) — full-board
Vor- und Nachsaison (VN) — outside the main holiday season
Wirtshaus — inn or public house
Zentralheizung — central heating
Zimmer frei/besetzt — Vacancies/No vacancies

Buildings and Gardens Open to the Public

Ansbach. Residenz
Open Tuesday to Sunday, April to September 9am–12noon and 2–5pm, October to March 10am–12noon, 2–4pm. Restaurant.

Aschaffenburg. Schloss Johannisburg
Open Tuesday to Sunday, April to September 9am–12noon,1–5pm, October to March 10am–12noon, 1–4. Wine bar.

Aschaffenburg. Schloss Schönbusch
Open Tuesday to Sunday, April to September 8am–1pm, 2–5pm. Restaurant.

Bamberg. Neue Residenz
Open daily 9am–12noon, 1.30–5pm (4pm October to March). Café in rose garden.

Bayreuth. Neues Schloss
Open Tuesday to Sunday, April to September 10am–12noon, 1.20–5pm, October to March 10am–12noon, 1.30–3.30pm.

Bayreuth. Markgräfliches Opernhaus
Opening times as Neues Schloss. Conduced tours (German).

Bayreuth. Eremitage
Fountains play May to mid-October at 10 and 11am, 2, 3, and 4pm; cascade 10am–12noon, 1–5pm. Extensive park. Café (closed Monday) in Neues Schloss, Restaurant (closed Tuesday). Altes Schloss open Tuesday to Sunday, April to September 9–11.30am, 1–4.30pm, October to March 10–11.30am, 1–2.30pm.

Burghausen. Burg and Art Gallery
Open daily 9am–12noon, 1–5pm (4pm October to March when also closed on Monday).

Coburg. Schloss Ehrenburg
Open Tuesday to Sunday 10am–12noon, 1–5.30pm (4.30pm October to March).

Dachau. Schloss
Open Saturday and Sunday, May to October 2–5pm. Café-Restaurant.

Eichstätt. Willibaldsburg
Open Tuesday to Sunday, April to September 9am–12noon, 1–5pm, October to March 10am–12noon, 1–4pm. Bar.

Garmisch-Partenkirchen. Jagdschloss Schachen
Open daily April to September 8am–1pm, 2–6pm. Restaurant.

Herrenchiemsee. Neues Schloss
Open dailyaaaapril to September 9am–5pm, October to March 10am–4pm. King Ludwig II memorial exhibition open 9am–5pm all year. Fountains play from mid-May until end-September. Hotel nearby.

Kulmbach. Plassenburg
Open Tuesday to Sunday 10am–4.40pm (3.30pm October to March).

Lauenstein. Burg
Open Tuesday to Sunday, April to September 9am–12noon, 1–5pm, October to March 10am–12noon, 1–3.30pm. Burghotel.

Linderhof. Schloss with Grotto and Moorish Kiosk
April to September open daily 9am–12.15pm, 12.45–5.30pm. Fountains play each hour on the hour. October to March *Schloss* only, open daily 10am–12.15pm, 12.45pm–4pm. Restaurant and café (Closed Friday in winter).

Mespelbrunn. Wasserschloss
Open Monday to Saturday 9am–12noon, 1–5pm, Sunday 9am–5pm. Restaurant nearby.

Munich – Nymphenburg. Schloss and Amalienburg
Open Tuesday to Sunday, April to September 9am–12.30pm, 1.30–5pm, October to March 10am–12.30pm, 1.30–4pm.
Marstallmuseum (carriages etc)
Open Tuesday to Sunday, April to September 9am–12noon, 1–5pm, October to March 10am–12noon, 1–4pm.
Badenburg, Pagodenburg and Magdalenenklause
Open Tuesday to Sunday, April to September 10am–12.30pm, 1.30–5pm. Café.

Munich – Schleissheim. Altes Schloss, Neues Schloss, Schloss Lustheim
Open Tuesday to Sunday 10am–12.30pm, 1.30–5pm (4pm October to March). *Schloss* restaurant.

Schillingsfurst. Schloss
Open May and October, Saturday, Sunday and holidays and June to September daily 9–11.30am, 2–5.30pm.

Schwangau. Burg Hohenschwangau
Open daily, summer 8.30am–5.30pm, winter 10am–4pm. Restaurant nearby.

Schwangau. Schloss Neuschwanstein
Open daily April to September 8.30am–5.30pm, October to March 10am–4pm. Inn.

Würzburg. Residenz
Open Tuesday to Saturday, April to September 9am–5pm, October to March 10am–4pm. Restaurant.

Würzburg. Festung Marienberg
Opening times as for Residenz. Bar and restaurant. See also Mainfränkisches Museum.

Museums

This alphabetical list by town excludes museums with very limited or irregular hours of opening and the many local '*Heimat*' museums unless these have exhibits of particular interest to the foreign visitor. In Bamberg, Munich Nuremberg and Regensberg, there are many other museums. Details from the respective tourist offices.

Aventinus-Museum
Karmelitenplatz 5,
8423 Abensberg
☎ 09443-421
Open: Wednesday, Friday, Saturday and Sunday 2–4pm.

Fränkisches Freilandmuseum
8832 Bad Windsheim
☎ 09841–5920
Open mid-March to mid-October, Tuesday to Sunday 9am–6pm, mid-October to 6 January, Tuesday to Sunday 10am–4pm. Open Easter and Whit Mondays, closed 24 and 31 December.

Naturkundemuseum
Fleischstrasse 2
8600 Bamberg
☎ 0951-4026230
Open Monday to Friday 8am–12 noon, 1–5pm, also first Sunday in month 9am–5pm. Natural history.

Diözesanmuseum
Domplatz 5
8600 Bamberg
☎ 0951-5021
Open Easter to October, Monday to Friday 10am–12noon, 2.30–6pm, Saturday 9am–1pm, Sunday 10am–1pm. Accompanied children free.

Richard-Wagner-Museum
Haus Wahnfried
8580 Bayreuth
Open daily 9am–5pm. Music at 10am, 12noon and 2pm.

Deutsches Freimaurer-Museum
Hofgarten 8580 Bayreuth
Open Tuesday to Friday 10am–12 noon, 2–4pm, Saturday 10am–12noon.

Deutsches Schreibmaschinen-museum
Bernecker Strasse 11
8580 Bayreuth
☎ 0921-23445
Open Monday to Friday 2–5pm. Advance confirmation requested. Admission free.

Jean-Paul-Museum
Wahnfriedstrasse 1
8580 Bayreuth
Open April to October daily 9am–12noon, 2–5pm, November to March Monday to Friday same times, Saturday and Sunday 10am–1pm.

Historische Fraunhofer Glashütte
Fraunhofer Strasse 2
8174 Benediktbeuern
☎ 08857-2512

Open Monday to Saturday 10am–12noon, 2–5pm, Sunday 1–5pm.

Museum Bodenmais
Bahnhofstrasse 1a
8373 Bodenmais
☎ 09924-656
Open weekdays 9–11am, 2–6pm, Sunday 10am–12noon. Closed Sundays in winter.

Historisches Erzbergwerk im Silberberg
BHS Bergwerk
8373 Bodenmais
☎ 09924-304
Open April to September 9am–5pm, October, Easter and Christmas 10am–4pm. Reduced admission charge for school parties.

Auto-Motorrad-Museum
Bleichstrasse 18
8672 Burgau
☎ 08222-1333
Open daily 10am–5pm.

Art Gallery Veste Coburg
8630 Coburg
☎ 09561-95055
Open daily April to October 9.30am–1pm, 2–5pm, November to March, Tuesday to Sunday 2–5pm. Restaurant, café.

Krügemuseum
Stadt Creussen
(14km S of Bayreuth on B2)
☎ 09270-607
Open Tuesday to Sunday 9.30am–12noon, 2–5.30pm.

Walhalla
Walhallastrasse 48
8405 Donaustauf
☎ 09403-1909
Open daily April to October 9am–6pm, November to March, 10–11.45am, 1–3.45pm. May be closed holidays. Accompanied children free.

Freilichtmuseum Bayerischer Wald

8391 Finsterau
☎ 08557-221
Open mid-December to April 1–4pm, May to September 9am–6pm, October 9am–4pm. Refreshments.

Glasmuseum

Am Museumspark 1
8371 Frauenau
☎ 09926-718
Open 20 December to 14 May 10am–4pm, 15 May to 30 October 9am–5pm.

Diözesanmuseum

Domberg 21
8050 Freising
☎ 08161-2432
Open Tuesday to Friday 10am–4pm, Saturday and Sunday 10am–6pm.

Waldmuseum

Steinbruchweg 9
8492 Furth im Wald
☎ 09973-609
Open daily 9am–12noon, 1–4pm.

Bauernmöbel-Museum

Kurpark
8352 Grafenau
☎ 08552-2085 (Verkehrsamt)
Open July and August daily 2–5pm, other months Tuesday, Thursday and Sunday only.

Schnupftabakmuseum

Spitalstrasse 4
8352 Grafenau
(In the Stadtmuseum)
☎ 08552-2081
Open 16 December to 31 October daily 2–5pm.

Freilichtmuseum des Bezirks Oberbayern an der Glentleiten

8119 Grossweil
☎ 08841-1095 or 1098
Open April to November Tuesday to Sunday 9am–6pm (5pm in November). Open Easter and Whit Mondays.

Automobil-Veteranen-Salon

Bächinger Strasse 68
8683 Gundelfingen
☎ 09073-2575
Open Easter to mid-October 9am–6pm.

Graphitbergwerk Kropfmühl

Langheinrichstrasse 1
8395 Hauzenberg
☎ 08586-2444
Open December to October, Tuesday to Sunday 9.30am–5.30pm.

Bayerisches Armeemuseum

Neues-Herzogs-Schloss
Paradeplatz 4
8070 Ingolstadt
☎ 0841-1370
Open Tuesday to Sunday 8.45am–4.30pm. Accompanied children free.

Befreiungshalle

Befreiungshalle-Strasse 3
8420 Kelheim
☎ 09441-1584
Open April to September daily 8.30am–5pm, October to March daily 9am–12noon, 1–4pm. Accompanied children free.

Deutsches Zinnfiguren-museum Plassenburg

Rathaus
8650 Kulmbach
☎ 09221-5550
Open April to September 10am–4pm, October to March 10am–3.30pm. Closed on Mondays.

Mineralien-Museum

Daxenhöhe 1
8496 Lam
☎ 09943-557
Open daily 8am–6pm.

Burg Trausnitz

8300 Landshut
☎ 0871-22638

Open April to September, Tuesday to Sunday 9am–12noon, 1–5pm, October to March 1–5.30pm only. Accompanied children free.

Stadtresidenz
Altstadt 79
8300 Landshut
☎ 0871-22638
Details as for Burg Trausnitz.

Flössermuseum Unterrodach
Kirchplatz 3
8641 Marktrodach
☎ 09261-885
Open Monday to Friday 8am–12noon, 2–5pm (advance confirmation requested) also Saturday and Sunday 2–4pm. Reduced admission charge for school parties.

Niederbayerisches Bauernhofmuseum
Schusteröd
8332 Massing
☎ 08724-451 or 784
Open Tuesday to Friday 10am–12noon, 2–6pm, Saturday, Sunday and holidays 2–6pm.

Deutsches Korbmuseum
Bismarckstrasse 4
8626 Michelau
☎ 09571-8046 and 88246
Open Monday to Friday 9am–12noon, 1–4pm and Saturday and Sunday by arrangement.

Geigenbau-Museum
Ballenhausgasse 3
8102 Mittenwald
☎ 08823-8418 and 8561
Open Monday to Friday 10am–12noon, 2–5pm, Saturday, Sunday and holidays 10am–12noon.

Historisches Nähmaschinen-und Bugeleisen-Museum
Heimeranstrasse 68–70
8000 München
☎ 089-503045

Open Monday to Friday 10am–4pm. History of sewing machines and irons. Admission free.

Deutsches Brauerei-Museum
St Jakobsplatz 1
8000 München 2
(In the Stadtmuseum)
☎ 089-2332370
Open Tuesday to Saturday 9am–4.30pm, Sunday and holidays 10am–6pm. Admission free Sunday and holidays. Children and school parties free at all times. History of beer and brewing. Models.

Photographic Museum, Fraunhofer Workshop
☎ 089-2332948
Other details as next above.

Siemens-Museum
Prannerstrasse 10
8000 München 2
☎ 089-2342660
Open Monday to Friday 9am–4pm, Saturday and Sunday 10am–2pm. Holidays closed. Admission free. Electrical engineering and electronics. Model railway with modern signalling.

German Museum of Science and Technology
Museumsinsel 1
8000 München 22
☎ 089-2179252
Open daily 9am–5pm but closed on 1 January, Good Friday, Easter Sunday, 1 May, Whit Monday, Corpus Christi, 17 June, 1 November, 24, 25 and 31 December. Restaurant and café.

BMW-Museum
Petuelring 130
8000 München 40
☎ 089-38953307
Open daily 9am–4pm (last admission). Technology, contemporary history. Art gallery.

Alte Pinakothek (Art Gallery)
Barer Strasse 27
8000 München
☎ 089-23805-216/215
Open Tuesday to Sunday 9am–
4.30pm, also Tuesday and Thursday 7–9pm. Open Whit Monday but
closed on 1 January, Good Friday,
Easter Sunday, 1 May, 17 June, 24
and 25 December. Admission free
on Sunday and holidays.

Neue Pinakothek (Art Gallery)
Barer Strasse 29
8000 München
☎ 089-23805-195
Open Tuesday to Sunday 9am–
4.30pm, also Tuesday 7–9pm.
Open Easter and Whit Mondays but
closed on Good Friday, 1 May, Whit
Sunday, Corpus Christi, 1 November, 24 and 25 December. On 31
December closes 12noon. Admission free on Sunday and holidays.

State Gallery of Modern Art
Haus der Kunst
Prinzregentenstrasse 1
8000 München
Open Tuesday to Sunday 9am–
4.30pm also Thursday 7–9pm.

Oberpfälzer Freilandmuseum
Perschen 13
8470 Nabburg
☎ 09433-486
Open Tuesday to Sunday 9am–
5pm. Closed 23 December to 6
January.

Trachtenpuppen-Museum
Hindenburgplatz
8632 Neustadt bei Coburg
☎ 09568-5600
Open 15 March to 15 October,
Tuesday to Sunday 9am–6pm.

Germanisches National-
museum
Kornmarkt 1
8500 Nürnberg
☎ 0911-203971

Open Tuesday to Sunday 9am–
5pm, also Thursday 8–9.30pm.

Spielzeugmuseum
Karlstrasse 13
8500 Nürnberg
☎ 0911-163164
Open Tuesday to Sunday
10am–5pm (9pm on Wednesday).

Verkehrsmuseum
Lessingstrasse 6
8500 Nürnberg
☎ 0911-2195428
Open Monday to Saturday
10am–5pm (4pm October to
March), Sunday 10am–4pm. For
holidays see local announcements.

Schloss-Museum
8359 Ortenburg
☎ 08542-596
Open May to September daily
10am–6pm and by arrangement.
Occasional concerts in banqueting
hall and inner courtyard.

Diözesanmuseum
St Emmeramsplatz 1
8400 Regensburg
☎ 0941-51068
Open April to October Tuesday to
Sunday 10am–5pm, November and
7 January to end-March open only
Saturday and Sunday 10am–4pm,
25 December to 6 January, Tuesday to Sunday 10am–4pm. Closed
1 to 24 December.

Domschatzmuseum
Kraterermarkt 3
8400 Regensburg
(Entrance through cathedral)
☎ 0941-53021
Open April to October, Tuesday to
Saturday 10am–5pm, Sunday and
holidays 11.30am–5pm, December
to March, Friday and Saturday
10am–4pm, Sunday 11.30am–4pm
but from 25 December to 6 January
as in summer until 4pm.

Museum der Stadt

Dachauplatz 2–4
8400 Regensburg
☎ 0941-2940/42
Open Tuesday to Saturday 10am–
4pm, Sunday and holidays 10am–
1pm. Closed on Good Friday, Easter
Monday, 1 May, Whit Monday, 1 November, 24, 25 and 31 December.

Städt. Galerie Leerer Beutel

Bertoldstrasse 9
8400 Regensburg
☎ 0941-5072872
Opening times as above.

Schiffahrtsmuseum

Werftstrasse
8400 Regensburg
☎ 0941-561660
Open mid-March to mid-October
daily 10am–5pm.

Fürstlich Thurn und Taxis Schloss und Marstallmuseum

Emmeramsplatz 5–6
8400 Regensburg
☎ 0941-50480
Guided tours only: *Schloss* and St
Emmerams Cloister, Monday to Friday 2 and 3pm, Sunday and holidays 10 and 11.15am. Marstallmuseum (carriages and stables),
Monday to Friday 2, 2.40 and
3.15pm, Sunday and holidays 10,
10.40 and 11.15am. Special arrangements possible for large groups.

Schloss Prunn

8422 Riedenburg
☎ 09442-1765
Open daily 9am–6pm (4pm October
to March when also closed Monday). Accompanied children free.
Terrace café.

Oberpfälzer Handwerks-museum

8463 Rötz-Hillstett
☎ 09976-423
Open mid-April to mid-October,
Tuesday to Sunday 10am–5pm.

Mittelalterliches Kriminal-museum

Burggasse 3
8803 Rothenburg
☎ 09861-5359
Open Summer 9.30am–6pm, winter
2–4pm, but closed January and
February.

Puppen- und Spielzeug-museum

Hofbronnengasse 13
8803 Rothenburg
☎ 09861-7330
Open January and February, 11am–
5pm, other months 9.30am–6pm.

Gäubodenmuseum

Fraunhoferstrasse 9
8440 Straubing
☎ 09421-16326
Open Tuesday to Sunday
10am–4pm.

Museumsdorf Bayerischer Wald

8391 Tittling
☎ 08504-8482
Open daily 9am–5pm. Inn.

Kristallmuseum

Spitalgasse 5
8374 Viechtach
☎ 09942-8107
Open summer daily 9am–12noon,
2–6pm. Closed in November. In
other winter months, Tuesday to
Saturday only at same times.

Stiftlandmuseum

Rathausstrasse 1
8595 Waldsassen
☎ 09632-811
Open spring to autumn daily 1–4pm
also 10–11am in main holiday
season.

Wegmacher-Museum

In der Strassenmeisterei
Herderstrasse 5
8090 Wasserburg/Inn
☎ 08071-7437

Open Monday to Friday 8–11am,
1–3pm. Admission free.

Stadtmuseum und Max-Reger-Sammlung
Kulturzentrum Haus Bauer
Pfarrplatz 4
8480 Weiden
☎ 0961-5051 and 262
Open Monday to Friday 10–11am,
2–3pm. Admission free.

Fichtelgebirgsmuseum
Spitalhof 1–2
8592 Wunsiedel
☎ 09232-2032
Open Tuesday to Saturday 9am–
5pm (9pm Thursday March to
October), Sunday and holidays
10am–5pm. General museum of
area with memorabilia of Max
Reger and Jean Paul.

Mainfränkisches Museum
Marienberg
8700 Würzburg
Open daily 10am–5pm (4pm
November to March). Restaurant.

Waldmuseum
Stadtplatz 29
8372 Zwiesel
☎ 09922-2041
Open mid-May to mid-October,
Monday to Friday 9am–5pm, Saturday and Sunday 10am–12noon,
2–4pm; other months Monday to
Friday 10am–12noon, 2–5pm, Saturday and Sunday 10am–12noon.

Churches

Altenmarkt (Chiemgau)
Klosterkirche Baumburg (1754–7).
Elevated position S of town.
Concerts in summer.

Altenstadt (Schongau)
Parish church of St Michael (from
around 1200). 2km W of Schongau.

Altötting
Heilige Kapelle. In town centre.
Pilgrimage church housing famous
'Black Madonna' (about 1300).

Andechs
Maria Verkündigung (Annunciation)
(1420–48).

Aschaffenburg
Collegiate church of St Peter and St
Alexander (tenth to seventeenth
century). In town centre.

Bamberg
Cathedral (1215–37). In town
centre.
St Michael (1121 with many later
additions). Elevated position above
town on Michaelsberg.

Banz
Former Benedictine abbey
(1710–19). 4km N of Staffelstein.

Benediktbeuern
St Benedikt (1680–6). In village.

Diessen
St Maria (about 1730). In town.

Dietramzell
Former collegiate church of Augustinian canons (1729–41). In village.

Dinkelsbühl
St George (1448–99). In town
centre. Some sections closed for
renovation until 1992.

Ettal
Benedictine monastery church
(1370), baroque re-modelling in
eighteenth century. 5km from
Oberammergau.

Freising
St Maria and St Korbinian Dom
(1160). Above town on Domberg.

Fürstenfeldbruck
Former Cistercian monastery
church of the Assumption (1701).

Kappel
Heilige Dreifaltigkeitskirche (Holy Trinity) (seventeenth century) 4km NW of Waldsassen on 628m (2060ft) Glasberg.

Kötzting
Pilgrimage church Weissenregen (about 1758). 2km W of Kötzting.

Landshut
St Martin's Minster (fifteenth century). In old town centre.

Limbach
Pilgrimage church Maria Limbach (1751–5). 6km SE of Zeil.

Munich
Jesuit church of St Michael (1583–9). In city centre, Neuhauser Strasse.
St Johann Nepomuk (The Asam Church) (1733–46). In city centre, Sendlinger Strasse.
Parish church of St Peter (1278–94). In city centre, Marienplatz.
Theatinerkirche St Kajetan (started 1663). In city centre, Theatinerstrasse.

Nuremberg
Parish church of St Sebaldus (1230–40). In city centre, Winklerstrasse.
Parish church of St Lorenz (thirteenth to fourteenth century). In city centre, Königstrasse.

Ottobeuren
Benedictine monastery church of the Holy Trinity (eighteenth century). In village centre.

Passau
St Stephan's Cathedral (1407–1520). In city centre.

Ramsau
Pilgrimage church of St Fabian and St Sebastian (sixteenth century). 10km W of Berchtesgaden.

Regensburg
St Peter's Cathedral (started about 1250). In city centre.
Former Benedictine monastery church of St Emmeram (tenth to eighteenth century). In city centre.

Reichenbach
Former Benedictine monastery church of the Assumption (1118–1200). 28km NE of Regensburg, 27km W of Cham.

Rinchnach
Former Benedictine priors' church, now the parish church (1438 with eighteenth-century baroque).

Rohr
Benedictine abbey church of the Assumption (1717). 11km SE of Abensberg.

Rothenburg
Parish church of St Jakob (1311–71). In town centre.

Rott am Inn
Former Benedictine abbey church of St Marinus and Anianus (1759–67).

Rottenbuch
Former Augustinian church of the Birth of the Virgin (eleventh to fourteenth century with eighteenth-century baroque).

Schäftlarn
Former Premonstratensian monastery church (1760). 25km S of Munich, 2km E of Ebenhausen.

Vierzehnheiligen
Pilgrimage church (1745–72). 3km S of Lichtenfels.

Weltenburg
Monastery church of St Georg and St Martin (1716–18). 6km SW of Kelheim on S bank of Danube.

Wessobrunn
Parish church of St Johannes
(1757–9)

Wies
Pilgrimage church (1746–57). 20km
S of Schongau via B17 or B23, 6km
SE of Steingaden.

Zoos and Wildlife Parks

Abensberg
Niederbayerischer Vogelpark
(Lower Bavarian Bird Park)
8423 Abensberg
☎ 09443-1215
Open daily April to October,
10am–5pm. Children's play area,
kiosk and beer garden.

Egloffstein (Fränkische Schweiz)
Wildehege Hundshaupten
8551 Egloffstein
☎ 09197-241 and 396
Open April to October, daily 9am–
6pm, November to March, Saturday, Sunday and holidays 11am–
3pm. Children under 5 free. Facilities for disabled. Refreshments.

Grafenau
Nationalpark Bayerischer Wald
Comprehensive information centre
8km NE of Grafenau. Extensive
animal and bird enclosures. Free.

Hesseneck
Wild Boar Park on road through
Odenwald towards Würzberg. Free.

Munich
Münchner Tierpark Hellabrunn
Siebenbrunner Strasse 6
8000 München 90
☎ 089-661021
5km S of city centre. Open daily
April to September, 8am–6pm, October to March, 9am–5pm. Children
under 4 admission free. Children's
amusements. Restaurant.

Nuremberg
Nürnberger Tiergarten
8500 Nürnberg
☎ 0911-571348
4km E of city centre. Open daily
March to October, 8am–sunset,
November to February 9am–
sunset. Additional charge for
dolphinarium. Restaurant and bars.

Riedenburg
Bayerischer Landes-Jagdfalken-Hof
Schloss Rosenburg
8422 Riedenburg
☎ 09442–1843
Open Tuesday to Sunday, 9am–
5pm. Headquarters of Bavarian
falconry. Free flying birds of prey at
3pm daily. Refreshments.

Straubing
Tiergarten
Regensburger Strasse
8440 Straubing
☎ 09421-21277
1km W of town. Open daily March
to September 8.30am–7pm,
October to February, 9.30am–5pm.
Children under 6 admission free.
Reduced admission for groups,
students, pensioners.

Railway Museums, etc

*= address for information

Bayrisch-Eisenstein
*Bayerische Localbahn Verein e.V.
Postfach 116
8180 Tegernsee
A museum devoted to Bavarian
local railways is being created here,
historical vehicles will be displayed
in authentic surroundings.

**Ebermannstadt-
  Behringersmühle**
Dampfbahn Fränkische Schweiz
Postfach 1
8553 Ebermannstadt
☎ 09131-65873

Operates steam passenger trains usually two Sundays each month May to September and on some holidays. Details in *DB Kursbuch* (timetable) Table 824. Connections from Forchheim by DB 'bus. Reduced fares for families, parties of 15 adults or more and those staying in Ebermannstadt, Gössweinstein and Behringersmühle (with *Kurkarte*).

Fünfstetten-Monheim
*Eisenbahnclub München e.V.
Oderstrasse 4
8000 München 80
Local address: Freunde der Bahnlinie Monheim-Fünfstetten, Eichstrasse 5, 8850 Donauwörth. Historic passenger trains operate on certain days. Details in *DB Kursbuch* (timetable) Table 916.

Lam-Kötzting: Blaibach-Gotteszell
*Regentalbahn AG.
8374 Viechtach
Historic steam passenger trains operate on certain days on both routes. Details in *DB Kursbuch* (timetable) Tables 864 and 867.

Munich
In the Deutsches Museum. Railway section including extensive model railway.
In Siemens-Museum. Model railway demonstrating modern signalling.

Neuenmarkt
Deutsches Dampflokomotiv Museum
8655 Neuenmarkt
☎ 09227–5700
Autobahn exit Bad Berneck then B303.
Open May to October, Tuesday to Friday 9am–12noon, 1–5pm and November to April, Tuesday, Friday, Saturday and Sunday 10am–12noon, 1–4pm. Many standard gauge steam locomotives, also narrow gauge locos, some in steam summer weekends.

Nuremberg
In the Tiergarten (zoo). Miniature passenger-carrying replica of first German railway Nürnberg-Fürth operates Easter to October.
In the Verkehrsmuseum (Transport Museum). Extensive display of railway vehicles and other equipment. Model railway.
In the Spielzeugmuseum (Toy Museum). Large model railway.

Prien-Stock
Chiemseebahn
*Chiemsee-Schiffahrt
  Ludwig Fessler
Postfach 21
8210 Prien
Steam trains between Prien DB station and Stock pier during summer months from mid-May.

Tegernsee-Schaftlach
Tegernsee-Bahn AG
8180 Tegernsee
Historic passenger train operates on certain days. Details in *DB Kursbach* (timetable) Table 955.

Weiden
Eisenbahnmuseum MEC Weiden Modelleisenbahnclub e.V.
8480 Weiden i.d.Opf
Adjoining DB station. Extensive model layout in operation on certain days, usually Sunday and holidays.

Mountain Railways

K = cabin cableway, Z = cog-wheel railway

Aschau
Kampenwandbahn (K)
Journey time 14 min.
Daily 9am–5pm (4.30pm in winter).

Bad Reichenhall
Predigtstuhlbahn (K)
Journey time 10 min.
Daily 9am–4pm.

Bayrischzell
Wendelstein-Seilbahn (K)
Journey time 6 min.
Daily 9am–4pm.

Berchtesgaden
Jennerbahn (K)
Obersalzburgbahn (K)
Journey time 20 min.
Daily 9am–4.30pm.
(4pm in December and January)

Bergen
Hochfelln-Seilbahn (K)
Section 1 - Journey time 7 min.
Section 2 - Journey time 4 min.
Daily 9am–11.30am, 12.30–4.30pm.

Brannenburg
Wendelstein-Zahnradbahn (Z)
Journey time 55 min.
Hourly 9am–3pm, upper station
  hourly 10am–5pm. May vary.

Füssen
Tegelbergbahn Schwangau (K)
Journey time 6-10 min.
Daily 8.30am–4.30pm.

Garmisch-Partenkirchen
  Zugspitzbahn (Garmisch to
  Schneefernerhaus) (Z)
Journey time 80 min.
Daily. Leaves Garmisch hourly
  7.35am–3.35pm and S'ferner-
  haus hourly 9am–5pm.
Seilbahn (S'fernerhaus to Summit)
  (K)
Journey time 4 min.
Daily 8.45am–4.45-pm (3.45pm in
  winter)
Seilbahn (Eibsee to Summit) (K)
Journey time 10 min.
Daily 8.30am–5.30pm (4.30pm in
  winter
Tiroler Zugspitzbahn (from Ehrwald
  in Austria) (K)
Section 1 - Journey time 6 min.
Section 2 - Journey time 6 min.
Section 3 - Journey time 2 min.
Daily. Approx hourly 9.15am–
  4.15pm.

Osterfelderbahn (K)
Journey time 9 min.
Daily 8.30am–5pm (4pm in winter).
Hochalmbahn (K)
Journey time 4 min.
Daily. At least hourly during
  operation of Osterfelderbahn
Kreuzechbahn (K)
Journey time 8 min.
Daily 8.14am–5pm (4.30pm in
  December and January).
Wankbahn (K)
Journey time 14min.
Eckbauerbahn (K)
Journey time 14min.
Hausbergbahn (K)
Journey time 5min.
All daily 8.30am–5pm.

Grainbach
Hochriesbahnen (K)
Journey time 5 min.
Daily 9am–4pm.

Lenggries
Brauneck-Bergbahn (K)
Journey time 17min.
Daily 8.15am–4.30pm.

Mittenwald
Karwendelbahn (K)
Journey time 10 min.
Daily 9am–5pm.

Oberammergau
Laber-Bergbahn (K)
Journey time 12 min.
Daily 9am–5pm (4pm November-
  April).

Oberstaufen
Hochgratbahn (K)
Journey time 15 min.
Daily 9am–5pm.

Oberstdorf
Fellhornbahn (K)
Sections 1 and 2 - Journey time 13
  min.
Daily 8.15am–5pm
Kanzelwandbahn (K)
Journey time 12 min.

Walmendingershornbahn (K)
Journey time 5 min.
Both daily 8.15am–4.45pm.
Nebelhornbahn (K)
Journey time 12 min.
Daily 8am–12noon, 1.20pm–5pm.

Pfronten-Steinach
Breitenbergbahn (K)
Journey time 11 min.
Daily 8.30am–12noon, 1–5pm.

Ruhpolding
Rauschbergbahn (K)
Journey time 4 min.
Daily 9am–5pm.

Schliersee
Schliersbergbahn (K)
Daily 9am–5pm.
Taubensteinbahn (K)
Journey time 15 min.
Daily 8.45am–4.15pm.

Tegernsee
Wallbergbahn (K)
Journey time 12 min.
Daily 8.30am–4.30pm.

Pleasure Parks

Märchen- und Freizeitpark
Sambachshof
8742 Bad Königshofen
Café-Restaurant
☎ 09762-2614 or 09765-284

Churpfalz-Park
8499 Loifling bei Cham
☎ 09971-30300
8km S of Cham on B20. Open daily
April to October 9am–6pm.
Restaurant.

Freizeit-Land
8602 Geiselwind
☎ 09556-234 and 357
Geiselwind exit on Würzburg-

Nuremberg *Autobahn* A3.
Open daily from around Easter to
mid-September 9am–6pm then
depending on weather Saturday,
Sunday and holidays only until end
of October. Café, restaurant, bars,
etc.·

Familien-Freizeitpark
Schloss Thurn
8551 Heroldsbach bei Forchheim
☎ 09190-555
6km W of Forchheim-Sud exit on
Nuremberg-Bamberg *Autobahn*
A73. Open daily from April to
October 9am–5pm. Restaurant,
wine-tasting.

Freizeitzentrum Hoher Bogen
Hohen-Bogen-Bahn
8497 Neukirchen bei Hl. Blut
☎ 09947-464 and 1078
Open all year. Cafés and bars.

Fränkisches Wunderland
Freizeitpark
8571 Plech
☎ 09244-451
Plech exit on Nuremberg-Bayreuth
Autobahn A9. Open daily Easter to
October 9am–6pm. Café.

Märchen-Familienpark
8222 Ruhpolding
☎ 08663-1413 or 08641–7269
3km SW of Ruhpolding in direction
of Brand. Open from about Easter
to end-October daily from 9am.
Refreshments.

Märchenwald im Isartal
Kräuterstrasse 39
8190 Wolfratshausen-Farchet
☎ 08171-18760
Wolfratshausen exit on Munich-
Garmisch *Autobahn* A95 then E of
town. Open daily 2 weeks before
Easter to mid-October 9am–6pm.
Restaurant and kiosk.

Official Holidays

Neujahr — New Year's Day
Heilige Drei Könige — Epiphany
Karfreitag — Good Friday
Ostern — Easter Day
Ostermontag — Easter Monday
Tag der Arbeit — May Day
Christi Himmelfahrt — Ascension
Day
Pfingsten — Whit Monday
Fronleichnam — Corpus Christi
Tag der Einheit — Day of German
Unity (17 June)
Maria Himmelfahrt — Assumption
of Mary (15 August)
Allheiligen — All Saints Day
Volkstrauertag — Remembrance
Day
Buss- und Bettag — Repentence
Day
Totensonntag — Remembrance of
dead relatives
Weihnachten — Christmas
(Many businesses and public
buildings close around mid-day on
31 December, *Sylvester*, New
Year's Eve.)

Local Events and Festivals

Bad Tölz. 6 November *Leonhardifahrt.* Best known of the St
Leonhard's Day rides. Similar
events in Rottenbuch and Waldkirchen.

Diessen. Ascension Day. South
German *Töpfermarkt.* Market for
every conceivable type of pot and
pan, vases, etc.

Dinkelsbühl. Mid-July, 1 week.
Kinderzeche. Historic festival
commemorating end of Swedish
siege brought about by children

during the Thirty Years' War.

Furth im Wald. Second Sunday
in August. *Drachenstich.* Historic
play and festival recalling a legend
going back to 1431, in which a
dragon plays a major role.

Grafenau. First Saturday in
August *Säumerfest.* Colourful folk
festival recalling the time when the
town was on one of the principal
salt-trade routes.

Kötzting. Whit Monday. *Pfingstritt.*
Colourful procession with religious
theme. Elaborate costumes and
splendid horses. Similar 'ride' in
Furth im Wald.

Munich. 16 days finishing 1st Sunday in October. *Oktoberfest.* Huge
processions on first and last days.
Beer tents and enormous fun fair.

Oberammergau. Mid-May to mid-
September every 10 years (1990
etc). Passion Play. Outstanding
religious spectacle. About 70
performances.

Pottenstein. 6 January. Festival
of the Three Kings. Unusual
spectacle with torchlight procession
and surrounding hills ablaze with
bonfires and lights.

Regen. 5 days around last Saturday in July. *Pichelsteinerfest.*
Unusual festival based on history of
famous local dish.

Staffelsee. Second Thursday
after Whitsun. *Fronleichnam.*
Corpus Christi procession of boats
on the lake.

Straubing. 2 weeks in mid-
August. *Gäubodenfest.* Based on a
large agricultural show supplemented by huge fairground, beer
tents, etc. A close second to the
better-known Munich *Oktoberfest.*

Long Distance Paths

Key: Ø= 'Hiking without Luggage'
(Wandern ohne Gepäck)
holidays.available. * See 'Cycling
and Cycle Hire' for addresses.

Liebliches Taubertal (100km)
Rothenburg to Wertheim on the
River Main through the charming
Tauber valley following the
Romantic Road. Also suitable as a
cycle tour avoiding main roads.

Lech-Höhenweg (120km)Ø
From Zollhaus north of Landsberg
through the Lech valley to Füssen.*

König-Ludwig-Weg (110km)Ø
From the Starnberger See, across
the Ammersee and through the
Pfaffenwinkel to Füssen.*

Prälatenweg (140km)Ø
Marktoberdorf (Allgäu) through the
Pfaffenwinkel to Kochel am See in
Upper Bavaria.*

Starnberger See Rundweg
(48km)
Circuit of the lake.

Über den Grat (60km)
High-level route (1522–2615m,
4992–8577ft) linking main peaks of
the Allgäu Alps, Oberstdorf to
Hindelang. Accommodation in
mountain huts. Not for beginners.

Ilztalwanderweg (70km)
A nature trail traversing both banks
of the River Ilz in a 'circular' route
with the south end at Passau.

Der Goldene Steig
Collective name for four walks in
the Bavarian Forest, often over the
historic salt caravan routes:
1. Prachatitzer Weg (28km): Röhrn-
bach, Waldkirchen, Bischofsreut.
2. Winterberger Steig (23km):
Hinterschmiding, Herzogsreut,

Philippsreut. 3. Bergreichensteiner
Weg (30km): Freyung, Kreuzberg,
Finsterau. 4. Gulden Strass
(12km): Grafenau, St Oswald,
Lusen. The various sections can be
combined for a longer tour.

Pandurensteig (174km)Ø
From Waldmünchen through the
Bavarian Forest to Passau on the
Danube. Fremdenverkehrsverband
Ostbayern, Landshuter Strasse 13,
8400 Regensburg.

**Der Nördlicher Hauptwand-
erung** (182km)
From Waldmünchen through the
highest mountains and the nature
reserve near the Czech border to
the Dreisessel.

Burgenweg (140km)Ø
From Friedenfels in the Steinwald
to Rötz visiting many ruined and
preserved castles. Address as for
Pandurensteig.

**Entlang Der Fränkischen
Saale und Sinn** (112km)Ø
Circular route Bad Kissingen,
Hammelburg, Bad Bocklet, Bad
Kissingen.
Tourist Information Rhön, Lan-
dratsamt, 8740 Bad Neustadt.

Quer Durch Die Rhön (225km)Ø
Circular route Fladungen, Bad Neu-
stadt, Bad Bocklet, Bad Kissingen,
Fladungen. Address as next above.

Cycling and Cycle Hire

From April to October cycles may
be hired at more than eighty railway stations of the DB or Munich
S-bahn; cyclists arriving by train
pay only half the normal charge.
Local tourist information offices can
provide addresses of private hirers.
Write to main tourist offices for
cycling suggestions in the areas

they cover. Organisations offering *Radeln ohne Gepäck* (cycling without luggage) holidays include Arbeitsgemeinschaft Fernwanderwege im Voralpenland, Von-Kühlmann-Strasse 15, 8910 Landsberg (particularly the area covered by König-Ludwig-Weg, Lech-Höhenweg and Prälatenweg — see 'Long Distance Paths'), the Fremdenverkehrsverband at the same address (Ammersee and Lech valley) and 'Leo'Aktiv Reisen GmbH, Söckinger Strasse 1, 8130 Starnberg (Upper Bavaria and Allgäu).

Youth Hostels

German youth hostels have a high reputation and there are many in Bavaria. A complete list of hostels in Germany can be obtained by sending eight International Reply Coupons to Deutsches Jugendherbergswerk, Hauptverband, Bülowstrasse 26, 4930 Detmold. YHA (England and Wales) has a publication giving details of continental hostels, including Germany. Write to YHA Travel Bureau, 14, Southampton Street, London WC2. US visitors should contact American Youth Hostels Inc, 1332 'I' Street NW, Washington DC, 20005,☎ (202) 783 61 61.

Hostels in Germany can be recognised by a green triangle with the letters DJH (Deutsche Jugendherberge). DJH has two conventional hostels in Munich with 645 beds together with a Youth Guest House (344 beds) for bed and breakfast at Miesingstrasse 4, 8000 München 70, ☎ 089-7236550/60. There are three other hostels within 35km of Munich. In the capital, further accommodation is available for young people at:

Haus International/Jugendhotel

Elisabethstrasse 87
8000 München 40
☎ 089-185081/82/83.
Underground line 8 to Hohenzollernplatz. 480 beds.

Christlicher Verein junger Männer (CVJM)
Landwehrstrasse 13
8000 München 2
☎ 089-555941.
Underground lines 1, 3, 6 or 8 to Sendlinger Tor or 5 minutes on foot from the *Hauptbahnnhof.* 80 beds. Similar to YMCA but women can also be accommodated. Reductions for groups.

Jugendhotel für weibliche Jugendliche
Goethestrasse 9
8000 München 2
☎ 089-555891.
At the *Hauptbahnhof.* 26 beds. Women only up to 25 years.

Sportschule Grünwald
Ebertstrasse 1
8022 Grünwald
☎ 089-641440.
Tram line 25, about 50 minutes journey from *Hauptbahnhof.* Only for pre-arranged groups.

In the *Oberpfälzerwald* in addition to youth hostels there are:

Tagungshaus Stützelvilla
Bahnhofstrasse 29
8486 Windischeschenbach
200m from station. Information and booking: Kreisjugendring, Landratsamt, 8482 Neustadt a.d.Waldnaab., ☎ 09602-79268. 50 beds. Suitable for school parties, holiday groups, conferences, etc.

Pfreimdtalhütte des Oberpfälzer Waldvereins
Augustin Waldtraud
Tanzmühle 2
8481 Tännesberg
☎ 09655-313

One family room (6 beds) and two 8-bed rooms for youth groups. Specially suitable as a base for rambling parties.

Useful Addresses

Aral Aktiengesellschaft
4630 Bochum
(For motoring maps)

DER Travel Service
18 Conduit Street
London W1
☎ 01 408 0111
(Package tours and travel)

Donauschiffahrtsgesellschaft
Wurm & Köck GmbH & Co.
Höllgasse 26
8390 Passau
☎ 0851-2066/2065
(Danube cruises based on Passau)

German National Tourist Office
61 Conduit Street
London W1R 0EN.
☎ 01 734 2600

German National Tourist Office
747 Third Avenue
33rd Floor
New York
NY 10017
☎ (212) 308 3300

German National Tourist Office
Broadway Plaza Suite 1714
700 South Flower Street
Los Angeles
CA 90017
☎ (213) 688 7332

German National Tourist Office
2 Fundy
PO Box 417
Place Bonaventure
Montreal
H5A 1B8
☎ (514) 878 9885

Fränkische Personen-Schiffahrt
Kranenkai 1
8700 Würzburg
☎ 0931-55356
(Cruises on River Main)

Fremdenverkehrsverband
Fuggerstrasse 9
8900 Augsburg
☎ 0821-33335
(Information about Bavarian Swabia and Allgäu)

Fremdenverkehrsverrband
Sonnenstrasse 10
8000 München 2
☎ 089-597347
(Information about Munich and Upper Bavaria)

Fremdenverkehrsverband
Postfach 269
8500 Nürnberg 81
☎ 0911-264202
(Information about Franconia)

Fremdenverkehrsverband
Landshuter Strasse 13
8400 Regensburg
☎ 0941 560260
(Information about Lower Bavaria and Upper Palatinate)

Gebr. Klinger
Personen-Schiffahrt
Jurastrasse 31
8409 Tegernheim
☎ 0941-55359
(Danube cruises from Regensburg)

Homes International Ltd
26 Bond Street
Edenfield
Bury BLO 0EW
☎ 0706 824334
(Self-catering accommodation in private homes, mainly in mountain villages)

North Sea Ferries
King George Dock
Hedon Road

Hull HU9 5QA
☎ 0482 795141
(Hull to Rotterdam and Zeebrugge)

Olau Line
Olau Line Terminal
Sheerness
Kent ME12 1SN
☎ 0795 666666
(Sheerness to Vlissingen (Flushing))

Personenschiffahrtsverkehr
Josef Schweiger
Rennweg 32
8420 Kelheim
☎ 09441-3402
(Danube cruises from Kelheim)

Sally Viking Line
Ferry Terminal
Ramsgate Harbour
Kent CT11 8RP
☎ 0843 595522
(Ramsgate to Dunkirk West)

Sealink UK Ltd
PO Box 29
London,SW1V 1JX
☎ 01 834 8122
(Harwich to Hook of Holland and cross-channel)

Townsend Thoresen
Eastern Docks
Dover
Kent CT16 3BR
☎ 0304 203388
(Felixtowe to Zeebrugge, Dover to Zeebrugge and Ostend and cross-channel)

GLOSSARY

Abtei — abbey
Autobahn (A-) — motorway
Bad (spa) — health resort with medical facilities/treatment
Bundesstrasse (B-) — Federal road
Burg — castle or fortress

Deutsche Bundesbahn (DB) — Federal railway
Dult — seasonal fair/market
Dom — cathedral
Fasching, Fastnacht, Fasnacht etc — carnival time prior to lent
Freibad (beheizt) — Open air swimming pool (heated)
Gaststätte — restaurant
Hallenbad — indoor swimming pool
Hallenwellenbad — indoor swimming pool with artificial waves
Hauptbahnhof — principal railway station
Heimatabend — traditional folk evening
Heimatmuseum — local museum
Hof — courtyard or sometimes superior hotel; often compounded with other words to mean court or royal, eg *Hofgarten*
Kapelle— chapel
Kirche — church
Kloster — monastery, nunnery, convent, etc. plural *Klöster*
Kurort/Luftkurort — health resorts with medical facilities/treatment
Münster — minster
Platz — square. Thus *Marktplatz, Stadtplatz,* etc.
Rathaus — town hall
Ruhetag — rest day for restaurant, etc.
Schloss — palace or residential castle, plural *Schlösser*
See — lake
Strasse — road/street
Tal — valley. Usually combined with river name, eg *Inntal*
Trimm-Dich or *Sport-pfad* — keep-fit circuit, usually in the woods
Wanderparkplatz — car park with access to walking area
Wanderweg — rambling route
Wallfahrtskirche — pilgrimage church
Wellenfreibad — open-air swimming pool with waves
Wildgehege — enclosure for deer, boars, etc

INDEX